D0984702

America's Global Advantage

For over sixty years the United States has been the largest economy and most powerful country in the world. However, there is growing speculation that this era of hegemony is under threat as it faces huge trade deficits, a weaker currency, and stretched military resources. *America's Global Advantage* argues that, despite these difficulties, the US will maintain its privileged position. In this original and important contribution to a central subject in International Relations, Carla Norrlof challenges the prevailing wisdom that other states benefit more from US hegemony than the United States itself. By analysing America's structural advantages in trade, money, and security, and the ways in which these advantages reinforce one another, Norrlof shows how and why America benefits from being the dominant power in the world. Contrary to predictions of American decline, she argues that American hegemony will endure for the foreseeable future.

CARLA NORRLOF is an Associate Professor in the Department of Political Science at the University of Toronto.

America's Global Advantage

US Hegemony and International Cooperation

CARLA NORRLOF

CAMBRIDGE
UNIVERSITY PRESS

CAMBRIDGE UNIVERSITY PRESS
Cambridge, New York, Melbourne, Madrid, Cape Town, Singapore,
São Paulo, Delhi, Dubai, Tokyo

Cambridge University Press
The Edinburgh Building, Cambridge CB2 8RU, UK

Published in the United States of America by Cambridge University Press, New York

www.cambridge.org
Information on this title: www.cambridge.org/9780521749381

First published 2010

Printed in the United Kingdom at the University Press, Cambridge

A catalogue record for this publication is available from the British Library

Library of Congress Cataloguing in Publication data
Norrlof, Carla.
   America's global advantage : US hegemony and international
   cooperation / Carla Norrlof.
   p. cm.
   ISBN 978-0-521-76543-5 (hbk.) – ISBN 978-0-521-74938-1 (pbk.)
   1. Hegemony–United States.   2. International cooperation.   3. International
   relations.   I. Title.
   JZ1312.N67 2010
   327.1′140973–dc22
   2009053753

ISBN 978-0-521-76543-5 Hardback
ISBN 978-0-521-74938-1 Paperback

To family and friends

Contents

Figures

Tables

Preface

When I began inquiring about the distribution of benefits from trade, I was first looking at countries' relative capacity for trade expansion, synergies between import and export growth, and the determinants of commercial bargaining power. After some time, I realized that evaluating countries' relative propensity for raising imports and exports, and any advantage tied to it, required a parallel assessment of countries' ability to absorb foreign investment and to invest in other countries. Analyzing commercial gains allocation meant getting to work on the politics of investment and monetary relations, and wading through more data than any scholar without a research assistant could possibly wish for. In the meantime, there was renewed interest in cross-border financial transactions in the economics discipline, a string of unprecedented current account deficits in the United States, euro success, and China's rise. One moment there was talk of America as empire, the next forecasts of American decline. But just how much systemic variation is there between the account of America the indispensable power and America the weak? This led me to consider the structural features at the basis of a country's relative standing in the world and the relationship between these features. Was there a bargaining advantage associated with being the largest power in the world, or was it better to be a free-riding smaller power, as so many scholars surmised? My research not only suggests that the United States benefits from being the most dominant power today, but that it will continue to be the greatest power for the foreseeable future. Not all gains are quantifiable in monetary terms but come in the form of an unusually wide policy autonomy window, i.e., a longer time horizon and a greater capacity for risk-taking. Because of the leverage the United States has over other states, it has considerable leeway to pursue policies that would be suicidal if undertaken by any other country. This is not to say that the United States is above all constraint or invulnerable, but rather that it is in a better position to gain from international economic relations than are other states – not all of the time, of course, but most of the time. This claim will seem obvious to many readers but is surprisingly controversial in the International Relations and Political Economy literature, where Olson's public goods argument has been completely internalized and where any finding that is not counterintuitive is frowned upon. While I understand that American decline is inevitable in the long run, my analysis adds a cautionary note to all the speculation about imminent decline, which is by no means restricted to our own time but goes back to the 1970s, and never quite seems to materialize in the thunderous fashion that would sound the end of the American era.

Watching the full dread of the financial crisis play itself out in the United States while waiting for reader reports added unwelcome suspense to the review process. Although clearly this is not a book about the credit crunch, it includes aspects of the crisis and fundamentals in the banking sector relevant to assessing America's clout, its relative position, and future prospects.

Acknowledgments

In writing this book I have benefited from the insight, kindness, and generosity of many people. My greatest debt is to Joseph Carens, who read several versions of this manuscript and offered piercing comments, along with unfailing friendship and support. The man deserves a medal for his mentoring and benevolent engagement. When few could see what I was up to, Jennifer Nedelsky took the time to sit down and talk to me about my project, gently pushing me to exhume the core of my argument. David Welch read several chapters several times and offered his expertise and enthusiasm from start to finish. David Welch and Melissa Williams opened their home and made me feel as good as I possibly could when nothing was going my way.

Three distinguished IPE scholars made a big difference. Duncan Snidal has offered advice and encouragement since I defended my thesis. In characteristic good-spirited fashion, he provided trenchant comments on an early version of the manuscript, and welcomed revisions to his model of hegemonic stability theory. Even though we had never met, I sent Benjamin Cohen a paper that engaged with his work, and he responded with unprecedented speed, delivering detailed challenging comments. With the same attention to specifics, and tremendous kindness, he then offered guidance on a subsequent paper. Likewise, Joseph Grieco graciously agreed to chair an APSA panel when I contacted him out of the blue. In his supportive, congenial way, he then provided incisive comments on my paper and gave me excellent advice on how to re-frame it. Robert Pahre also agreed to participate on the same panel. His thorough criticism helped improve my paper and another one as well. Other participants on the panel, Frank Grundig and Hugh Ward, also offered insightful comments and support. Vinod Aggarwal gave me a critical but sympathetic reading of an early draft of the introductory chapter, which helped me advance my project. Louis Pauly and Steven Bernstein delivered thoughtful comments on the introductory chapter as well. Martin Osborne shared his reflections on a game-theoretic model. Mark Brawley gave me extremely useful comments on a paper on the IPE of investment, and invited me to talk on the rivalry between the dollar and the euro at McGill. Csaba Nikolenyi offered useful pointers and a generous reading of a paper on America's external liability position. Carol Bertaut sent me a dataset, and a co-authored paper, on cross-border securities, and took the time to answer a series of questions in very precise terms. Cedric Tille looked at a rough draft on external imbalances and offered valuable feedback including recommendations for further reading. In response to e-mail, Pierre-Olivier Gourinchas took the time to clarify some of the criticism that economists at the Federal Reserve Board of Governors had leveled against his work with Helene Rey. I also owe a special thanks to three political economists at the Graduate Institute of International Studies – Urs Luterbacher, Cedric Dupont, and David Sylvan – where I did my PhD. My supervisor, Urs Luterbacher, gave me what game-theoretic tools I have, and the attention and space I needed to develop my own ideas. His views on my work, his encouragement, and his friendship have been invaluable. Cedric Dupont shaped my way of thinking about international institutions and offered me an affiliation, a desk, and moral support at a critical juncture of this book project. David Sylvan taught me to question assumptions in the IPE literature, and gave me incredibly useful advice on the very first proposal for this book project.

Several colleagues at the University of Toronto, in addition to the ones already mentioned, offered advice and encouragement. Many thanks to: David Cameron, Ran Hirschl, Matt Hoffman, Rebecca Kingston, Nancy Kokaz, Neil Nevitte, and Grace Skogstad. I would also like to acknowledge Robert Vipond, Ragnar Buchweitz, John Miron, and John Coleman, for giving me the time and resources to complete this project.

The editors at Cambridge University Press have been terrific. John Haslam was quick on the mail and reassuring when I was impatient for the reviews. Equally fast to turn things around, Carrie Parkinson provided patient, gentle reminders for approaching deadlines, including the ones that I missed. Rosina Di Marzo facilitated every step of the production process, and Juliet Doyle did a great job editing the text. I am also immeasurably grateful to the anonymous reviewers who offered illuminating and constructive commentary.

I would also like to officially acknowledge previous publications. Parts of chapters 4 and 5 appeared earlier, in different form, in the *Canadian Journal of Political Science*, and parts of chapter 7 in *Cooperation & Conflict*.

Finally, special thanks to my family, Eva-Carin, Claes, Sofia, and Håkan, as well as Karl and other members of my extended family for love and support, and to Isabelle and Marwa for feedback on these chapters and impeccable friendship. This book is for you.

1 | *Introduction*

Short on cash before his ship comes in, Antonio seals a bond with Shylock to sustain the profligacy of loyal, dear Bassanio. Cunningly, Shylock extends the credit with the proviso that, should Antonio fail to honor the bond, Shylock is entitled to a pound of Antonio's flesh. Predictably, Antonio's fortune is not homeward bound. With unmitigated glee, Shylock claims the bond. But enforcing the bond proves difficult. The rules of the game are interpreted in such a way that Shylock must forego his bond unless he claims it in a way which spills no Christian blood – a way which is clearly impossible. All ends well except for Shylock. Antonio is richer by Shylock's misfortune and so, indirectly, is Bassanio, having used the loan to conquer princess Portia, who is as good a catch as anyone ever was.

The main themes of Shakespeare's play, *The Merchant of Venice*, are familiar. Friendship juxtaposed to love, greed to sacrifice. But it is literally a story of debt, and figuratively an account of the possibility of taking advantage of debt when being in debt is as fluid and deceptive as the Seas of Venice.

In sixteenth-century Venice, Christian rules favored Christian borrowers over Jewish lenders. Shylock tried to bring that order down by funding the untenable spending habits of Bassanio, whom Antonio felt obliged to protect. Much by way of commercial and financial interactions has changed in the course of half a millennium yet there are striking parallels to mull over. This book argues that American liabilities are strategic because the prevailing order in trade, money, and security makes it possible for the American people – the Bassanios of this world – to enjoy a cornucopia of foreign goods. Alarmist bells notwithstanding, if, by financing American consumption, China is banking on the demise of American hegemony, it is betting on the same terrible odds that sealed the fate of poor Shylock.

The United States has been the most powerful country in the world for more than sixty years. Throughout this period, it has had the world's largest economy and the world's most important currency. For most of this time, it had the world's most powerful military as well – and its military supremacy today is beyond question. We are truly in an era of US hegemony, a unipolar moment, a Pax Americana, which has enabled Americans to enjoy the highest standard of living in human history.

Is this privileged position being undercut by serial trade deficits? The pessimists are growing more numerous by the day. They see the country's spendthrift ways as a disaster waiting to happen. They warn that the cavernous gap in merchandise trade, well above 6 percent in 2006, is an ominous sign of competitive slippage. In 2008, the liabilities acquired to finance the shortfall in exports reached an amazing 29 percent of GDP. A falling dollar, military overstretch, the rise of the euro, the rise of China, and progressively deeper integration in East Asia are among the factors that many believe herald the imminent decline of American hegemony.

In my view, the doomsayers are mistaken. I argue that American hegemony is stable and sustainable. While the United States certainly does face a number of challenges, an analysis of the linkages between trade, money, and security shows that American power is robust.

This book is a story about why and how American hegemony works, and what other states would have to do to emulate or, on other grounds, thwart, America's power base. As I will show, the United States benefits from running persistent trade deficits as a result of its special position in the international system. I will argue that any comparably situated country would choose to pursue the same cyclical deficit policy as the one encouraged by the US government. A series of size advantages cut across trade, money, and security: the size of the American market, the role of the dollar, and American military power interact to make a trade deficit policy rewarding and buffer the United States from the extreme consequences that a sustained deficit policy would otherwise have.

Based on new research in economics on valuation adjustments (i.e., capital and exchange rate gains), and data analysis of my own, this study draws attention to the economic advantages for the United States of having the key currency. In addition to benefits in the form of seignorage, the United States gains substantially from valuation adjustments, reinforcing policy autonomy and the gains derived from the asymmetry in the structure of borrowing and lending. I also lean on new economic research on valuation adjustments to supplement the conventional view of why military preeminence is necessary for key currency status. Military power has been seen as important in enforcing debt repayments, but there is clearly a need to rethink the connection between reserve status and military power in the present systemic context where the reserve currency country has the world's largest external liablities.

We have seen erroneous predictions of American decline before. In the 1970s, the combination of high inflation, high interest rates, high unemployment, the Vietnam War, political and military challenges from China and the Soviet Union, and the economic rise of Japan led to eerily similar forecasts. Pessimists then, as today, underestimated the longevity of American power. The main reason the United States has continued to occupy a unique place in the international system is because a sufficient number of major and lesser powers have a strong interest in maintaining America at the top of the hierarchy. To bring America down would take a deliberate, coordinated strategy on the part of others and this is simply not plausible. As much as the United States benefits from the space it has carved out for itself in the current world order, its ability to reap unequal gains will remain unless and until allies start to incur heavy losses under American dominance. Even that, by itself, will not be sufficient to sink American hegemony. A strong alternative to American rule will have to come into view for things to fundamentally change. At present, no credible alternative is in sight. The United States is not invincible but its dominance is currently steady.

Those who are inclined to think that American hegemony will persist – at least for a while – tend to dwell on the claim that the United States is providing a range of public goods to the benefit of all at its own expense. This is a chimera. The United States is self-interested, not altruistic. The illusion of benevolence has meant that very little attention has been given to uncovering the mechanism through which the United States gains disproportionately from supplying a large open market, the world's reserve currency, and a military machine capable of stoking or foiling deadly disputes. This book exposes the mechanism through which the United States reaps unequal gains and shows that the current world system, and the distribution of power that supports it, has built-in stabilizers that strengthen American power following bouts of decline. Although all dominant powers must eventually decline, I will show that the downward progression need not be linear when mutually reinforcing tendencies across various power dimensions are at play. Specifically, I will demonstrate how the United States' reserve currency status produces disproportionate commercial gains; how commercial power gives added flexibility in monetary affairs; and, finally, how military preponderance creates advantages in both monetary and trade affairs.

The puzzle

This book grows out of my attempt to understand a particular puzzle in international political economy, the ongoing American trade deficit. In absolute terms, the American deficit, which in 2006 amounted to $753 billion, is the largest ever.[1] Net external liabilities also exploded, starting in the middle of the 1990s, and peaked at $4.2 trillion in 2008. Even as a share of GDP, these figures (5.7 percent and 23 percent respectively) are high in comparison with other industrialized countries. Is it a coincidence that the country with the most potent military force and the largest capital and consumer market is able to get away with accumulating deficits and debt? If not, why is the American experience a coup instead of the usual curse?

Large sustained trade deficits are usually seen as a liability and a sign of weakness in an increasingly competitive international economy. When countries in Africa, Southeast Asia, South and Central America run deficits for prolonged periods something of a national emergency is proclaimed as private investors pick up and leave. In order to be persuaded to stay, official investors – both governments and international institutions such as the World Bank and the IMF – demand reform and attach different levels of conditionality to their policy prescriptions. Caught in this bind, deficit countries are forced to sacrifice significant policy flexibility to prevent massive capital outflow. Given the inherent tendency of all governments to maximize policy autonomy, developing countries often choose import-restricting policies as a way of eschewing excessive deficits. Middle-rank traders, consisting of super-developing countries such as China, Brazil, and India on the one hand, and advanced economies such as Japan (and until recently, the euro-zone) on the other, have looser constraints. But they have for the most part reaped big benefits by prioritizing

[1] BEA 2009a, BEA 2008a, BEA 2009b.

exports over imports, since it enables them to use world markets to compensate for slack domestic demand or to expand their industrial base and absorb excess labor.

If it is generally wise to shun a deficit policy, why has the single most dominant state in the international system opted for policies which have systematically provoked a shortfall between exports and imports for twenty-seven of the thirty-seven years of the post-Bretton Woods era? Answering this question requires an understanding of how and why the United States enjoys a privileged position in the modern international economic order.

The argument

In sketching my argument, I will show that the United States gains both materially and in terms of policy autonomy from running persistent deficits because of its multi-purpose power base. It gains economically by absorbing more capital and goods from the rest of the world and through capital and exchange rate gains on the international investment position (IIP).[2] It also gains in terms of policy autonomy. Because foreigners have a wide range of incentives to invest in dollar-denominated assets (in the United States) and, when necessary, help soft-land the economy, the United States can adjust imbalances over a longer time horizon. The gain in policy flexibility means it can adjust imbalances using its preferred policy instruments, and that its 'policy error' threshold is higher than it is for other countries. Therefore, it can more easily avoid the kind of shock therapy that is normally associated with a consistent pattern of trade deficits and high external liabilities.

My claim is not merely that America has benefited from its hegemonic position but that it has benefited disproportionately, and that the system through which it benefits is sustainable. By disproportionate I mean that it has received more than what it 'pays' for the public goods it provides, and that it reaps a higher benefit than other states. I argue that the United States reaps increasing returns in trade, money, and security – in other words, that it gets more back than it puts in. In the trade realm, it systematically absorbs more imports than it gives

---

[2] The net international investment position (NIIP) is the difference between American claims on foreigners and foreign claims on Americans.

back to the world in the form of exports. In the monetary sphere, it makes more money from its lending than it pays on its borrowing. In the security domain, it is well known that the United States spends more on security than all other states combined. Just how much mileage the United States gets on its military spending is not common knowledge, however. At least part of the reason the United States has been able to attract capital on a grand scale is that it provides a safe investment environment, which is tied to a strong tradition of property rights protection, and the ability to secure American territory militarily. A portion of defense spending has also been used to protect and expand foreign investments, and to protect allies. The economic return on this stabilizing role has been huge in terms of allied support for dollar adjustment.

Methodology and value added

In this book, I adopt the analytical framework from economics that treats agents as rational actors seeking to achieve economic gains and avoid economic loss. The primary agents in this case, however, are states, not firms, and I am particularly interested in exploring the logic of economic action for a state possessing attributes that the United States has today, namely the largest domestic economy, the key world currency, and the strongest military. I argue that these attributes give the United States certain positional and structural advantages in the international economic system, including advantages in shaping the institutions of the international economic system, and that, as a result, the United States gains disproportionately from international economic institutions and interactions. This notion of disproportionality will be assessed in precise theoretical and empirical terms.

To avoid misunderstanding, let me make three points clear right away. First, I am not claiming that the United States is the only state to gain from international economic activity. For reasons that will be explored in more detail later, all states gain from cooperating in an international economic system in which trade across state borders is relatively free, in which there is a stable, abundant, and liquid currency that can be used for purposes of international exchange, and in which relations between states are peaceful rather than violent. These three goods interact. Even if trade is permitted, it will not take place to any considerable extent unless there is a viable international currency and relations between states are peaceful. The existence of an international currency does not matter much unless there is a lot of trade and the viability of such a currency is in various ways dependent on military backing. Finally, peace and security have economic benefits. So, the question is not whether all gain from international cooperation but rather how the gains from economic cooperation (and any costs associated with cooperation) are allocated among various states. My claim is that the United States is able to get other states to bear some of the costs that one would expect it (or any other similarly situated state) to bear on its own, that it gains in ways that others cannot, and that it is more able than other states to structure the rules and institutions of international economic life to its advantage. In sum, the international economy is a system of asymmetrical cooperation in which the United States has an advantaged position and enjoys disproportionate gains as a result. Some might see this as a proposition so obvious as not to be worth stating, but I will show in chapter 2 that it is not a view that has been embraced by the majority of scholars in international relations and that even those who are sympathetic to the view rarely spell out the precise ways in which the United States enjoys a position of privilege or how it is able to achieve disproportionate gains.

Second, the purpose of this book is not to criticize or praise the United States for its policies. I seek merely to understand and explain, or, more cautiously, to show the close fit between what a rational state actor, seeking to achieve economic gain and avoid economic loss, would do if positioned like the United States and what the United States has actually done. The whole point of the underlying framework is that any rational actor would pursue a similar course, so there is no purchase within this framework for praise or blame. Instead, the obvious question is why other states, which are presumably seeking their own economic advantage as well, do not try to challenge the positional advantages of the United States. I try to show that the courses pursued by other states are also economically rational, given the constraints they face and the obstacles in removing those constraints. Chapter 7, in particular, considers what major actors in Asia and Europe would have to do to reduce or even take over the positional advantages enjoyed by the United States and why it is so difficult for them to do so, although they can make a little headway in some areas, and where they can, they do.

Finally, I want to emphasize that this is a book about international political economy, not a book about all aspects of international relations. I am not claiming that states are only seeking economic gains in their policies or that this would provide a good framework for thinking about, say, international security issues. Although I do pay attention to the ways in which the dominant military position of the United States contributes to its positional advantage in the international economy and yields direct and indirect economic benefits, I do not claim that the United States' military policy is primarily driven by the pursuit of economic advantage. This book does not attempt to give a full account of the motivations for military expenditures, nor am I claiming that all military expenditure is economically rational in the sense that the economic benefits gained from those expenditures always outweigh their costs. In the same vein, I do not view national security as reducible to economic strength or foreign policy as reducible to the pursuit of economic gain. In assuming that states are rational economic actors in the sphere of international political economy, I do not rule out that states sometimes pursue values in their foreign policies, nor do I mean to suggest that international life is reducible to international political economy.

Plan of the book

This book consists of seven chapters, apart from this introduction and a conclusion. The next chapter (chapter 2) offers descriptive indicators of America's hegemonic position and places the argument in relation to the literature on hegemony in international political economy.

Chapter 3 is conceptual. It models cooperation under hegemony and shows that the hegemon is often in a good position to reap disproportionate benefits from providing public goods as a result of its ability to credibly threaten exclusion. Its ability to shift gains in its favor is, however, variable and depends at least as much on the relative power gap between other Great Powers as on its own preponderance. Paradoxically, the hegemon actually acquires a greater capacity to shift gains in its favor as it declines.

Chapter 4 examines the sources of trade according to different theories – Traditional (the Classical and Neo-Classical approach) and New Trade theories. The analysis will be familiar to political economists but I have included it for the benefit of readers not well

versed in the economics of trade. I have left out class-based theories, such as Dependencia and World Systems theories because of their
uneasy fit with mainstream economic theory. Some of the critiques
voiced by these perspectives – for instance, the difficulty in rectifying
unequal gains from trade and the politicization of commercial interactions – are, however, echoed in the analysis. The aim of chapter 4
is to demonstrate how firm and country size determine trade policies
and patterns, and to explain the significance of trade deficits. After
unpacking the trade deficit, relating it to other deficits (and external
liabilities), and emphasizing the danger associated with them, I argue
that they have been beneficial for the United States and even a source
of bargaining power, which has been used to advance American commercial interests.

Chapter 5 explains the rationality of American hegemony, and
demonstrates how the United States benefits from serial trade deficits
and from having net external liabilities. I argue that American privilege cuts across trade and monetary matters (currency and investment)
and look at the interactive effects between trade and monetary affairs.
The chapter provides a thorough examination of how the United
States' special position in the monetary domain has produced commercial advantages, and how commercial power has enhanced monetary gains. For example, a strong dollar has subsidized American
imports while only minimally affecting American sales from foreign
locations, partially offsetting the negative impact on American export
performance. A weak dollar, on the other hand, has increased exports
from the United States with imports declining relatively slowly despite weakening terms of trade. This is because foreign producers are
ready to lower their prices in order to compensate for the implicit tax
which a low dollar represents. This allows foreigners to maintain and
expand exports to the United States. I discuss the extent of the gains
that flow from the structure of America's trade and investment links
with other countries, and in what measure these gains are generalized, rewarding other countries as well. At the end of the chapter, I
discuss to how this advantage might be exhausted in the future.

Chapter 6 relates military and economic power. According to prevailing wisdom, the special currency country must also be the dominant military power so that it can persuade countries to repay loans in
case they default. But if this rationale is correct, countries should not
be willing to lend extensively to the United States since in addition to

having the world's largest external liabilities, it is the world's biggest military power. The fact that military power cannot be used to collect American debt does not preclude a connection between military, monetary, and commercial power. I make a different argument about how the United States has used military power to promote economic interests. The claim is in four parts. First, military means were used to keep the European Great Powers out of the western hemisphere in the late nineteenth and early twentieth centuries. As a result, American lending, including the dollar, could be extended over a large area. Second, widely regarded as safe, foreign investors have been willing to pay a security premium to invest in the American market. Third, the United States has intervened militarily for economic reasons, both for narrow economic purposes, in support of American business interests, and for broader economic goals in order to provide a stable political context in which economic exchange can take place, and in order to safeguard the current capitalist structure from Communist encroachment. Fourth, and last, the United States is obliged by treaty to defend roughly fifty countries. These interventions, whether to push back aggressors, or for humanitarian reasons, have purchased goodwill and provided Great Powers with an interest in preserving an American-centered world order.

Chapter 7 examines two trends in world affairs that could prove damaging to the United States. The rise of the euro and heightened military cooperation in Europe on the one hand, and, on the other hand, stronger commercial links in East Asia, which could create viable alternatives to American power over the long term. In their current form, however, neither development is likely to upset the status quo because of internal rivalries, institutional deficiencies, and dilemmas of sovereignty. For reasons explained in chapter 3, it is not sufficient for the combined power base of the European Union and East Asia to exceed that of the United States. To create an alternative to American power, a cohesive entity, whether in the form of a single state or a cooperative effort, must alone command greater resources than the United States. Barring this, the only other trigger for change is for Great Powers to experience substantial and painful loss as a result of American policies, provoking them to openly defy American hegemony. More exploitative policies on the part of the American government could change the calculus of strategic interaction.

2 | *The forms and consequences of hegemonic leadership*

Everyone knows that the United States is special but there is little agreement as to whether being special has been a net positive for the United States and even less agreement about what it has meant for the world. The default position is to view America as unique because, unlike Great Powers in the past, it has used its dominance to everyone's benefit.[1] The claim is not simply that there are positive externalities as a result of the hegemon's supply of public goods but that most of the benefits accrue to other states who, even though they do not pay for public goods, cannot be excluded from enjoying the benefits associated with them.[2] This is known as hegemonic stability theory, and is a belief in the benevelont hegemon. While this approach has been challenged in the past under the headings coercive, malevolent, and exploitative hegemony, none of these labels fits easily with the incentives behind American hegemony or its consequences. Although the literature is replete with objections to the characterization of the United States as a benevolent hegemon, I am not aware of any other work that gives a theoretically and empirically grounded account of precisely how the United States reaps disproportionate benefits across multiple issue areas.[3]

In this book, I understand American hegemony as being broadly beneficial and especially beneficial for the United States. To be sure, my claim is not that the United States comes out ahead in every imaginable situation but that it benefits disproportionately most of the time, and as a direct result of structural advantages. The challenge for me is to devise appropriate measures for disproportionality and to uncover the mechanism through which the United States promotes its interests. While the United States has declined relative to some states, and it is inevitable that it will one day lose its dominant position, its

---

[1] Keohane 1984; Kindleberger 1981.   [2] Olson 1965.
[3] For two classics, see Russett 1985 and Strange 1987.

ability to extract unequal gains implies that the shape of its power curve is a lot more irregular than the debate about its superpower status suggests.

I start this chapter with a discussion of the standard benevolent hegemon thesis and contrast it with other varieties of hegemonic leadership – the coercive and exploitative strands of hegemony – and point to the problems these approaches have in capturing essential features of American hegemony. As a second and related point, I will argue that these models of hegemony do not give a convincing account of the repercussions of American leadership in the world system. My goal in this book is to dispel the idea that other states have had more to gain from American hegemony than America itself. To the contrary, I will show that the United States has gained relative to other states, and that these gains are due to its special position within the international system across three key issue-areas – trade, monetary relations, and security affairs – as well as the interactive effects between these. To make this point, I begin the section on the consequences of American hegemony by sketching a rough portrait of the United States' basic strategy within these domains. The common enabling factor across different spheres is size. A number of hegemonic indicators are presented in order to demonstrate that the United States is uniquely large in the security and economic arena. These descriptive statistics, tables, and graphs cover a period ranging from a quarter of a century to nearly half a century, and offer a clear view of how the United States' hegemonic position has evolved. The subsequent section explores different ways to think about disproportionality and highlights some drawbacks with certain intuitive measures.

The forms of hegemonic leadership

Following the seminal work of Charles Kindleberger, international relations scholars have largely accepted the idea that the United States is a benevolent hegemon that provides public goods.[4] Such goods involve non-rival benefits which states cannot be prevented from enjoying. This notion has had a profound impact on how we conceive the relationship between the United States and other countries. Because states gain whether or not they contribute to international

[4] Kindleberger 1973, 1986a.

public goods, a hegemon, willing and able to take on disproportionate costs, is needed to solve the free-rider problem.

A state that is prepared to contribute more than any other state, although it benefits less than other states, would certainly count as benevolent if some other more profitable course of action is available. This would correspond to the colloquial use of the term 'benevolent', which suggests a dose of altruism. In the literature, however, the precise meaning of benevolence is ambiguous. By emphasizing that a *responsible* actor is needed to maintain an open market for distress goods, provide long-term lending and a stable system of exchange rates, coordinate macro-economic policies, and perform lender of last resort functions, Kindleberger suggests that the leader is not only motivated by its own interests but by others' interests as well.[5] Leadership, "thought of as the provision of the public good of responsibility, rather than exploitation of followers or the private good of prestige … remains a positive idea."[6] Indeed, most of Kindleberger's writings seem to go in the direction of a responsible hegemon claiming immaterial rewards in the form of moral high-ground.

As Brawley has argued, one can also interpret Kindleberger as seeing the hegemon as benevolent on the grounds that "a significantly large state would consume enough of [the] public good that it would be willing to provide it by itself."[7] This solves the free-rider problem. Kindleberger borrows the idea "that a leader is prepared to bear more than a proportionate share of maintaining the cost of the system" from Frohlich and Oppenheimer,[8] although he disagrees that the leader's willingness to bear these costs hinges on being "paid in … prestige, or glory."[9] Nor is Kindleberger[10] satisfied with the neoliberal understanding of leadership, that a benevolent hegemon is motivated by its long-term self-interest, as Keohane advised.[11] Unlike Kindleberger, Keohane finds that "explanations based on empathy can also be reinterpreted in ways consistent with egoistic theories," thus "the trick is not to ignore self-interest but to redefine it, to make it less myopic and more empathetic."[12] On this reading, it is the hegemon's

---

[5] Kindleberger 1973.   [6] Kindleberger 1973.
[7] Brawley 1995.   [8] Frohlich and Oppenheimer 1970.
[9] Kindleberger 1986a.   [10] Kindleberger 1986b.
[11] Keohane 1984.
[12] For Keohane, an actor that incorporates others' preferences in its utility function violates the "assumption of egoism, not that of rationality."

long-term preference (for cooperative outcomes) that is benevolent. In this case, what is really meant by benevolence is that, under certain circumstances, an agent's pursuit of its own interest serves the interests of others as well – not only in the way that is characteristic of all market transactions, but in a more specific way, namely the production of goods with net positive externalities. Essentially, short-term goals are being sacrificed for longer-term ones. This may indeed be rational but it is misleading to call it benevolent. Instead, Kindleberger believes that a leader (he is reluctant to use the term hegemon) is motivated by "conscience, duty, obligation, or such old-fashioned notions as noblesse oblige ... [both] by ethical training and by the circumstance of position."[13] But this language of responsibility is hard to reconcile with rational actor analysis where the basic premise is that parties are motivated by self-interest.

Even if we were to accept the looser, semantically improper, meaning of benevolence in the sense of everyone being better off, two implausible assumptions are necessary in order to make rational choice compatible with benevolence, namely that cooperation does not affect gains distribution and that small states do not mind being organized by the hegemon.[14] In other words, if cooperation impinges on gains distribution, and contributes to the hegemon's relative decline, as the theory assumes, the hegemon is benevolent but not rational. If, on the other hand, the hegemon benefits disproportionally economically and politically from cooperating with smaller states, such cooperation serves the hegemon's interests, and so is rational, but small states would hardly characterize it as benevolent.

The term benevolent also speaks to style. In contrast to the benevolent hegemon, a coercive hegemon primarily relies on forceful means to foster international cooperation. A coercive hegemon is not necessarily, but could be, exploitative. If coercion is required to solicit contributions from states that are otherwise inclined to free-ride, the hegemon is merely exercising leadership to keep the system

---

Although economists have started to incorporate the idea that a utility function is not necessarily bounded around an individual actor's preferences, this line of research, drawn to its logical conclusion, pushes rational choice in the direction of holism, vitiating its very purpose. It is in this sense that I see it as ultimately incompatible with rational choice. Keohane 1984; Becker 1997; Becker and Murphy 2001.

[13] Kindleberger 1986b.   [14] Grunberg 1990.

intact.[15] The real difference lies in the distinction between a benevolent or coercive hegemon on the one hand, and one that is exploitative on the other. Different authors come to different conclusions about what counts as exploitation.

According to Kindleberger, the hegemon is exploitative if it uses power to extract rents.[16] But if everyone gains, the hegemon is not necessarily being exploitative when using its bargaining power to shift gains. Although this is not the only way to think about hegemony, a number of authors assume it. Gilpin's position, for example, is very similar to Kindleberger's.[17] In Snidal's illustration of the theory, lesser great powers always experience net gains on cooperation (if the United States cooperates), so the hegemon is, according to this definition, never exploitative.[18]

Few International Relations (IR) scholars characterize American hegemony as coercive or exploitative, especially not when pursuing its interests in the international economy. The default position has rather been to see the United States as benevolent. As I will argue, this label is not only inappropriate because of the definitional problems that surround it and because of the difficulty in reconciling it with rational choice analysis, but because it does not explain what drives American hegemony or its implications.

The consequences of American hegemony

The spread of liberal democracy and economic liberalism in the postwar era has created unprecedented amounts of wealth and lifted more people out of poverty than any other political or economic system. Although income is still very unevenly distributed (in some countries more so than in the past), more people enjoy a higher standard of living than during any other era. As a way of organizing relations within and between societies, the American model of strong market freedoms backed by robust institutions is largely responsible for generating the tremendous growth in GDP, trade, and cross-border securities that the world has witnessed in the last sixty-five years.

---

[15] Lake 1993.   [16] Kindleberger 1981.
[17] Exploitation and benevolence coexist somewhat uncomfortably in Gilpin's analysis, since the hegemon does not take measures to forestall its long term decline: Gilpin 1981.
[18] Snidal 1985.

At the domestic level, a market-based economy protects private ownership, determines resource-use through the price mechanism and puts in place credit institutions so that income can grow beyond the underlying resource base. Safeguarding political freedoms, primarily through free and general elections, is not only a good in itself but should, in theory, limit the ability of elected officials to use their political power to manipulate market outcomes for private gain. In practice, political freedoms have been less widely accepted than market freedoms, in part because the United States has historically been less effective in promoting political reform than market reform. In addition, the prospect of being thrown out of office has not always deterred politicians from abusing their position, especially – but not exclusively – in developing countries. The unequal distribution of resources and wealth within societies is in large part due to the failure to promote political and economic freedoms in equal measure and to prevent agents higher up in the hierarchy from using their power for economic gain.

Internationally, institutions such as the World Trade Organization, the IMF, the World Bank, and more informal arrangements such as the G-7-plus meetings have encouraged the free flow of goods, services, and capital across countries. As one would expect, states at the top of the international power ladder have been more successful in pursuing their economic interests than less powerful states. As the single largest producer, trader, and financial power, the United States has commanded the greatest authority in the economic field and consequently been in a good position to further its economic interests. In the security field, the United States has been the most powerful state for most of the postwar era, and when it shared superpower status with the Soviet Union during the Cold War, it had even more leverage over those who scoffed at the barter terms available with the Soviet Union. The United States has, through its military and naval presence in different parts of the world, helped safeguard economic activity in areas where property rights are weak and guaranteed the free flow of goods at sea. Since enforcing the right to ownership is a prerequisite for efficient production and enforcing the right to safe passage is necessary for exchange, all states with a stake in the functioning of the current economic order are well served by the United States' self-appointed role as global policeman. However, an examination of cases where the United States has rolled out its military and naval machinery, unsurprisingly reveals that the primary consideration has been the protection of American business and political interests.

Although all of this may seem obvious, this perspective cuts against the grain of international relations theory and the standard assumption that "the small exploit the large."[19] Looking at that literature, I do not dispute the claim that American hegemony has been generally beneficial, but I do take issue with the fact that it has been more beneficial for other states than for the United States. In reality, the path of hegemonic leadership has been extremely irregular, with possibilities of growth in the face of decline, and this explains the many false alarms predicting the end of the American era. Decline can be advantageous for the hegemon as long as it retains the number one position in the international system in absolute terms. In some circumstances, a closing of the relative power gap gives the hegemon a greater capacity to distribute gains in its favor as well as a preference for more non-cooperative policies.

The evolution of the United States' hegemonic position

Given my goal in this book – which is to show both analytically and empirically that the United States is unique, that its special position is a function of its size, and that this is what allows it to gain more than others, and often more than it contributes to make international cooperation work – I provide statistics that track the United States' hegemonic position in a twenty-five- to forty-five-year perspective. The discussion is completely data-driven (with the conceptualization of hegemony left to the next chapter). After a cross-country comparison of the various size measures, I then go on to give a brief overview of how I plan to support my disproportionality claim empirically and discuss the measures I propose to use.

Size measures

Scholars who try to get at the United States' unique position in the international system implicitly talk about size. However, what precisely makes the United States special has been difficult to establish and the subject of intense debate for a long time. In the mid-1980s,

---

[19] Olson 1965.

scholars agreed that the United States was the most powerful actor in the system, in absolute terms, although they disagreed about how much surplus power it needed to have in order to remain a hegemonic power.[20] The British political economist, Susan Strange, argued that hegemonic indicators such as trade to GDP or monetary reserves were inappropriate, vague, and almost irrelevant; what really mattered was the United States' structural power.[21] She was right to discount trade to GDP, which is rather a measure of a country's trade dependence. Instead, I use world trade shares, although, as I will argue, the tendency for commercially successful states to disperse their production and sales creates problems with this measure as well.

Strange emphasized five sources of power, the United States' ability to protect allies, its lead in the knowledge industry, its reserve currency status, its share of production, and its agenda-setting power.[22] This catalogue is still a good starting point for assessing American privilege, although Milner and Snyder criticized Strange for not being clear about the meaning of the indicator, world production shares.[23] I meet this criticism by using shares of world GDP to compare economic size and world trade shares to assess commercial performance (in chapter 4, I discuss multinational sales). Strange saw that multinational activity was a source of power but she did not explain how such production benefited America. More generally, although Strange's list has intuitive appeal, she did not clarify how excelling in these domains made the United States special. Although Strange understood that control over the decision-making framework across various issue-areas gave the United States a hold on other countries, she never demonstrated how power was exercised or how the United States benefited from organizing the world economy.[24] From Strange's list, I will use only measures that are readily quantifiable, and thus leave out things like agenda-setting power, which in any case is mostly derivative of other, "harder," more tangible structural capabilities. To gauge American financial power, I use capital market size rather than reserve currency status, since the latter is partly a function of the former. A consideration of America's key currency status is merely deferred to chapter 7, which offers a fully-fledged analysis of prospects for the dollar to

---

[20] Russett 1985.   [21] Strange 1987.
[22] Strange 1987.   [23] Milner and Snyder 1988.
[24] Russett 1985.

remain hegemonic with the arrival of the euro. Currently, approximately 65 percent of the world's currency reserves are held in dollars. I have also avoided using more subjective categories, such as "lead in the knowledge industry," although a quick count of the world's largest firms reveals that American firms still account for half of the top twenty-five slots and also dominate the 2000 list using any measure (see chapter 4). In short, the key indicators for countries' relative capability that I will use are military spending, GDP, capital market size, and trade performance.

As illustrated in table 2.1, the United States is by far the largest military spender and has actually increased its share of world military spending in the last twenty years. Moreover, the United States' lead over its nearest competitor is actually stronger in the security arena than it was in 1988. The Soviet Union was the closest rival in 1988, accounting for 18 percent of the world total, whereas China, the country with the second largest share today, only accounts for 5 percent of the world total. Counting coalitions as potential balancers, the euro area still accounts for a lower share today than did the Soviet Union in 1988. The European Union, on the other hand, accounts for a larger share than did the Soviet Union in 1988. But the European Union's share does not amount to even half of the United States' share of the world total. Without even throwing the technological sophistication of American weaponry (or the collective action problems that many states confront when deciding to act in the national interest) into the balance, it is clear that the United States is peerless in the security sphere and has strengthened its lead in the last two decades. Because of the superiority of American military power, and other states' dependence on it for effective action, the United States faces very few constraints in the security arena. The 2003 invasion of Iraq is a case in point but there are plenty of other examples. As I will also show in chapter 6, there are also economic advantages associated with this privileged position in the security field.

Although some question the utility of armed force, few will contest that the United States is in a league of its own when it comes to security affairs. But what about the economic realm? The real test is whether the United States still towers over other countries economically, and is able to reap economic benefits as a result of its hegemonic position. This is the claim that is likely to be the most carefully scrutinized.

Table 2.1 *Cross-country comparison of military expenditures*

Share of world military expenditures	1988*	2007	2008
US	41%	44%	45%
Euro-16	...	15%	15%
EU-12/EU-27	16%	22%	21%
China	1%	5%	5%
Japan	3%	4%	3%
Soviet Union/Russia	18%	3%	3%
India	1%	2%	2%

Notes: *1989 figures for China; ... = not applicable.
Source: SIPRI 2009a, 2009b.

Before turning to the idea that hegemony is economically advantageous, let us start with comparative economic measures of the size of the American economy. As mentioned, I will use the most obvious data points – shares of world GDP, world trade, and world capital markets.

Table 2.2 lists the top ten countries in terms of their share of world GDP in 2008 and compares their current position with their 1965 position in six-year intervals forward, i.e., 1971, 1977, and so on, up to 2007 and 2008.[25]

One notices three things. First, the United States has consistently had the highest share of GDP. Second, its share of GDP has been declining, although not steadily, since shares actually increased between 1977 and 1983 and then again between 1995 and 2001. Third, while countries like Japan and China have improved their relative position, in terms of GDP shares, vis-à-vis the United States, they only command a third of the United States' share. Consequently, there is no single competitor around to oust the United States from its number one position. The only existing challenger in this domain is the euro

---

[25] There are, of course, a lot of problems with GDP as a measure of prosperity. For one, there is huge variation in the reliability of the official data, so cross-country comparisons are difficult. For another, GDP is not a good proxy for how an entire country is faring, since it masks productive and income disparities within them. Third, in our highly integrated world economy, a country's productivity depends on productivity elsewhere, often in the form of imported inputs, which nonetheless is deducted from GDP.

Table 2.2 *World GDP shares*

	1965	1971	1977	1983	1989	1995	2001	2007	2008
United States	36.7%	35.0%	28.3%	30.8%	27.8%	24.7%	31.8%	25.4%	23.4%
China	3.6%	3.1%	2.4%	2.0%	1.7%	2.5%	4.2%	6.0%	7.1%
Japan	4.7%	7.2%	9.7%	10.4%	15.0%	17.7%	12.9%	8.1%	8.1%
India	3.0%	2.1%	1.7%	1.9%	1.5%	1.2%	1.5%	2.2%	2.0%
Germany	...	7.6%	8.2%	6.6%	6.9%	8.5%	6.0%	6.1%	6.0%
Russian Federation	...	...	...	...	2.6%	1.3%	1.0%	2.4%	2.7%
France	5.3%	5.2%	5.7%	4.8%	5.1%	5.3%	4.2%	4.7%	4.7%
United Kingdom	5.2%	4.4%	3.6%	4.0%	4.3%	3.8%	4.5%	5.0%	4.4%
Brazil	1.1%	1.5%	2.5%	1.8%	2.2%	2.6%	1.7%	2.4%	2.7%
Italy	3.5%	3.8%	3.5%	3.8%	4.6%	3.8%	3.5%	3.9%	3.8%
Euro area	21.2%	22.2%	24.3%	20.7%	23.1%	24.5%	20.0%	22.4%	22.4%

Note: ... = not applicable.
Source: IBRD 2009.

area, and a whole chapter is dedicated to analyzing the prospects for euro-zone countries to replace American hegemony.

The next size measure, world trade shares, is on display in tables 2.3 and 2.4. As can be seen in table 2.3, the United States was clearly the largest exporter in 1965 but was only the third largest exporter in 2008 behind Germany and China. From table 2.4, we see, however, that the United States has maintained its lead as the world's largest importer. These statistics get to the heart of the argument in this book, which is that commanding large import shares is more relevant for hegemonic status than commanding large export shares. As I will also argue in chapters 4 and 5, importing more than one exports, i.e., sustaining trade deficits, is desirable as long as negative consequences in the form of an unmanageable buildup in external liabilities can be avoided.

In gauging the relative size of the United States' capital market, I use the selected indicators from which the IMF derives capital market size. Table 2.5 takes into account a country's stock-market capitalization, its bond market, and its bank assets, which are all added up to arrive at a single measure for capital market size. As can be gleaned from the table, the United States has a stronger lead in equities and bonds than in bank assets. I will return to this observation in chapter 7, in talking about the financial crisis and in thinking about how it will affect the pattern of financial power. From table 2.5 it is also clear that, in 2008, the size of America's closest rival, Japan's, capital market, was significantly lower than what it was in 1995 (see columns 10 and 12). These figures suggest that no single country can challenge the United States' dominance in the financial field, although, as with world trade shares, we need to consider to what extent the group of countries that now constitutes the euro area is a threat to American hegemony (see chapter 7).

Measuring disproportionality

While these size measures tell us that the United States still enjoys a considerable lead in the world economy, my claim is also that it benefits disproportionately compared to other states. Assessing unequal gains is fraught with difficulties, and my measure will necessarily be imperfect, but I will try to make the case that it is not so flawed that it cannot tell us who comes out on top in the international political economy.

Table 2.3 *World export shares*

	1965	1971	1977	1983	1989	1995	2001	2007	2008
United States	14.5%	12.5%	10.9%	11.1%	11.7%	11.3%	11.8%	8.3%	8.0%
Germany	9.4%	11.0%	10.5%	9.2%	11.0%	10.1%	9.2%	9.5%	9.1%
United Kingdom	7.3%	6.2%	5.0%	5.0%	4.9%	4.6%	4.4%	3.1%	2.9%
France	5.4%	5.9%	5.8%	5.1%	5.8%	5.8%	5.2%	4.0%	3.8%
Japan	4.4%	6.8%	7.2%	8.0%	8.8%	8.6%	6.5%	5.1%	4.9%
Italy	3.8%	4.3%	4.0%	3.9%	4.5%	4.5%	3.9%	3.5%	3.3%
Netherlands	3.9%	4.5%	4.4%	3.5%	3.5%	3.9%	3.7%	4.0%	3.9%
Canada	4.5%	5.2%	3.9%	4.2%	3.9%	3.7%	4.2%	3.0%	2.8%
China	1.4%	1.0%	0.9%	1.4%	2.0%	2.9%	5.3%	8.7%	8.9%
Belgium	0.0%	0.0%	0.0%	0.0%	0.0%	0.0%	3.1%	3.1%	3.0%

Source: WTO 2009a.

Table 2.4 *World import shares*

	1965	1971	1977	1983	1989	1995	2001	2007	2008
United States	11.7%	13.2%	13.7%	14.3%	15.4%	14.6%	18.2%	14.2%	13.2%
Germany	9.1%	11.0%	10.4%	8.1%	11.1%	8.7%	7.6%	7.4%	7.3%
China	1.1%	0.6%	0.6%	1.1%	1.8%	2.5%	3.8%	6.7%	6.9%
Japan	4.1%	5.4%	6.1%	6.7%	6.6%	6.4%	5.4%	4.4%	4.6%
United Kingdom	8.1%	6.5%	5.4%	5.3%	6.2%	5.1%	5.3%	4.3%	3.8%
France	5.2%	5.8%	6.0%	5.6%	6.0%	5.5%	5.1%	4.3%	4.3%
Italy	3.7%	4.4%	4.1%	4.2%	4.8%	3.9%	3.6%	3.5%	3.4%
Netherlands	2.3%	2.4%	1.5%	2.8%	1.9%	2.0%	2.9%	1.5%	3.5%
Belgium	...	...	...	...	...	...	2.8%	2.9%	2.9%
Canada	4.3%	4.5%	3.6%	3.4%	3.7%	3.2%	3.5%	2.7%	2.5%

Source: WTO 2009a.

Table 2.5 *Rivals' share of the United States' capital market (indicators)*

	SMC 1995	SMC 2007	SMC 2008	Bonds 1995	Bonds 2007	Bonds 2008	Bank 1995	Bank 2007	**Bank 2008**	Total 1995	Total 2007	Total 2008
United States	100%	100%	**100%**	100%	100%	**100%**	100%	100%	**100%**	100%	100%	**100%**
Japan	53%	23%	**27%**	48%	31%	**14%**	148%	70%	**72%**	71%	36%	**44%**
France	8%	14%	**13%**	13%	15%	**5%**	58%	78%	**75%**	22%	26%	**29%**
Germany	8%	11%	**9%**	20%	19%	**7%**	75%	58%	**47%**	28%	23%	**23%**
United Kingdom	21%	19%	**16%**	7%	13%	**5%**	48%	99%	**88%**	20%	31%	**32%**

Notes: SMC = stock-market capitalization; bonds include private and public debt securities.
Source: Author's calculations based on IMF 1997, October 2009.

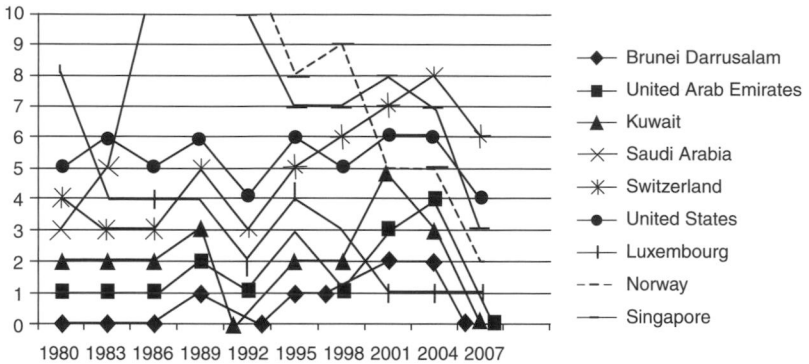

Figure 2.1 Ranking of GNI per capita, PPP
Note: Zero values indicate non-existent data.
Source: IBRD 2009.

An intuitive approach to how the United States fares in the world economy is to attempt a correspondence between the size of the gains and the evolution of the indicators discussed above. One might expect a state that benefits more than others to increase or at least maintain its lead over others in the various areas discussed here. Looking at disproportionality this way, however, misses the point that these size measures are as much influenced by a state's domestic policies as by its foreign policy and most of the time it will be difficult to disentangle the different policy effects. In addition, the relative size of, for example, say a country's capital market can be influenced by the domestic policies of other states (e.g., Japan) or collective action among other states (e.g., the European Union or the euro area).

The next chapter explores different ways of thinking about how the gains from cooperation might be divided. Should they be divided according to countries' size or equally, and what precisely should be divided – the total gains from cooperation or the surplus over what countries can realize individually? Taking the first measure and scaling countries' gross national income (GNI) to size (i.e., population) and adjusting for purchasing power parity (PPP), figure 2.1 ranks the top performing countries from 1 to 10. Where the data does not exist, the entry is plotted as zero. A word of caution is in order for interpreting the years 1980, 1983, 1986, 1992, and 2007, where there is no data for a handful of countries (Brunei Darussalam, the United Arab Emirates, and Kuwait). While this has the effect of changing the number position of countries in the figure, it does not change their relative position in the hierarchy. As another caveat, there are a number of countries where we should expect GNI per capita to be very high, but for which there is no data at all, or where the data is too incomplete to work with (Bermuda, the Channel Islands, Liechtenstein, Monaco, and Qatar). Except for Qatar, with a population of 1.5 million people, all the rest have populations under 100,000 and specialize in financial services, often with some form of financial safe-keeping function. Typically, these are single-cell economies, with no geopolitical role whatsoever. Stripped of their custodial accounts, it is not clear how they would be ranked, or otherwise invent themselves, or even begin to elbow their way through the world economy. With foreign tax authorities cracking down on offshore accounts in the wake of the financial crisis, one of the pillars of the wealth generated by these financial repositories may be in jeopardy.

With these qualifiers in mind, the United States has consistently ranked between fourth and sixth in terms of GNI per capita, as measured by three-year intervals between 1980 and 2007. With the exception of Brunei Darussalam (for which data is lacking), the position of all other countries who made the top five during this period is much more variable. This gives some support to the third leg of my argument about the relative stability of American power, and the fact that it tends to grow following decline. Arguments relating to the waxing and waning of American hegemony are pursued more fully in chapter 3.

Countries ranked above the United States are either oil-producing nations (e.g., Norway, Kuwait, Saudi Arabia, and the United Arab Emirates) or countries that specialize in offering custodial accounts (e.g., Luxembourg and Switzerland), or serve as a financial center and entrepot for trade (e.g., Singapore). With the exception of Saudi Arabia, which ranked above the United States only in 1980 and 1983 and was ranked number 29 in 2007, these are all small countries with populations below 5 million. We can take this as evidence that, under certain circumstances, there is some truth to the claim that small states gain disproportionately from international economic cooperation. This claim has very limited validity, however, since most of these countries, with the exception of Singapore, are not significant players in international trade and monetary cooperation. Their gains come from the resources and services they offer but do not extend to other areas, certainly not to the political realm. Missing from this list are small- to medium-sized European countries, the countries which International Relations scholars have chastized for acting as free-riders. Even as a group, the euro area does not make this list and was ranked number 21 in 2007.

Despite the fact that figure 2.1 lends support to my argument about how the United States gains disproportionately from the international economy, some of the criticisms I raised earlier about tracking statistics that depend on domestic and international cooperation apply here as well.

Another way to think about whether the United States gains more from international cooperation than other states is to examine to what extent it can pursue its preferred policies without assuming the negative consequences that any other country pursuing the same course of action would have to face. This would indicate some special advantage encompassing both political and economic gain. In this book, I will demonstrate how the United States' reserve currency status produces disproportionate commercial gains; how commercial power gives added flexibility in monetary affairs; and, finally, how military preponderance creates both monetary and commercial advantages.

First, despite recurrent trade deficits to the tune of 7 percent of GDP, foreign investors have not fled the dollar to the extent typical of countries running up substantial and sustained deficits, and when financial crisis fell upon the world economy, foreign investors actually fled to the dollar. Import expansion has also supplied American negotiators with a bargaining chip – the ability to offer access to a huge market – in the World Trade Organization (WTO) and conclude trade agreements that for the most part reflect American interests. Although, consistent with my claim that American dominance is just as contingent upon the relative size between other actors as on its size relative to other actors, there is variation across different periods.

Second, I show how the United States benefits economically from its position as monetary hegemon, i.e. as the supplier of the key currency for international financial transactions and reserves. Using new datasets (my own and others'), I will show that the United States is the only country, with a positive investment relationship with the rest of the world, that is able to combine a positive return differential on the international investment position (IIP) and on the income balance with ongoing trade deficits. I will explain how the American capacity to maintain this unique and advantageous pattern derives from its position as monetary hegemon. I will argue further that other countries' dependence on the American market for trade and investment helps us to understand why the United States has been able to maintain its position as the dominant monetary power in the world over the past few decades despite periodic weaknesses in the American economy and relative gains by other economic powers. This leads me to predict that it will remain the dominant monetary power in the immediate future despite current financial and economic difficulties.

Third, I demonstrate how military power has supported American foreign investment and how it has helped attract foreign investment to the United States. In addition, because so many countries rely on American security provision, governments are sometimes willing to go the extra mile with economic assistance and adjustments when the United States finds itself in economic trouble.

Conclusion

Political economists often quip that there is no such thing as a free lunch. While this suggests that a benevolent actor doling out free meals does not exist, there is an implicit assumption in much of the literature that small states benefit disproportionally from hegemonic provision of common goods. At first glance, this conception of hegemony does not appear to have a rational basis, although Duncan Snidal constructed a model to illustrate the logic of smaller states taking advantage of a dominant state pursuing its own interests. In the following chapter, I discuss the assumptions driving the model, and show that replacing them with other, in my view more realistic, assumptions, produces the opposite result, a hegemon benefiting more than smaller states. One of the key modifications I make is to use a curve that more accurately depicts how size impinges on the production of public goods. So while the hegemonic indicators presented in this chapter point to America's continued lead in every issue-area when measured against any single country, and foresee a close draw when measured against groups of countries such as the euro-zone countries (see chapter 7), the following chapter offers a theoretical account of how cooperation among states of various sizes affects gains distribution. Interestingly, the hegemon sometimes stands to benefit from a reduction in the power gap to principal rivals.

3 | *Cooperation under hegemony*

The main defining feature of the international system is anarchy. There is no world government. And ours is not an imperial world. No country today, not even the United States, directly controls the foreign or domestic policies of other states. When states cooperate, they do so in the absence of a formal governing authority to mediate their interests and enforce agreement. Despite the emergence of a decentralized system in which states are not formally subservient to each other or any other entity, a plethora of international institutions exists to organize states. Why do these institutions, or "regimes", exist? Who benefits, and to what extent; who bears the cost, and to what extent?

In this chapter, I provide some answers based on a plausible model of interactions among one large state and several smaller states. I turn first to conventional explanations for the emergence of international institutions (as well as interaction within them). In this section, I also examine gains allocation and the neorealist challenge, identifying problems with both the neoliberal and neorealist account of international institutions. Second, I review how size and public goods have been analyzed in the literature. Third, I briefly outline how one might model international cooperation in the context of a hegemonic power. The proposed model is a revised version of Duncan Snidal's size model and I justify why this is a suitable starting point for considering gains allocation and why modifications are needed in order to do so.[1] Fourth, I present model results. Specifically, I contrast what the revised model tells us about the stability of the current American-centered world order, and offer some counterintuitive insights about the distributive and systemic effects of hegemonic decline.

---

[1] Snidal 1985.

The emergence of international institutions and the neorealist challenge

The economic historian, Charles Kindleberger, captured the imagination of political scientists for more than a generation by characterizing international institutions as public goods from which every state benefits but from which no state can be excluded.[2] The immediate question that arises from conceptualizing international institutions this way, i.e., as public goods, is why anyone would contribute to collective action if they can reap cooperation benefits even if they do not contribute. For Kindleberger, an actor that is large enough will want to provide the good singlehandedly even if it bears the cost alone. But if one actor has an interest in supplying the good on its own, other states will not contribute, if they cannot be excluded. They will free-ride. Because these smaller actors enjoy benefits from public goods without paying for them, they benefit more than the hegemon. This perspective on international cooperation, where there are regular interactions between one dominant state and many smaller states, is known as hegemonic stability theory (HST) in the IR literature.

If an actor can ensure unilateral provision of public goods because of its dominance, why do institutions persist when that actor declines? This question preoccupied scholars in the 1980s, when the United States seemed to be in relative decline. In a classic piece, Snidal constructed a model of HST and showed that the theory was wrong to assume that hegemonic decline would reduce public good provision.[3] Instead, he demonstrated that international institutions would persist even if the hegemon were to decline because others would be more inclined to contribute to public goods. In a seminal contribution, Robert Keohane also argued that there would be continued demand for international institutions despite the hegemon's decline.[4] According to Keohane, various features like repeated interaction, transparency, and monitoring would intervene to solve the collective action problem. In a key contribution, Robert Pahre showed that even if states were operating in a non-cooperative setting, without these cooperation-generating attributes, hegemonic decline would not result in lower levels of public goods (i.e., international institutions),

---

[2] Kindleberger 1981, Kindleberger 1973. His theory is based on Olson 1965.
[3] Snidal 1985.   [4] Keohane 1984.

because smaller states would have incentives to increase their contributions as the leading state contributed less.[5] Despite the different setup, this conception gets close to Snidal's representation of HST and his interpretation of hegemonic decline within that framework. Ikenberry adds another element to these general efforts and shows why international institutions will continue to exist in the face of decline.[6] He argues that the United States' interest in international institutions is constant. By setting up facially neutral structures, which have some independence from other actors in the system, the United States effectively hedges against its own decline, and thereby maximizes long-term benefits.

While these seminal contributions specify the conditions under which international institutions exist, they do not propose to tell us how the gains from cooperation are allocated when public goods are fully provided.[7] Joseph Grieco, however, has drawn our attention to the important consequences of gains distribution.[8] Arguing against the neoliberal creed that states have incentives to cooperate as long as they are better off, he suggested that states are also concerned about how well they do relative to other states. His proposition triggered one of the fiercest debates in the IR literature. Eventually, the controversy about "absolute versus relative gains" boiled down to the question of whether or not the incentive to seek relative gains would inhibit cooperation and thereby thwart international institutions.[9]

But the neorealist complaint about neoliberals' lack of attention to gains distribution is not contingent upon whether states are motivated by relative gains. The problem with the neoliberal account, from a neorealist perspective, is that it does not assume that the dominant state will gain relatively more from international institutions than other states in the system.[10] The neorealists are striking

---

[5] To prove these results Pahre relies on Cournot conjectures: Pahre 1999.
[6] Ikenberry 2001.
[7] Snidal (1985) introduces the problem but chooses not to pursue it fully. Pahre (1999) discusses gains distribution by contrasting a quantitative (Cournot) and qualitative (Stackelberg) interpretation of hegemony. If the hegemon is able to move like any other actor (Cournot), smaller states benefit disproportionately. If the hegemon moves first (Stackelberg), the hegemon benefits disproportionately, as it is able to transfer costs onto other actors, but this also diminishes the supply of public goods.
[8] Grieco 1988, 1990.   [9] See Grieco, Powell, and Snidal 1993.
[10] Grieco 2002.

back by revisiting the distributional consequences of each state doing the best it can. Neorealists, not associated with hegemonic stability theory, believe that the strongest state is well-positioned to gain more than other states. In this chapter, I will show that they are right.

I will argue that in an international context, and under certain plausible assumptions, in which there is one dominant power and one or more lesser powers, the hegemon will gain more than other states from international institutions such as trade regimes or monetary regimes that involve multilateral agreements, and will gain more than it could from pursuing alternative courses of action such as unilateral provision or bilateral coalitions. Counterintuitively, the hegemon often gains more from these international institutions as its power declines. In contrast to accounts by Keohane, Snidal, and Pahre, who explain support for international institutions in terms of the greater interests of smaller states to contribute to the good, my account emphasizes the dominant power's interest to continue working through international institutions.[11] This explains why the United States has been a strong proponent of international institutions and why, despite its recent decline, its support for international institutions remains strong.

Limitations of the neoliberal and neorealist approaches

The neoliberal approach assumes strategic interaction among many states of equal size, and is very helpful in explaining why international institutions emerge in that particular context.[12] The high transaction costs involved with devising agreement between many states across many issue-areas may impede collective action unless there is a system of rules and procedures to guide state behavior. Other barriers to cooperation also exist when a multitude of similarly sized states attempt to collaborate. The lack of information about each other's interests and actions can be a real problem, which institutions can help overcome by providing an arena for regular interaction and a secretariat with monitoring functions. Many smaller states also have a harder time creating effective coalitions because they cannot

---

[11] Keohane 1984; Snidal 1985; Pahre 1999.
[12] See Keohane 1982.

combine to reach the requisite size to make cooperation work without introducing collective action problems. Regimes play an important role in promoting cooperation under these conditions. They facilitate interaction by providing a setting for informal and formal negotiations and framework agreements that regulate state behavior along with mechanisms that increase transparency. Sometimes, as in the case of the WTO, they even establish procedures to punish recalcitrant members.

This idealized setting is a far cry from the international system of the twentieth and twenty-first centuries, when international institutions were set up, and possibly from any given time since the Peace of Westphalia in 1648, when the modern system of sovereign states was introduced. Throughout this period, the main actors have consisted of a few very large and powerful states, or state-like entities such as the European Union (EU), and many much weaker states. This is of great significance because conventional explanations for institutions are not very compelling if what really matters is the interaction between a few large, powerful states. When large power differentials characterize the international system, a small number of powerful states dominate international relations and exercise a disproportionate influence on regime rules and outcomes. In a setting where the essential interaction takes place between limited numbers of actors, transaction costs are significantly reduced, and information shared on unequal terms. With substantial size differentials, states can build bilateral coalitions that are effective threats to a multilateral process. Modeling these features of the international system and the behavior it generates, one can arrive at more realistic predictions about how gains will be allocated in the multilateral arena.

While my position is closer to the neorealist perspective in emphasizing the largest state's interest in institutions, I am not as skeptical as are they about "international arrangements hav[ing] strong independent effects on the preferences, policies, or interactions of states."[13] Instead, I will show that larger states are better off when institutions support cooperative agreements from which they benefit more than from ad-hoc bilateral agreements. While institutions also serve the interests of smaller states, larger states tend to gain much more than them.

---

[13] Grieco attributes this view to Mearsheimer 1994.

Size matters

Most people feel intuitively that a larger, more powerful actor will have a set of distinct advantages when interacting with smaller, weaker actors. In International Relations, the opposite view – that smaller states can free-ride on larger ones and 'get something for nothing' – is a common one. One measure of its success is the litany of criticism leveled against it. Another is the tenacity of the finding that small states fare better than large states in international relations. Before discussing the problems that scholars see in this theory, let me first give a sense of the various size models that exist in International Relations.

In a seminal contribution, Robert Gilpin uses an S-shaped curve to explain the growth and outward extension of hegemonic and imperialist powers.[14] The hegemon or empire can extend its power base quite easily at first. Eventually, however, its economic lead begins to erode and the cost of policing the system becomes more and more expensive, limiting its further expansion. Alesina and Spolaore explain a state's expansion in terms of the trade-off that exists between the benefits tied to providing public goods over a large area and the benefits associated with providing public goods over a homogenous (and therefore smaller) area.[15] Lake and O'Mahony link the type of political system (federal and unitary democracies) to the size of states and use increasing returns to scale to explain the advent of large federal democracies.[16] In common, these accounts focus on explaining why and how a particular state expands. Only Gilpin is interested in how this affects other states but only because he is thinking of a particular kind of state, a hegemon. Here, the impact on other states is just a byproduct of the hegemon's outward extension and the incentives of other states do not figure prominently in the analysis. Instead, the availability of public goods is a function of where on the S-curve the hegemon is located.

Several size models do, however, depict strategic interaction among states. Olson and Zeckhauser derive reaction curves to show that small states have incentives to free ride on a large state that (because of its larger size) attaches a higher value to the public good.[17] Snidal

---

[14] Gilpin 1981.   [15] Alesina and Spolaore 2003.
[16] Lake and O'Mahony 2004.
[17] Olson and Zeckhauser 1966.

develops a computational model of HST in order to criticize it on its own terms.[18] Boyer proposes comparative advantage-based alliances as a way for free-riders to start contributing.[19] A careful treatment of how public goods provision relates to strategic interaction is the analytical framework developed by Aggarwal and Dupont.[20] Theirs is a systematic account of how the problem of cooperation changes with variations in resources, benefits and costs. As I will discuss further on, I attempt something similar, although my objective is to expose how sensitive strategic interaction is to both the functional form that determines public good provision and the threat of exclusion.[21] Pahre uses Cournot and Stackelberg conjectures to explore how benefits are distributed among interacting states of various size (as represented in quantitative and qualitative terms). As a special case, he considered the effect of assuming scale economies in the production of the public good.[22] Pahre's Cournot analysis is closest to the approach used by Snidal, and as a result, the approach used here. There are important differences, though. In Pahre's framework, contributions are a function of income and the contribution levels of others. An actor experiencing an increase (reduction) in income will raise (lower) contributions. The argument produces a nice twist. An asymmetrical distribution of resources is not required for public good provision because, as states with higher income raise contributions, states with lower income contribute less, leaving the total level of contributions constant. Clearly, in this model, introducing scale economies does not alter the result that large states contribute disproportionately to public goods. Pahre's model has the advantage of considering a continuum of contribution levels, which vary according to income. But this also imposes certain limitations. Since contributions are a function of income, no one ever

---

[18] Snidal 1985.   [19] Boyer 1989.

[20] Aggarwal and Dupont 1999.

[21] Because our concerns (and therefore assumptions) are different, it is not surprising that our results are different. While we agree that public goods can potentially be provided when power asymmetries are large, and on the tendency for one actor to acquire Chicken instead of PD preferences when resources are unevenly distributed, our models offer different predictions on who acquires these (Chicken) preferences, as I find only limited support for smaller actors' ability to free-ride on the hegemon and plenty of opportunities for the hegemon to shift the burden of cooperation onto smaller actors.

[22] Pahre 1999,31.

really free-rides, everyone just pays what they can.[23] The leading state contributes the most and poorer states contribute less. Thus, there is little room for the idea that an actor might face incentives not to contribute even though it is able to contribute, as would be the case if a state's free-ride exceeded its net benefits from contributing.

I assume instead, as did Snidal, that the strategic choice, to contribute or free-ride, depends on the total payoff from cooperation. Thus, states will contribute if their payoff (i.e., the benefit derived from their own contribution plus other states' contributions less costs) exceeds their free-riding payoff. With these assumptions, others will not necessarily have incentives to fully compensate for the leading states' contributions if it declines, and will not necessarily be able to provide the good. Because costs and benefits are scaled to size, rising states may not experience sufficient net benefits to provide the good as the leading actor reduces its contributions. In Snidal's HST model, rising states never experience sufficient benefits to jointly and singlehandedly provide the good as the leading state declines. By contrast, when an S-shaped curve is used to describe benefits from public good provision, a coalition of rising states can provide the good alone. Under these circumstances, an ascending state will only contribute *if* another rising state contributes. Only in this case will the good be provided at the same level as the leading state. Thus, in certain cases, states will be more prepared to contribute when others contribute. Incorporating significant scale economics changes the logic of strategic interaction when using these assumptions.

The core proposition in this literature is the finding popularized by Kindleberger, but already developed by Olson and Zeckhauser, that a large state is needed to provide public goods and that small states have incentives to free-ride on the large state's provision, enabling them to reap benefits but avoid costs.[24] The wedge issues separating those who subscribe to this view and those who do not are the nature of hegemony (which I talked about in the last chapter),[25] the public goods assumption, and its central prediction that dominance is a necessary condition for stability.

---

[23] Unless what is meant is that a leading state, which by definition has the highest income, never can free-ride, whereas poor states always tend to the free-riding spectrum of this continuum.

[24] Olson and Zeckhauser 1966; Kindleberger 1981.

[25] As a reminder, the coercive and exploitative strands of hegemony are responses to hegemonic stability in so far that they challenge the idea that a

The public goods assumption

Several scholars criticize hegemonic stability theorists for using a public goods framework to describe the problems tied to international cooperation. Public goods are characterized by jointness of supply and non-exclusion. Jointness of supply ensures that once the good is supplied to one actor it is supplied to all, and that the utility one actor derives from consuming the good does not detract from the utility others derive from consuming it. Non-exclusion means that it is prohibitively costly to exclude actors from enjoying the good. If actors can benefit from public goods without contributing to them, public goods will be under-provided, and a hegemon with a sufficiently large interest in providing the good is needed. However, the whole idea of free-riding states benefiting from a hegemonic state pursuing its own interests hinges on the characterization of international collaboration as a public goods problem. If an important class of international problems does not fit the public good description, a hegemon is not needed to solve the public goods dilemma.

Conybeare did not see free trade as a public good but a Prisoner's Dilemma, in which parties are able to exclude each other from free trade benefits, especially the hegemon, which has especially strong incentives to shift gains in its favor by imposing the optimal tariff.[26] Despite his critique of HST, Conybeare concludes that the hegemon will forego the opportunity to capture disproportionate benefits in order to ensure a cooperative outcome. Gowa, on the other hand, viewed the public goods framework as appropriate, emphasizing the difficulties involved in excluding potential free-riders from public good benefits. To address Gowa's concerns about free-riding, I propose to model international collaboration as an imperfect public good – i.e., not a club good where perfect exclusion is feasible but a good – where excluding members by forming bilateral coalitions still allows the excluded member to enjoy significant free-ride benefits.[27]

Snidal also made the case that the public goods framework has limited applicability to international matters.[28] In effect, although

benevolent hegemon has no choice but to let other states take advantage of it. In other words, coercive means or other uses of political power can be used to shift the gains in its own favor.
[26] Conybeare 1984.   [27] Gowa 1989.
[28] Snidal 1985.

his authoritative analysis of strategic interaction among various sized states is known as a proof of the possibility of cooperation despite hegemonic decline, it is a thinly veiled criticism of the pure public goods edifice as applied to international relations. He suggested that many so-called public goods are public only in so far as the hegemon has an interest in making them so. Two passages illustrate his reservations concerning the two defining attributes of public goods: non-rivalry (i.e., jointess of supply) and non-exclusion. First, with respect to non-rivalry, he warns, "as distributional questions ... become important ... the presence of a regime will not itself suffice to ensure the presence of jointness."[29] Second, with regard to non-exclusion, he argues, "typically we would expect a hegemonic power – even in the benevolent leadership model – to have some minimal ability to exclude other states and for the regime's institutional arrangements to reflect this ability."[30] While Snidal worried about gains distribution and how the threat of exclusion would affect public good provision, he did not model this critique of HST. Instead, his strategy was to disprove the theory, especially its predictions about the consequences of hegemonic decline, by modeling the theory on its own terms. Picking up where Snidal left off, the next section points to possibilities for cooperation once Snidal's own criticism of the theory is taken seriously.

More recently, Lloyd Gruber has shown that the threat of exclusion may even induce cooperation when states are worse off cooperating than under the status quo, because the status quo may no longer be accessible and cooperating may therefore be better than being excluded from agreement.[31] If, to avoid exclusion, states are prepared to accept agreements that are less beneficial than the agreement in force at the start of negotiations, it follows that actors capable of devising exclusionary arrangements have incentives to threaten exclusion to impose benefit-sharing schemes that work to their advantage. However, I adopt a less stringent requirement for the threat of exclusion to be effective. In so far as there are public aspects to the good being provided, and therefore institutions in general, states are not necessarily worse off when locked out of bilateral arrangements, since the worst that can happen is that they obtain their free ride. Consequently, in order for a stable equilibrium to exist in which the hegemon is able

---

[29] Snidal 1985, 591.   [30] Snidal 1985, 592.
[31] Gruber 2001.

to claim a disproportionate share of the surplus from multilateral cooperation, weaker states cannot systematically reap higher gains from unilateralism or bilateralism than from multilateralism.[32]

While the specification of assumptions is to some extent irreducibly arbitrary, the purpose of this section was to show that the adjustments presented in the next section are theoretically defensible. As I will show in subsequent chapters, they also yield results that provide a good empirical fit. In the following section, I will explain the adjustments I offer to Snidal's model and provide appropriate justifications.

Revised size model

In a revised version of Snidal's HST model, I assume the following, each of which I will justify in turn:

- An S-shaped curve with a significant segment of increasing returns in the production function, reflecting magnified benefits with size increments.
- Some rivalry in consumption.
- Credible and effective threats of exclusion when these offer superior rewards to multilateral cooperation.

First, I leverage the intuition that an S-shaped curve can and should be used to model public good *benefits* when states of varying size interact. The S-shaped curve subsumes all the possible returns from cooperation – the possibility of increasing returns, constant returns, and decreasing returns to scale. This modification allows me to offer a comprehensive account of what different sized states, and combinations of states, can achieve when promoting international institutions. Second, I conceptualize international institutions as imperfect public goods, with some fluidity on the rivalry and exclusivity dimension. These goods nonetheless remain public with positive externalities and possibilities to free-ride. They are not subject to complete rivalry, or complete excludability, which would turn them into private or club goods. Specifically, I allow parties to exclude each other from cooperation.

---

[32] For Gruber, smaller states are worse off with multilateral agreements than from unilateral action.

These changes yield interesting insights. First, once these assumptions are used, the problem of cooperation switches from one of inducing Great Power cooperation when Great Powers gain more from free-riding than cooperating to one of preventing the United States from claiming a disproportionate share of gains. The widespread impression that the United States has developed non-cooperative preferences – its intransigence in Security Council negotiations over Iraq, its refractory posture in the Doha Round negotiations, openly threatening bilateralism by declaring to solely deal with "will-do nations" – does not fit with the image of the United States as a benevolent hegemon that one finds in much of the literature, but fits comfortably with the reconstructed model. Second, while one might intuitively suspect that dominant states would shift the burden of cooperation onto less powerful ones, the reconstructed model counterintuitively demonstrates that the United States has greater incentives to do this as a result of its relative decline. Unless other great powers suddenly become uncharacteristically assertive and risk-acceptant, we should therefore expect American hegemony to be stable. These results depend critically on adopting *both* refinements together, i.e., adopting an S-shaped curve while relaxing exclusivity.[33]

The assumption of increasing returns in the S-curve

Throughout, I assume that all states consume all of the good. As a result, the production function is also the utility function. If size confers a unique advantage, this should be reflected in the production function. It is fairly standard to assume that output can expand disproportionately to inputs with increased size. Economists use scale economies (i.e., increasing returns to scale) to describe a production process that is able to enhance capabilities more than proportionally through successive size increments.

Applied to public goods provision, the concept of scale economies suggests that states need to acquire a critical mass before collaboration

---

[33] Allowing for exclusivity without the possibility of more than proportional gains will not permit effective coalitions to form, and incorporating the potential for increasing returns without introducing some exclusivity will not allow actors to threaten bilateral coalitions in order to practice gains shifting. Thus, the results presented in this chapter do not contradict the result that small states gain disproportionally to large ones if we introduce increasing returns in a Cournot framework, as argued by Pahre.

pays off. This brings implicit assumptions in much of the literature into the open. The hidden assumptions are that a hegemon gains much more than it contributes to cooperation and so is willing to bear disproportionate costs, and that benefits are magnified as additional states join in. Applied to trade, for instance, benefits are amplified as free trade is practiced over a larger area. However, although increasing returns are present over a segment of the function, every process has a limit, and so we should expect benefits eventually to level off. At some point, increasing returns from pooling capabilities increase at a decreasing rate and gains begin to recede as more members combine. Substantively, this suggests that, as the number of states grows, there is greater room for disagreement about what form cooperation should take, and also fewer benefits per state. So, the greater the number of states, the more likely it is that any particular state will enjoy higher gains from free-riding than from cooperating, leaving the group worse off. Initial improvements in collective action will generate more than proportional returns in the public good but, sooner or later, with more states involved, states will reap less than proportional gains. Thus, we should expect to see a "weak S" curve, not the kind of steeply decreasing returns associated with a logistics curve. The fact that returns do not decrease precipitously but rather tend to level off with a carrying capacity of more than 200 states (see figure 3.1) is a plausible assumption for most public goods since the entire world is often the optimal area.

The particular curve used to represent public good provision is a special form of the Gompertz curve, which is asymmetrical around the inflection point.[34] This function lends itself to analysis of international public goods because it suggests that there are benefits to including all states even though most benefits materialize once a quorum is reached. As shown in figure 3.1, public good benefits first increase rapidly, then slowly, before reaching an asymptotic limit, and eventually flattening out as the group expands. The inflection point can be found at E_1, where the curve switches from being slightly convex to being concave with marginal benefits declining.[35] Although benefits are decreasing at an increasing rate at this point, there are

---

[34] See Winsor 1932. A similar curve has been used to model arms race dynamics: see Lambelet, Luterbacher, and Allan 1979.

[35] More precisely, the inflection point is at 4 units of the good and a utility level 7.4.

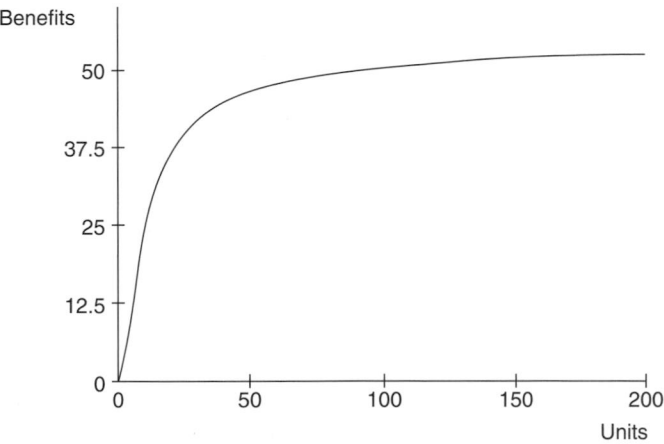

Figure 3.1 Production curve for public goods
Note: The inflection point is at 4 units of the good, and 7.4 benefits.

additional gains to be had from expanding group size. When the functional form used to represent public good (g) provision exhibits increasing returns, e.g., $e^{\beta-\frac{\phi}{g}}$, with marginal benefits $(\phi/x^2)e^{(-\beta-\phi/g)}$, all states gain more from cooperation than from free-riding if everyone cooperates.

Figure 3.2 relates total benefits to costs and shows that public good benefits start to outstrip provision costs when an actor achieves size four or more or is able to pool resources through a coalition of aggregate size four. If, as Snidal assumed, the aggregate size of the Great Powers influencing the international system was 12, this would for instance mean that the United States' size in the postwar era up until the 1970s was 8, whereas the size of smaller Great Powers (i.e., Germany and Japan) was 2, for a size ratio of 8:2:2. One thus arrives at different configurations of power by varying these size ratios. In terms of the numerical simulation undertaken here (and in Snidal's 1985 article), this means that in a three-actor model, two smaller Great Powers are able to produce benefits net of costs if the leading actor is twice their joint size. Thus, the two smaller Great Powers do not have to build a coalition of the same size as the leading actor in order to produce public goods at a net benefit. It suffices that their joint size is half the hegemon's size. In this sense, the function used here constrains the hegemon more than the one used by Snidal to represent HST. Using

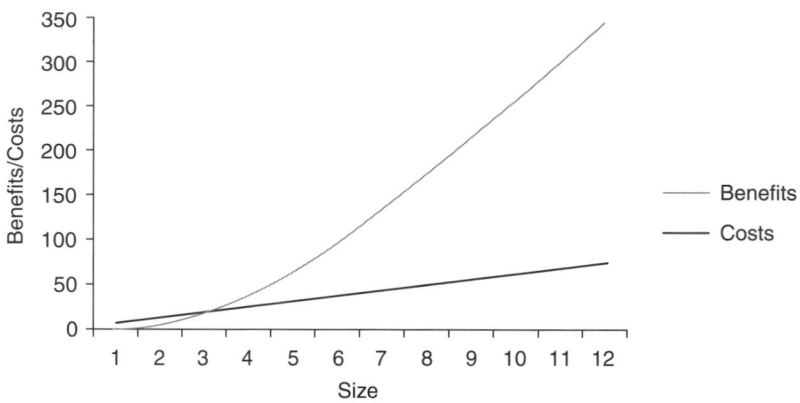

Figure 3.2 Public good benefits and provision cost

a standard decreasing returns function, the two smaller Great Powers are unable to jointly provide the good even if they reach the same size as the hegemon. The effect of using this particular function is to introduce more competition in the process of public good provision across different size distributions.

The modification of the functional form of the production function changes the logic of collective action in ways that will turn out to have important consequences. The good remains public, supplied to everyone, even those who do not contribute. A larger initial effort is however needed for collective action to produce the good. This particular modification brings size to the fore of the analysis. Preventing small states from free-riding becomes a minor challenge when size determines interaction among states, whereas accommodating the largest actor's demands becomes a major challenge.

The assumption of rival gains

Most situations in international relations present states with opportunities to pursue mutual gains. All states benefit if there is an international order that is peaceful, that respects property rights (so that economic actors are willing to trade and invest), that contains relatively few barriers to trade, and that has a reliable medium of exchange. Notwithstanding these shared gains, there is some degree of rivalry in realizing common goals. All states may benefit from a stable order in which interstate relations are harmonious and markets open, but some states will benefit more than others because they are better able to influence the terms of an open world order, and their firms are better able to benefit from that order.

If states commit to the cooperative equilibrium, how much should they expect to receive over and above what they are able to achieve when playing non-cooperatively? I propose to resolve the bargaining dilemma by considering what each actor is able to obtain by threatening a viable (bilateral) coalition.

The assumption of exclusion

My last assumption is that threats of exclusion are credible and effective when all members of the coalition are better off than under multilateralism. This represents an intermediate category between public and club goods, since states have variable and limited capacity to exclude each other. States' capacity to exclude one another depends on their pooled size. Not all dyads command sufficient resources to credibly threaten exclusion. Some bilateral coalitions are prohibitively costly. Exclusion is also limited in the sense that non-members cannot be entirely excluded from benefits. Members of the coalition can exclude non-members from member benefits but cannot exclude non-members from free-riding benefits. Thus, there is some fluidity in the measurement of both rivalry and exclusion.[36]

Benefit sharing

Snidal proposed four ways of allocating benefits: distribute payoffs according to contributions (PC); distribute payoffs according to equal shares (PES); distribute joint gains according to contributions (JGC); distribute joint gains according to equal shares (JGES). Each of these represents a possible benchmark of fairness. As I will demonstrate, there are always opportunities for the hegemon to gain more than

---

[36] One way of understanding excludability is to decompose a good with an externality into a private and public good, $G_e = G_p + G_q$, and to empirically assess the size of the excludable good G_p/G_e. This approach makes sense if actors cannot use G_p/G_e strategically to influence the substantive effect of G_e and the relative size of G_p and G_q. If, however, one suspects that strategic use of G_p/G_e affects bargaining outcomes, there is a need to incorporate the possibility of exclusion in explaining cooperation under hegemonic leadership. I thank Robert Pahre for this comment, which also is the view taken by Russett (1985).

according to the scheme that distributes joint gains according to contributions, and sometimes more than distributing payoffs according to
contributions. When the hegemon realizes an allocation that exceeds
distributing joint gains according to contributions, it is in effect taking a greater share of the surplus from cooperation than any other
actor and, in particular, a share of the surplus that is disproportionate
to what it contributes.[37]

Below, I report what the model predicts in terms of how benefits are
shared.[38] The model points to two sources of bargaining power, the
"power of initiative" and "gains-shifting power." The power of initiative is the power to propose a distribution, which depends on which
outcome is equilibrium. Gains-shifting power is the power to propose
a distribution, which is disproportionately beneficial and self-enforcing. According to model results, the hegemon's bargaining power, as
defined by these two different forms of power, is much larger than
commonly assumed and also much more context-dependent – in other
words, much more contingent on how power is distributed between
itself and other actors in the system as well as on the distribution of
power among other actors in the system.

When the United States is twice as large as the two other Great
Powers (Germany and Japan) combined (i.e., under the size ratio
8:2:2), the United States is alone in having the "power of initiative,"
since a single stable solution can be found where the United States'
multilateral offer is the equilibrium. If, in addition, the United States
can induce other states to participate in a multilateral coalition at
relatively low cost (by compensating for actors' unilateral alternatives and offering modest side-payments), the United States can actually realize an allocation that is higher than distributing joint gains
according to contributions, which is its second most preferred alternative. Roughly, this corresponds to the period prior to the early 1970s,
before the first oil price shock.

---

[37] Notice that the hegemon always stands to gain more from sharing payoffs
according to contributions than from sharing joint gains according to
contributions. This is because its share of contributions is higher than its
share of baseline gains.
[38] For a full discussion of how public goods provision translates into strategic
interaction in a non-cooperative environment, and how benefits are shared
(under different size ratios) in a non-cooperative setting of bilateral threats,
see Norrlof 2008.

However, American bargaining power declined somewhat as Europe organized and the Japanese economy took off in the early to mid-1970s. With the two smaller Great Powers equally sized, and together accounting for capabilities equal to the United States', this would correspond to a size ratio of 6:3:3. In this new situation, the United States is no longer unique in having "power of initiative". Instead, all states have the capacity to propose a distribution given that there are three equilibria: one where the United States decides the distribution, one where the EU decides, and one where Japan decides. However, the equilibria where the EU's and Japan's offers are accepted are not as stable as the equilibrium where the United States' offer is accepted: as they depend on the size of the side-payment. It is nevertheless important to note that the United States loses this form of bargaining power in this particular phase of decline. The United States is, however, in as good a position to extract gains from the bargaining process as either of the smaller Great Powers. If the outcome where the United States decides the distribution materializes, it again receives more benefits than if joint gains had been distributed according to contributions (i.e., its second preferred distribution scheme). For comparison, if the outcome where either the European Community or Japan proposes how to allocate benefits materializes, either one of them (but not both simultaneously) is able to achieve an allocation that is better than distributing payoffs according to equal shares (i.e., is their second preferred distribution scheme). However, even under these unfavorable conditions, the United States still does better than in the HST model, where it is exploited as it declines.[39]

As Europe continues to grow stronger at Japan's expense (i.e., a size ratio of 6:4:2), American political and economic power receives a boost, even though the joint capability of smaller Great Powers remains constant. Both the United States and the European Union have the power of initiative with this change in the configuration of power. Only if the side-payment remains within a particular interval can Japan also decide the distribution. In other words, the European Union gains the power of initiative at Japan's expense. The European

[39] Using my figure 3.5, and table 5 in Snidal (1984, 609), yields a game with an equilibrium where the United States is exploited in the specific sense of receiving negative benefits from multilateral cooperation if $\alpha < 7.2$. If $\alpha > 7.2$, the United States forms an alliance with either the EC or Japan and receives negative benefits from bilateral cooperation.

Union also acquires "gains- shifting" power and, more unexpectedly, so does the United States. If the United States is able to decide the distribution, it not only gains disproportionately to distributing *joint gains* according to contributions but disproportionately to distributing *payoffs* according to contributions, its most preferred distribution principle. This result is contingent upon a very small side-payment. If the European Union decides the distribution, it also gains more than under its most preferred distribution principle.

In a second phase of hegemonic decline, the United States is no longer as strong as the other two Great Powers combined. Here, we can imagine that America declines relative to Japan or China, whereas the European Union's power base remains unchanged, so that the size ratio is 5:4:3. Normally, we would expect America's bargaining power to diminish significantly at this critical threshold. However, the analysis yields unexpected results. There are three equilibria, so all three Great Powers have power of initiative. However, each outcome is not equally likely to obtain. The outcome where the United States decides the distribution is most likely to materialize, since it is viable under a wider range of possible side-payments, and the outcomes where either the European Union or Japan/China propose a self-enforcing distribution are equally likely to occur. If actors require very large side-payments in addition to receiving their best unilateral course of action as compensation, the outcome where the United States decides how to distribute benefits in a bilateral coalition with the European Union may also emerge as a stable equilibrium. From a distributive perspective, so in terms of the second form of bargaining power, such a coalition is not beneficial to the United States. What the United States must offer the European Union in such a bilateral alliance far exceeds anything the European Union could achieve through any of the distribution principles. A bilateral alliance with the European Union is a drag on its resource base, producing an allocation much below the United States' baseline of providing the common good unilaterally.

If instead the multilateral outcome – where the United States has the power of initiative – materializes, and as long as coalition formation is relatively inexpensive (i.e., side-payments are small), the United States can gain disproportionately to the principle that distributes payoffs according to contributions (its most preferred distribution principle) and can for higher side-payments also realize an allocation which is disproportionate to the principle that distributes joint gains according to contributions (its second most preferred distribution scheme). With the power of initiative, the best that either the European Union or Japan/China can do, in terms of extracting gains from the bargaining process, however, is to reap gains disproportionate to the principle that distributes joint gains according to contributions. The European Union is able to do this by offering lower side-payments than Japan/China and also receives a more favorable distribution than Japan/China, achieving gains that are disproportionate to its second *most* preferred distribution scheme rather than, as in the case of Japan/China, their second *least* preferred distribution scheme. An interesting aspect of American decline is that the United States can actually reap benefits disproportionate to the principle that distributes joint gains according to contributions (its second most preferred distribution scheme), even if the European Union or Japan/China propose the distribution. America's potential scope for gains shifting continues to increase with decline.

Systemic stability and hegemonic decline

The flipside of the HST argument that dominance breeds stability is that the hegemon's decline will wreak systemic havoc. What is particularly chilling about this prognosis is that decline is seen not only as inevitable but also as imminent. The hegemon must weaken relative to other states, given the theory's predictions about smaller states not contributing to public goods and the capacity this gives smaller states to benefit disproportionately from international cooperation.

Keohane and Snidal's predictions – that the waning of American power did not have to jeopardize cooperation – were in this context reassuring. As mentioned at the outset of this chapter, Keohane explained the persistence of cooperation in terms of states' continued demand for regimes.[40] Snidal demonstrated that collective action depends as much on the hegemon's size, as it does on the size of other actors in the international system. By paying attention to the size of all Great Powers, not just the hegemon, Snidal opened up the possibility that a more symmetrical distribution of power might enhance the prospects for the provision of public goods, thus offering a potential explanation for the otherwise puzzling persistence of cooperation in

[40] Keohane 1982.

the 1980s despite America's relative decline. The likelihood for cooperation increases with American decline because the hegemon can no
longer singlehandedly provide the good as it declines, so smaller states
have to chip in for the good to be provided. If one were to use Snidal's
production function in the revised model (i.e., by plugging the numbers from his production function into the revised model), the waning
hegemon continues to be taken advantage of. While Snidal was modeling a theory he did not believe in, these distributional implications
haunt the literature and cast decline as inescapable and continuous.

Predictions of American decline have been pervasive since the 1970s.
A product of the dollar, the multinational corporation, and nuclear
weapons, US hegemony was, according to Gilpin, surprisingly fragile.[41]
The particular brand of hegemony touted by the United States and
the United Kingdom, prioritizing foreign investment at the expense
of domestic investment and therefore exports, would necessarily lead
to decline. With all the excitement these days about American exposure to the whims of foreign investors, it is ironic that thirty years ago
the increased dependence of American investors on host governments
was a "source of political vulnerability."[42] For Gilpin, the hegemon's
relative decline was linked to the process of technological diffusion, a
phenomenon exacerbated by openness, since foreign investment relo-
cates to areas where resources including labor can be acquired at low
cost.[43] Gilpin suggests that Pax Americana has made a difference, that
the government insisted on national treatment for American firms,
implemented favorable tax laws, and "provided the security and political order for the expansion of MNC activity." Gilpin sees these
actions as purposefully pursued but nonetheless conspiring against
the United States in the long run. The only way for the United States
to stay on top is to innovate itself out of the capitalist bind which
"plants the seeds of its own destruction in that it diffuses economic
growth, industry, and technology, and thereby undermines the distribution of power upon which the liberal, independent economy has
rested."[44] In the political realm, however, Gilpin saw the hegemon's
decline as being brought on by deliberate gains calculations on the
part of rivals.[45]

---

[41] Gilpin 1975.   [42] Gilpin 1975.
[43] Gilpin 1975.   [44] Gilpin 1975, 45. For discussion, see Sylvan 1981.
[45] Gilpin 1975.

While Kennedy too worried about American hegemony not being sustainable from an economic point of view, he saw decline as a function of upbeat political ambitions, not the loss of economic verve.[46] On his account, the hegemon's security tasks chipped away at its economic foundations. Like other Great Powers, the United States was likely to decline relative to other countries because of the tendency of economically dominant states to expand and over-extend themselves militarily. Kennedy was right that unilateral foreign policy campaigns could undermine American hegemony, although, for reasons I develop in chapter 6, it will probably take more than the present war in Iraq to alter the configuration of power in the world. Kennedy's overstretch argument, however, presumes a unidirectional link between economic and military power. Although economic performance is the bedrock of military might in Kennedy's analysis, the relationship is not reciprocal. Twenty years on, it is still commonplace for neoliberals to downgrade the role of military power for economic cooperation in much the same way that neorealists downplayed the significance of economic interactions for military cooperation. Emphasizing the non-military aspects of American rule, Keohane solicited a conversation about whether military power matters for economic power.[47] Still, for the most part, those who acknowledge the United States' military primacy see it as a second-rate economic force with military overstretch compounding economic decline. Seldom are economic and military power seen as mutually reinforcing.

In today's debate on American decline redux, scholars continue to assume a substitute relation between economic and political power. Bacevich, for instance, sees the United States as a global enforcer that uses new advanced means to practice old-style gunboat diplomacy, a development he laments and sees as more or less irreversible.[48] Ferguson draws a similar conclusion concerning America's role as global policeman but instead of worrying about it, he applauds it, and warns that the empire may be in trouble if it does not get its economic house in order. Lal believes the United States is an empire, and like Ferguson he thinks it ought to be one, with the prospects of remaining one limited only by its reluctance to live by Queen Elizabeth I's maxim "not to make windows into men's souls."[49] American meddling with

---

[46] Kennedy 1987.   [47] Keohane 1982, 41.
[48] Bacevich 2002.   [49] Lal 2004, 213.

the mores and practices in other countries is seen as especially devastating for its dominance. While Mann too sees the United States as a "military giant," he does not think military power is of much use, and disparagingly calls it an economic "backseat driver."[50] Mann clearly sees the United States as a power in decline. In two books, Chalmers Johnson describes the proliferation of American bases around the world, the resentment they create, and how it might provoke decline.[51] The French analyst Emmanuel Todd indicts the United States for outright banditry, "the mugging of Europeans by Wall Street," but does not believe the United States has the military wherewithal to ensure that it can continue to reap disproportionate economic benefits, or that it is capable of the kind of political (non-discriminatory) rule that attracts dependable followers.[52]

Not everyone has been convinced that the United States has declined in any meaningful way. As several authors have pointed out, the relative ascendancy of Europe and Japan was not only to be expected, but an explicit aim of American policy after the war.[53] Critics charged that those who believed that the United States had declined in significant ways had failed to grasp important changes in the international economy and the prominent role played by multi-national corporations.[54] To appreciate the full extent of America's reach one had to take into account the functioning of the world economy, the vitality of the American economy, the diversity of its population, and its military preponderance. Samuel Huntington was particularly prescient in identifying what kept America on top and in spelling out challenges to its lead position. He saw the country's multi-dimensional power base as difficult for others to replicate and understood that the dynamism of the American economy would take a blow if consumer overstretch got out of hand, even though he believed that the most serious challenge to American power would come from a coalition of European states.[55] While Huntington correctly perceived that America's preeminence is anchored across a wide range of issue-areas, he did not connect these different sources of power.

In elaborating an alternative way of thinking about the hegemon's power arc, I show how various forms of power mutually reinforce

---

[50] Mann 2003.   [51] Johnson 2000, 2004.
[52] Todd 2003.   [53] Russett 1985; Huntington 1988/89.
[54] Gill 1990; Nye 1990.   [55] Huntington 1988/89, 88.

one another as the hegemon travels up and down the power ladder. As I have already suggested, the consequences of relative decline are potentially favorable to the hegemon and can in some circumstances activate power.

What then are causes of hegemonic decline within my framework? The hegemon's relative slippage may be the result of other states' devising cooperative schemes from which the hegemon is excluded, the euro area for instance, or could be the result of internal problems within the hegemonic state, unproductive spending on the part of citizens or government. Although the hegemon can afford to mismanage its economy to a greater extent than others, accumulating greater liabilities than other states could ever get away with, debt in combination with poor domestic or foreign policies could still whittle down its power base. Yet, in contrast to several authors on American hegemony, I do not believe international cooperation is likely to diffuse power, in ways that fundamentally change the distribution of power, unless states adopt riskier, more assertive, policies deliberately to thwart American hegemony.

Just as complementarities between different power dimensions – trade, money, and security – placed the United States in a position of dominance, a negative power loop could eventually trigger its demise if strong, defiant opposition appeared. I will argue, however, that the system is stable as long as key countries are not weighed down by heavy loss, and as long as credible alternatives to American hegemony do not exist. Indeed, the United States has "sticky power" as other countries have become large stake-holders in the American economy, both commercially and financially.[56] The decline of America's soft power would be a potential threat to both its hard and sticky power. If the United States were to lose its power to attract, it would increasingly have to substitute hard for soft power. Countries would be less and less persuaded of the merits of depending on the American market and leadership. These power types reinforce each other negatively (not only positively). Without sticky power the American economy would have to abide by the same laws as other countries, making it difficult to simultaneously boost investments and military spending. Without hard power, the United States would no longer benefit from the security premium that countries are willing to pay when investing in the American economy,

[56] Mead 2004, 52.

and governments would not be quite as eager to smooth sail the economy if the United States were unable to enforce a stable world order.

Conclusion

The conventional wisdom on public goods provision in a system dominated by a single power presupposes that the manner in which gains are distributed is *not* advantageous to the hegemon. By allowing free-riding, or in order to mitigate free-riding, the hegemon accepts a distribution of gains that favors smaller powers, and thus stabilizes the system at some cost.

By specifically addressing issues that Snidal viewed as problematic in hegemonic stability theory, yet bracketed for purposes of his analysis, such as the question of gains distribution and the possibility of exclusion, I show that a leading state can benefit disproportionately from public good provision by threatening to supply club goods instead of public goods as long as it enjoys an absolute size advantage. This allows me to revisit Grieco's important insight that states care about how the gains from cooperation are distributed, and that a dominant actor creates and acts through international institutions because it stands to gain more from them (than any other actor in the system).

The revised model reveals that the leading power always has the *possibility* (i.e., the power of initiative) to extract a disproportionate share of surplus benefits, and sometimes a disproportionate share of the total benefits, from international cooperation, although whether it will succeed also depends on the power of initiative vested with other actors and their ability to extract gains from the bargaining process. Under certain structural conditions, the leading power is in an exceptionally good position to gain disproportionately, explaining its interest in furthering cooperation while possible balancers put up with a (disproportionately) lower share of gains from cooperation lest they be excluded from public goods should the leading power seek bilateral solutions to common problems.

In discussing different ways to share benefits, and disentangling who gains what, I make a distinction between two different forms of bargaining power – the power of initiative and the power of gains-shifting. The United States occupied a privileged position, in terms of its power of initiative, and its capacity to extract benefits from international cooperation up until the early 1970s, when it towered over other states, and its power base was twice as large as Germany and Japan's combined.

In a first phase of decline, as Germany and Japan together were able to match America's capability (i.e., the size ratio looked something like 6:3:3), the United States had to start to share its agenda-setting power with these smaller Great Powers, and its ability to extract gains from the bargaining process suffered. American bargaining power took a hit in the specific sense that it was now equally poised to enforce its second most preferred distribution (as were smaller Great Powers). This situation persisted until the early 1990s. From that time until the onset of the third millennium, American capability remained constant, whereas the European Union grew stronger, at the expense of Japan, representing the size ratio 6:4:2. This development was beneficial for both the United States and Europe. Both the United States and the European Union acquired agenda-setting power, although the United States had this form of power under a wider range of circumstances than the European Union, whereas Japan only had agenda-setting power in very limited circumstances. Predictably, the European Union acquired gain-shifting power as the United States declined, although, surprisingly, so did the United States. Both the United States and the European Union are able to gain disproportionately to their most preferred distribution scheme. American support for European integration can be understood in light of the model and thus on other than ideological or cultural grounds. Rather than viewing Europe as a potential balancer, American governments might have suspected that they had more to gain from a strong Europe than from a diffusion of power between Europe and Japan.

A second phase of American decline took place as China thundered onto the world scene in the third millennium, and American domestic and foreign policies were mismanaged. With European power remaining constant, the distribution of power could be represented by the size ratio 5:4:3. Unexpectedly, the model predicts a greater capacity of the hegemon to practice gains shifting at this critical juncture. All three Great Powers have the power of initiative but prospects for the different outcomes vary, with the United States' proposal most likely to be entertained and equal prospects for the two smaller Great Powers' proposals to be entertained. When the bargaining process is conflict-ridden, and characterized by intense rivalry (i.e., high side-payments), a bilateral coalition between the United States and the European Union, (unfavorable to the United States), could materialize (see Uruguay Round negotiations, chapter 4). The United States, however, is able to propose a self-enforcing multilateral coalition and to benefit disproportionally to its most preferred distribution scheme, whereas smaller Great Powers are only able to make multilateral offers from which they gain disproportionately to their second *most* preferred (i.e., the European Union) or second *least* preferred (i.e., China) distribution scheme. In addition, even if the European Union or China proposes the distribution, the United States can still reap benefits disproportionate to the principle that distributes joint gains according to contributions, its second most preferred distribution scheme. America's potential scope for gains shifting, more specifically to enjoy a disproportionate share of the surplus and even total cooperation benefits, continues to increase with decline.

A major implication of the revised model is that American leverage is variable across different size ratios, and at least as contingent upon the relative size between other states as on its power gap to other states.

American hegemony, and the order it generates, is surprisingly stable. What makes the system stable is the hegemon's interest in achieving disproportionate gains through international cooperation and other Great Powers' interest in achieving gains above what they can achieve through unilateral action. A benevolent hegemon would not seek disproportionate benefits whereas an exploitative hegemon uses force to seek disproportionate benefits, and risks turning allies into balancers and adversaries. There is at present no prospect of this. Pax Americana persists, despite a gradual increase in American exceptionalism and a rising sense that the United States no longer carries the burden of underwriting global order in a manner commensurate with its size and role. This shifts our focus from the question of whether collective action *will* take place to *how* different forms of cooperation are connected (bilateral and multilateral) and how the gains from multilateral cooperation are distributed. In the following chapters we will see how this theoretical proposition rhymes with collaboration in the trade area (chapter 4), in monetary and financial affairs (chapter 5), and in the security field (chapter 6), and we also examine where today's collective action to circumvent American power might take us (chapter 7). Will it lead us to a new world order or right back to the American-centered system in which we live?

4 | *International trade cooperation*

A common assumption in the IR and PE literature is that international institutions, and the policies they embody, are public goods. What does the economics literature say on this score? That is the topic of the first section of this chapter, in which I review traditional and new trade theories and look at how one might represent the "good" of free trade. In a second section, I relate the trade deficit to the balance of payments and the international investment position, and examine different perspectives on their origin, and why they are normally shunned. A third section explores how running serial deficits has been good for America, allowing consumers to enjoy goods beyond the production and export possibility frontier, while allowing firms to expand the production and sale of final goods by importing cheap intermediate inputs. A fourth section suggests that import expansion has been a source of bargaining power, benefiting American firms by offering them opportunities to extend their global reach. By expanding imports, the American government has been in a good position to exchange access to the American market for American access to foreign markets. The last section of this chapter demonstrates how the United States has benefited from the trade regime and how it has used the threat of exclusion to advantage under various configurations of power. As I will show, and as argued in the model presented in chapter 3, the United States has been well placed to reap disproportionate benefits in international economic negotiations although its bargaining power is structurally contingent and depends at least as much on the relative size difference *between* other Great Powers as on its own preponderance.

Trade theories

From an economic point of view, it is well established that open exchange is potentially welfare-enhancing at both the national and international levels. Elaborated in the long window from the eighteenth to the twentieth century, classical and neoclassical theories have had a profound impact on the postwar system regulating trade, and are the basis of international institutions such as the General Agreement on Tariffs and Trade (GATT) and its successor, the World Trade Organization (WTO).

Both the classical and neoclassical approaches view trade among different countries as being potentially welfare-enhancing. The north and south have complementary economies, and can therefore gain substantially from trading with each other. The north has a comparative advantage in producing capital-intensive goods while the south has a comparative advantage producing labor-intensive goods. By trading goods, countries are indirectly trading differences in factor endowments and technology, and stand to gain mutually.

Classical trade theory

In *The Wealth of Nations*, Adam Smith showed that countries should specialize in producing goods which they can turn out at lower cost than other countries, that is, in goods where they have an absolute cost advantage:[1]

Whether the advantages which one country has over another be natural or acquired is in this respect of no consequence. As long as the one country has those advantages, and the other wants them, it will always be more advantageous for the latter rather to buy of the former than to make.[2]

Differences in technology are, for Smith, a source of trade which, through the division of labor, creates joint rewards limited only by the extent of the market.[3] According to Smith, countries should trade freely, except for when the imposition of an equalization tax is necessary to offset domestic taxes or safeguard a country's defense industry: "of much more importance than opulence, the act of navigation is, perhaps, the wisest of all the commercial regulations of England."[4]

Smith not only provided us with a systematic way of thinking about the division of labor, but was also politically astute, recognizing the

---

[1] Smith 1991.   [2] Smith 1991, 401–2.
[3] Buchanan and Yoon 1994.   [4] Smith 1991, 407.

importance of reciprocal threats and promises in sustaining free trade: "[t]here may be good policy in retaliations of this kind, when there is a probability that they will procure the repeal of the high duties or prohibitions complained of..."[5] Smith was also attuned to the fact that there might be circumstances under which countries were better off with a gradual move towards free trade: "[h]umanity may in this case require that the freedom of trade should be restored only by slow gradations, and with a good deal of reserve and circumspection."[6]

Almost half a century would pass before any major revision to Smith's magisterial work. In the early decades of the nineteenth century, David Ricardo proposed that countries should trade not on the basis of absolute but comparative advantage, an idea which had been circulating among the most prominent economists of the time, and which Paul Samuelson would eventually extol as "the most beautiful idea in economics." According to the economic historian Douglas Irwin, Ricardo received all the credit for a theory that had really been elaborated by Robert Torrens and James Stuart Mill, as well as James's son, John Stuart Mill.[7] We nevertheless see the concept of comparative advantage – the idea that a country can gain from trade even if it can produce all goods more efficiently than others – expressed clearly in Ricardo's *Principles of Political Economy and Taxation* from 1816:[8]

because it would be advantageous to her rather to employ her capital in the production of wine, for which she would obtain more cloth from England, than she could produce by diverting a portion of her capital from the cultivation of vines to the manufacture of cloth.[9]

The leap taken by Ricardo was to reason in terms of opportunity cost. What a country was best suited to produce would depend on what it had to give up in terms of one good if it were to produce another. The famous example given by Ricardo himself was to imagine that Portugal not only produces wine more efficiently than cloth but produces both goods (wine and cloth) more efficiently than England. Whereas "Smithian" absolute advantage does not imagine trade between Portugal and England under these conditions, Ricardo

[5] Smith 1991, 410–11. [6] Smith 1991, 410–11
[7] Irwin 1996, 89–92. [8] Ricardo 1996.
[9] Ricardo 1996, 94.

saw that trade could still be profitable. If Portugal were to funnel all her resources into wine production, she could, by selling surplus wine, get more cloth from England than she could produce at home. Comparable levels of Portuguese cloth could only be produced by giving up some of the wine that Portugal could have enjoyed by importing the desired amount of cloth (now unwisely produced in Portugal) from England. Thus, according to the law of comparative advantage, a country (Portugal) should export the good (wine) where its sacrifice, in terms of the other good (cloth) – i.e. its opportunity cost – is lowest. The law of comparative advantage reinforced the case for free trade by demonstrating that as long as countries were relatively better at producing different goods, they could gain mutually by exchanging differences in technology. This idea that we should measure ourselves not against others but according to what we are capable of, goes back a long way, and at least to emperor Marcus Aurelius's "Meditations" in the second century, but had never been given a precise economic formulation before Ricardo.

From a theoretical perspective, the law of comparative advantage was the final nail in the mercantilist coffin. Mercantilists advocated restrictions on trade because they saw all the gains from trade as stemming from surplus exports. A stable system of trade cooperation could never emerge given this perspective since the sum of all surplus exports must be the sum of all surplus imports. A belief in mercantilism was a belief that some countries had to lose in order for others to gain. First in a letter to Montesquieu, and then in his 1752 publication, *Of Balance of Trade*, David Hume showed the logical impossibility of this zero sum perspective. A permanent trade surplus could not be sustained because the resulting inflow of gold, coveted by mercantilists, would create inflationary pressures that would make exports more expensive, equilibrating the trade position and ultimately bringing it into balance or deficit. Just because prominent thinkers cast indefinite surpluses as a non sequitur, the temptation to prolong them artificially did not vanish. As a digression, notice that what makes continuous surpluses impossible, according to this framework, also makes regular deficits impossible.[10] The theory of

[10] They are, but there is hard evidence of trade deficits being sustained for considerable periods, as in the case of the United States, although this is exceptional, as I argue in the text.

comparative advantage largely contributed to removing the *theoretical* incentive to avoid imports by pointing to the better resource allocation attainable through imports. This emphasis on the benefits derived from imports was taken to another level by James Mill, who in 1821 stated: "The benefit which is derived from exchanging one commodity for another arises, in all cases, from the commodity, not the commodity given."[11]

Neoclassical trade theory

While classical economists saw differences in labor productivity as a source of trade, the neoclassical economists of the early twentieth century emphasized how differences in factor endowments determine trade patterns.

The main prediction of Heckscher-Ohlin theory, or as it is also called the factor-proportions theory of trade, is that countries export the good which draws intensively upon the abundant factor and import the good which draws heavily upon the scarce factor.[12] A number of theorems are tied to this conception of trade, most notably the Rybczynski theorem, the factor price equalization theorem, and the Stolper-Samuelson theorem. Rybczynski showed that increasing the supply of the abundant factor not only raises the production of the good drawing intensively on the well-endowed factor, but actually does so disproportionately, thus accentuating the potential benefits of international trade.[13] Before trade is opened up, countries are able to supply more of the good that draws intensively on whatever factor they are well endowed with at any given price (of the "abundant factor" good relative to the "scarce factor" good). Under autarchy, countries are therefore able to offer the good that draws intensively on their abundant factor more cheaply than countries that are scarce in the factor. When countries start trading, they will tend to export the good that draws intensively on the abundant factor and import the good that draws intensively on the scarce factor. With greater international demand for whichever good a country is exporting, the price of the exported good will rise, whereas the price of the imported good, which now comes from a cheaper source,

[11] Mill 1844.
[12] Heckscher 1950; Ohlin 1933; Krugman and Obstfeld 2000.
[13] Rybczynski 1955.

will decline. This convergence in relative prices also leads to factor price convergence, at least in theory. Trade generates greater demand for whichever good draws heavily on the abundant factor; therefore, demand for the abundant factor increases relative to the scarce factor. At the same time, the reward to the scarce factor declines, since trade makes available cheap substitutes to the domestically produced good, causing demand for the import-competing good along with the factor used intensively in its production, to fall. This result is known as the factor price equalization theorem.

The impact of trade on factor prices has political implications, both domestically and internationally. Domestically, trade will tend to reward owners of the abundant factor and harm interests tied to the scarce factor, a result known as the Stolper-Samuelson theorem.[14] According to traditional theories, we should expect interests tied to the abundant factor to support free trade and interests tied to the scarce factor to ask for protection.[15] Since countries are variably endowed with production factors, trade will favor different groups in different countries. Capitalists are better off in capital-abundant countries but worse off in capital-scarce countries, and, similarly, workers are better off in a labor-abundant (rather than labor-scarce) environment. Neoclassical trade theory therefore speaks against a Marxist-imperial drive. To be sure, class cannot motivate capitalists (workers or landowners) in all countries to mobilize for the same cause, when their interests are uniquely determined by the domestic distribution of factors. If, however, factors are not perfectly mobile, but "stuck" in certain industries as in the Ricardo-Viner "specific factors" model, political coalitions will be sectorally determined and not based on factor belonging. More realistically, relative factor mobility will determine whether coalitions form along factor- or industry lines.[16] The effect of trade on the relative price of goods and factors across countries should not be exaggerated, however. In reality, the impact has been less striking than the factor proportions theory of trade would suggest. Whatever distributional conflicts exist domestically, a central result of the classical and neoclassical framework is that countries gain more from implementing free trade and compensating losers than from introducing protection.

---

[14] Stolper and Samuelson 1941.   [15] Rogowski 1989.
[16] Hiscox 2002.

As a broad body of thought, the main prediction of classical and neoclassical trade theory is that trade among countries with different technologies or factor endowments is mutually welfare-enhancing. Trade is not exclusively motivated by such differences however. Instead, a significant amount of trade takes place among similar industrialized countries. The United States, for instance, trades more with the European Union and Japan than it does with Ethiopia or Bangladesh.

New trade theories

While traditional trade theories predict trade among countries with different technologies and factor endowments, most of the United States' trade is with other advanced or semi-advanced countries with significant trade happening within the same industry. Economists first noticed that American trade patterns deviated considerably from the predictions of the factor proportions theory of trade in the 1960s.

Through a close examination of the factor content in American trade, Wassily Leontief discovered that America's imports were relatively more capital-intensive than its exports.[17] Since the factor proportions theory of trade predicts just the opposite, that the United States, the most capital-abundant country in the world, should be exporting capital-intensive goods, the finding that its exports were relatively more labor-intensive became known as the "Leontief paradox." Numerous explanations were put forward to account for this factor reversal. First, it was suggested that American exports seemed more labor-intensive than American imports because exports were produced using innovative technologies and therefore required labor in the form of human capital. Second, some scholars suspected that the American government had actually been quite effective in keeping labor-intensive goods out of the country through protectionist measures. Third, wages were still much lower in Europe than in the United States in the 1960s, and it therefore made sense for the United States to import capital-intensive goods from Europe.

As this puzzle was being considered, other scholars, such as the Swedish economist Staffan Burenstam-Linder, were struck by the extensive trade among similar industrialized countries more generally

---

[17] Leontief 1953, cited in Krugman and Obstfeld 2000, 81.

not just involving the United States. This made it increasingly difficult to dismiss the factor reversal in America's trade as an anomaly.
Going back to the work of the economists of the late nineteenth and
early twentieth centuries, new trade theorists would show that market imperfections could be a major source of trade.

Alfred Marshall was the first economist to imagine a competitive process with both increasing and decreasing returns to scale.[18]
Marshall introduced the concept of external economies to show that
a monopoly would not necessarily form if scale economies applied
to the entire industry. Instead, the process would remain competitive as long as the firm itself faced constant or diminishing returns
to scale.[19] In the first decades of the twentieth century, Piero Sraffa[20]
started to explore what exactly limited the size of the firm, and suggested that by offering a slightly different product, each firm was
operating in a separate niche (i.e., product differentiation), which
placed a limit on its expansion, a concept later developed by Joan
Robinson[21] and Edward Chamberlin.[22] In their work on imperfect
and monopolistic competition, both Joan Robinson and Edward
Chamberlin showed that increasing returns at the firm level could
yield a unique competitive equilibrium.[23] These were the main
theoretical findings on imperfect competition up until the Second
World War, and it would take many decades before the concepts
were applied to the area of trade.

In the late 1970s, a series of papers started to appear which demonstrated that scale economies along with similarities in taste can
be a source of trade, and that these give rise to greater consumer
variety and income gains.[24] This work combined scale economies at
both the internal and external level with traditional explanations of
trade. Under internal scale economies, the firm itself is able to expand
more than proportionally, and reap magnified benefits for any given
effort. As a result, firms can gain disproportionately through successive size increases. A large firm can, for instance, force a drop in the
price of a good by raising output, thus deterring small firms from
entering the market, a practice known as limit pricing. Threatened

[18] Marshall 1895.   [19] Buchanan and Yoon 1994; Schultz 1993, 20–1, 27.
[20] Sraffa 1926.   [21] Robinson 1933.
[22] Chamberlin 1933; and see Hicks, 193–4.   [23] Buchanan 1994, 7.
[24] Dixit and Stiglitz 1979; Ethier 1982; Krugman 1979; Yoon 1994, 360.

price reductions are often enough to bar competitors from entering the market.[25] Through strategic control of market variables, firms can expand and protect market shares by preemptively increasing supply to dissuade market entry. Monopolistic and oligopolistic firms that enjoy internal scale economies have strong incentives to expand beyond national borders because a single country is too small to make optimal use of advanced technologies and production processes. Because firms are better able to compete when they are close to the market where they sell, firms producing differentiated products also have strong incentives to enlarge their scale of operation and locate in other countries.

Scale economies need not be internal to the firm, however, but can occur at the industry level and extend throughout the whole economy with the concentration of firms in a particular area, such as the garment industry in New York or the electronic industry in Silicon Valley.[26] External economies imply that firms gain from the actions of other firms through the diffusion of knowledge, and experience decreasing costs in proportion to the size of the industry.[27] Again, firms concentrated in a particular location can gain more from open international markets than if they were confined to the domestic market, and, as a direct result of the superior gains from trade, can raise wages and welfare domestically. Monopolistic and oligopolistic firms thus have strong incentives to support free trade.

Through their emphasis on scale economies and product differentiation, new trade theories explain America's demand for similar products from other countries, and the outward-oriented commercial strategies that have sustained high import demand.

Product differentiation and scale economies

New trade theories underscore that much trade is in differentiated products. By making fine distinctions within functionally equivalent product categories, firms have tapped into individuals' perceived needs and created consumption possibilities for them.

Monopolistically competitive firms sell similar but differentiated products, such as cars or stereos, that are practically similar but can

---

[25] Ekelund and Tollison 1997, 289; Gabszewicz 1999, 35–7.
[26] Krugman 1991b, cited in Van Bergeijk and Kabel 1993.
[27] Krugman 1986.

easily be distinguished in terms of quality. By catering to slight variations in consumer preferences – by offering customers a particular product or service, or by offering superior quality or an otherwise similar good in a nearby location, and by working on consumer taste through advertisement campaigns and brand names – firms can raise demand for their products.[28] A firm's capacity to produce and compete in differentiated goods and services depends on intangible advantages, i.e., organization skills, investments in technology and advertising.[29] Wealthy, advanced countries therefore have a higher probability of being home to such firms, since they are better able to provide public goods of various sorts, such as the accumulation of human and physical capital, and social stability (in the face of market uncertainty).[30] Large firms can also afford to take greater risks to tap new markets, and in many cases, the firm is unable to expand internationally unless it is able to assume considerable risk. The ability of the US government to protect its firms' interests by exerting pressure on foreign governments and by safeguarding the right to property militarily, has provided American firms with some padding compared to peer competitors in foreign destinations (see chapter 6).

American firms have been extraordinarily successful in branching out internationally. Combining mobile firm-specific assets with locational advantages, American firms have had more to gain from internalizing operations by setting up shop locally than from pursuing licensing arrangements.[31] Firm-specific assets are wide-ranging. They include technological and organizational expertise, scale economies, brand names, and patents, which come together to create entry barriers, enabling the firm to lock in market shares. And by locating offshore, firms can design and market products to meet specific cultural needs. The foreign affiliate has an advantage over domestic competitors since it can draw on the assets of the home company. Similarly, it has an advantage over foreign rivals who will find it hard to compete with "sell where you make" tactics. By cannibalizing firms in foreign locations or creating a foreign subsidiary, the firm is able to internalize the benefit of servicing that particular market, and to position itself strategically to service other markets. Scale economies

[28] Ekelund and Tollison 1997, 263–7, 288; Van Bergeijk and Kabel 1993, 177.
[29] Stopford, Strange, and Henley 1991, 74–5, 89.
[30] Garrett 1998, 822–4.   [31] Dunning 2002.

are also facilitated when the firm is able to control all strings in the supply chain, and take advantage of country differences in sourcing inputs. While benefits in the form of employment, productivity, and technological diffusion accrue to host countries, American companies are distinct in so far as they prefer to retain most of their R&D activity at home, in an institutionally familiar environment.[32] Operating in a research-friendly milieu shaped by domestic institutions, firms have taken advantage of external scale economies throughout the American economy by keeping their technological base at home.

Increasingly, firms take pride in catering to specific consumer tastes and in many ways actually define what consumers want. By offering superior quality in specific products and luring individuals to identify with a particular image through advertising campaigns and brand names, firms manipulate consumer satisfaction. This demand for a renewed selection of easily attainable goods is not exclusively an American phenomenon but the size of the American market is unique, and this has placed the American government in a particularly good position to extract concessions from other countries. By offering a large market able to absorb other countries' export products on the one hand, and a consumer-oriented population with an insatiable appetite for foreign goods on the other, the United States has emerged as the indispensable trading partner.

What 'good' is free trade?

Traditional trade theorists and new trade theorists come to different conclusions about whether free trade is a pure public good, whether trade benefits are non-rivalrous and non-excludable. Free trade is a pure public good according to traditional trade theories. They believe free trade creates mutual non-rival benefits. All countries stand to gain from the optimal allocation of resources, freely exporting and importing goods based on where they are most efficiently produced. What one state enjoys when exporting a good another enjoys when importing it. There simply is no rivalry. Furthermore, although states can raise trade barriers and exclude each other from trade benefits, there is no incentive to do so, because states are better off importing what others can produce more cheaply than diverting resources to

[32] Doremus *et al.* 1998.

more costly domestic production. By implication, gains from trade are higher, the greater the number of countries engaged in open trade relations, making free trade non-excludable. If free trade has pure public goods characteristics from an economic point of view, domestic political considerations turn states into free-riders, unwilling to contribute to maintaining open domestic markets, while trying to benefit from open markets elsewhere. The reluctance of governments to contribute fully to the public good of free trade is due to the uneven distribution of trade benefits within countries. Whereas all citizens gain in their consumer capacity, certain producer interests lose in the short term because of stiffer competition, and certain classes lose factor income. Because who wins and who loses from international trade will vary as firms adjust to international competition, it is difficult for governments to adopt effective redistribution schemes. They are in any case seen as more inclined to exchange protection for political favors.[33] While a small state may correctly think it can get away with a free ride – taking advantage of open markets while excluding others from sectors where it does not have a comparative advantage – the basis for trade is quickly wiped out, and protectionism soon in full swing, if all states make the same calculation. In a nutshell, this is the collective action problem, associated with characterizing free trade as a public good. If the good is to be provided at all, a large state must have a sufficient interest in a liberal trade order, and maintain an open market despite the free-riding incentives of other states.[34]

Not all analysts have been persuaded that free trade is non-rival, however. Free trade has instead been characterized as a prisoner's dilemma, with competitive gains and strong incentives to exploit trade partners.[35] Scholars emphasizing these rival aspects have argued that asymmetries in size are important for understanding unequal gains from trade, and point to one of the few exceptions to free trade in which a large country, a hegemon, instead of solving the collective action problem by practicing free trade, is able to gain more than other states by imposing an optimum tariff that skews terms of trade in its favor.[36] Because trade partners want continued access to the hegemon's market, they lower export prices to compensate for the tariff. The hegemon's terms of trade (i.e., the relative price of exports to imports)

[33] Grossman and Helpman 1994.   [34] Kindleberger 1981.
[35] Conybeare 1984.   [36] Johnson 1953.

improve as a result. For several reasons, however, a hegemon might nevertheless choose to pursue free trade rather than impose the optimal tariff. To encourage free trade policies, other large states, or a coalition of smaller states, may threaten retaliation against the hegemon.[37] This can quickly degenerate into a protectionist trade war, leaving all countries worse off.[38] The Smoot-Hawley tariff, which was introduced by the United States in the 1930s, is the nightmare example of this kind of tariff war. In order for the hegemon's use of the optimal tariff to be effective, other countries must be unable to retaliate, whether individually or collectively. Other factors also complicate resort to the optimal tariff. For one thing, it is difficult to maintain the levy at the particular level that improves terms of trade. On the other hand, if the tariff is nonetheless set up properly, the 'terms of trade effect' that gives rise to cheap imports by inducing other countries to lower their export prices, undermines the hegemon's relative export performance.[39]

According to new trade theories, free trade is an imperfect public good. While there are complementary gains from trade, there is also some rivalry. When states try to maximize market shares, and promote their national champions, the expansion of one firm occurs at the expense of other firms. In this case, the benefits that accrue to one country clearly impinge on the benefits that accrue to other countries. This outward extension also excludes some countries from trade benefits, and government policy may aggravate this lock-out effect. While free trade is not a perfect public good, neither is it completely rivalrous or excludable; the idea is rather that there is some fluidity along these dimensions. From the literature on imperfect markets, political economists borrow the idea that a large actor is able to benefit from scale economies and gain market shares by charging lower prices than competitors. Thus, rather than setting up the optimal tariff, the hegemon is seen as having an interest in following a strategy of 'limit pricing' and creating an environment where its firms are able to expand.[40] Here, limit pricing translates into a policy of free trade, or in any case a low tariff regime, which prevents the deterioration in external competitiveness that is the result of adopting the optimal tariff. By escaping the competitive backlash from the optimal tariff, this strategy keeps export prices low enough to allow firms in the

---

[37] Conybeare 1984.   [38] Conybeare 1987.
[39] Conybeare 1987.   [40] Gowa 1989.

hegemonic country to expand foreign market shares.[41] There are other ways in which governments can help firms compete in international markets. Using strategic trade policy, governments may, for instance, subsidize exports, or invest in R&D to give firms a competitive edge over foreign counterparts.[42] On this interpretation, the government is performing a careful balancing act between pursuing a policy of limit pricing and interventionist policies that contradict such a strategy. At best, it can achieve a nearly free (also referred to as a "managed") trade system and switch between different policies.

The United States can be seen as alternating between an optimal tariff strategy and a strategy of limit pricing. A cheap dollar can be assimilated to an import tax in the optimal tariff model, which foreigners accommodate by lowering their prices. By maintaining prices that make goods affordable to American consumers, their sales to the United States do not suffer as the result of a weaker dollar. Foreign producers' readiness to adjust has the added virtue of reducing the inflationary impact of the dollar's decline. As with the optimal tariff, the de facto improvement in America's terms of trade is a good thing unless it undercuts American producers' international competitiveness. In order for the latter effect to outweigh the former, the cheaper exports made available to the American market must also be made available elsewhere, which is not necessarily the case. A high-powered dollar, on the other hand, can be thought of as a limit-pricing strategy to the extent that it encourages imports, and in particular inexpensive intermediate inputs, to keep the price of exported (final) goods down, reinforcing American firms' ability to produce for a large market. The scope and size of American business makes it possible for American consumers and outward-oriented American firms to enjoy the advantages of a weak dollar without the attendant negative effects on American buying power and inflation. Under a strong dollar, on the other hand, cheap imports can be enjoyed without internationalized firms losing sales to other countries.

American tariffs are relatively low by international standards and its market relatively easy to access. Administrative procedures to block

---

[41] Smaller countries cut their export prices in response to the protectionist measures adopted by the hegemon which has an incidence on the hegemon's ability to sell its products.
[42] Brander 1995.

imports when necessary without contravening GATT/WTO rules have given the American government the latitude to oscillate between an optimal tariff and a limit-pricing policy. Foreigners have been able to offload their products on the American market with relative ease although import-competing interests have had recourse to administrative measures during times of distress. The ability to block out imported goods under certain circumstances, and in a way that is consistent with GATT/WTO legislation, to a large extent explains domestic support for free trade (see the next section for a discussion of these procedures).

In more explicit ways, too, the American government has imposed tariff and non-tariff barriers on imported goods, by making use of its trade policy powers, and more recently by retaliating through the WTO's Dispute Settlement Body. While the WTO empowered small states by giving them the capacity to retaliate effectively against large advanced trade partners, this institutional device does not level the playing field to the extent that one might think, since retaliation by a state with a large market hurts more than retaliation by a country with a small market. Because large states have a stronger retaliatory threat, small states are not likely to restrict trade with large states in the first place. Conversely, small states depend on world markets for a wider range of products than do larger ones and they might not find it in their interest to retaliate by closing off their market. The threat of closing off one's market is effective to the extent that other countries want to access it. The American government is well placed to threaten protectionism because the American market is the world's favorite export destination. We often think of protection as something practiced by governments, but firms can also give rise to certain forms of protection by raising natural barriers to entry in the form of scale economies, product differentiation, high start-up costs, and high risk.[43] Because the United States is home to the world's largest firms, often equipped with the most advanced technologies, American firms are more likely to raise such natural barriers to entry, giving them a competitive advantage at home and abroad. Before sharing profits with new entrants, firms operating under imperfect market conditions have been able to protect their initial advantage to gain a strong future lead, allowing them to amass considerable wealth at both the firm and country level.

---

[43] Ekelund and Tollison 1997; Gabszewicz 1999.

The United States has for the most part maintained an open market, which has enabled it to push for trade liberalization in other countries. With American firms spreading their production throughout the world, they have increasingly lobbied government for open markets. As carefully detailed by Helen Milner, this outward orientation of American firms has four distinct sources.[44] First, export-oriented firms with extensive foreign production will support free trade to avoid retaliation from import-restricting policies. Second, multinational companies have incentives to oppose protection at home in order to facilitate intra-firm trade. Third, firms dependent on intermediate inputs will resist trade barriers. Fourth, export-oriented firms engaged in intra-industry trade will oppose protection at home since this will favor competitors whose sales only target the domestic market. Organized consumer groups looking out for a broad range of cheap products have also become a bastion of free trade.[45] The inclination of American firms to use the whole world as playing field along with the consumer culture that is a hallmark of American society has unambiguously favored free trade over protectionist interests.

The significance of trade deficits

This section unpacks the trade deficit, and offers a general macroeconomic overview. I also discuss why trade deficits are normally avoided, why they are usually seen as harmful, and why they have arisen and persisted in the American case.

Different kinds of deficit

A "deficit" can refer to different things. In this book, and unless otherwise specified, the deficit refers to the current account deficit, or loosely the trade deficit which is a surplus of imports over exports. The current account deficit is the balance of trade (exports minus imports) plus the balance of income (the difference between the income the United States receives on overseas investment and what it pays on investments made by foreigners in the United States). The trade deficit and the current account deficit are almost identical since the balance of income is trivial in comparison with the balance of trade. This is

[44] Milner 1988.   [45] Destler 1995.

true in general since the balance of income measures profit, whereas the balance of trade measures revenues from net exports.

A brief examination of the macroeconomic relationships as they appear from a national income accounting perspective tells us that the trade deficit is equivalent to the investment-savings gap in the economy.[46]

Whatever is produced (Y_{prod}) or imported (Z) in an open economy is directed towards consumption (C), investment (I), government purchases (G), or exports (X), and is identical to the country's national income (Y_{inc}):

$$Y_{prod} + Z = Y_{inc} \tag{1}$$

$$Y_{inc} = C + I + G + X$$

$$Y_{prod} + Z = C + I + G + X$$

The private sector, roughly households and firms, spend (i.e., consume) what they do not save (S^p) or pay in taxes (T):

$$C = -(S^p + T) \tag{2}$$

Similarly, the government "consumes" or spends the difference between what it receives in taxes and what it saves:

$$G = T - S^g \tag{3}$$

Substituting (2) and (3) into (1) therefore yields:

$$Y_{prod} + Z = -(S^p + T) + I + (T - S^g) + X \quad \text{which can be written as}$$

$$Z - X = I - (S^p + S^g) \tag{4}$$

This expression tells us that trade deficits occur when domestic investments exceed national savings, although there is not much consensus about the causality behind this relationship.

---

[46] See Krugman and Obstfeld 2000.

There are a variety of views on what is driving the current account deficit.[47] First, there is the domestic "savings deficit" view, according to which the dearth of savings in the United States, whether by the private sector or government, is covered by foreigners who invest in the American economy. Second, there is the foreign "savings glut" view, espoused by the Federal Reserve chairman, Ben Bernanke. On this reading, excess foreign savings find their way to the American market in search of good investment opportunities. Attracted by the most advanced capital markets in the world, and exceptionally high growth rates, investors comb the American market for high risk-adjusted returns. Trade imbalances are the starting point for the third perspective on the current account deficit. According to this outlook, Americans have a stronger preference for exotic goods, and more income than other countries to spend on imports, resulting in chronic deficits.

These perspectives are more a question of emphasis than stark incompatibilities. The view one is inclined to adopt, however, says something about whether the deficit is a sign of weakness or of strength. While I do not mean to minimize the unprecedented size and longevity of American deficits, my angle is a variation on the second theme.

Thus, consistent with the second perspective, America's central role in money and security gives us a fuller picture of why the United States is more prone to deficits than other countries. On the one hand, the United States attracts the lion's share of foreign capital because of its key currency functions, central to which is providing the world with liquid dollar assets. World demand for liquid assets allows banks and other credit institutions to borrow at preferential rates, i.e., to sell bank deposits and financial instruments to foreigners, and to pass on easy money to American households in the form of credit cards and cheap loans (including mortgages).[48] On the other hand, American military might is also part of this equation. The American market is viewed as a secure investment environment and has been essential for drawing in vast amounts of money from the rest of the world (see chapter 6). Of course, if what is meant by the former perspective is simply that there are more investment opportunities in the United States than can

---

[47] Levey and Brown 2005; Mann 2002.
[48] McKinnon 2001b, 5.

be taken up by what Americans are willing to save, there is virtually no difference between the first and the second view, just a matter of who to blame for the deficit – Americans saving too little or foreigners saving too much. This does not seem to be a very interesting or even answerable question. What is sometimes implied, however, is that the shortfall in savings creates a trade deficit, which then requires for-eigners to foot the import bill through a corresponding capital inflow, which seems sequentially problematic. The United States is not receiv-ing emergency assistance to balance payments – it rather seems that surplus imports have been cleared and paid for *with* foreign savings.

The trade deficit and external liabilities

The counterpart of a current account deficit is a surplus on the finan-cial account. The two accounts can balance naturally, thus offsetting a balance of payments crisis. As long as more capital is being imported than exported, the country can also import more goods and services than it exports. But there is a limit to how deep the current account deficit can run, since it implies that more and more assets are sold. As the sale of American assets grows in proportion to American acquisi-tion of foreign assets, the net foreign asset (NFA) or net international investment position (NIIP) also rises, triggering fears that the United States has become excessively dependent on foreign capital and may not be able to honor liabilities.

The risks associated with the United States' net liability position are said to be twofold and to interact.[49] First, there is a limit on the size of liabilities. Second, there is a danger that the flow of funds to the United States is insufficient to cover the current account deficit. These two phenomena are seen as closely linked, since any limitation on the stock of liabilities implies a problem funding the deficit.[50] While there is a threat to asset stock levels, threats to current account "financing" dissipate on the second view of the deficit (discussed above). At the margin, there may be some need to sell Treasury notes in order to balance payments, but if foreign investment is really what is fueling the deficit, the capital surplus that is the counterpart to the deficit has already made an appearance on the financial account. The most likely consequence associated with large-scale outflow of foreign capital is

[49] Cline 2005.   [50] Cline 2005, 153–64.

a decline in the deficit (but not an inability to fund it) along with higher interest rates. There is, however, a cap on how large external liabilities can loom. Even though markets have been more tolerant towards liabilities in equity, there is a danger of saturating foreigners' willingness to add on American assets due to a home bias and a global portfolio constraint that kicks in because of the size of the American economy. Looking at the different ways of measuring the United States' portfolio constraint gives us an idea of how far it is pushing liabilities.

While American liabilities are large by international comparison, they are small when measured against the domestic economy. This size advantage is crucial for understanding the United States' ability to amass debt. For instance, in 2002, when America's NFA reached a high-point (before peaking again in 2008), external liabilities were 40 percent of all countries' gross liabilities and 13 percent of world gross financial assets, whereas the share of America's net foreign liabilities was 11 percent of its net financial assets and only 5 percent of its net wealth.[51] The United States has been claiming a substantial amount of world capital available for investment purposes, however, and may soon bump up against a liability ceiling. Given investors' home bias and the significant amount of funds already invested in the United States, there will come a point when investors are unwilling to buy more American assets, although predicting precisely when that will happen is fraught with difficulties. Cline draws on the work of Karen Lewis, which shows that home bias only leaves 30 percent of world financial assets for foreign investment, and predicts that American external liabilities will amount to 16 percent of gross world financial assets by 2010, and therefore argues that the United States has some leeway in expanding external liabilities.[52] The 14 percent valve is not just reserved for American investments though; all countries compete for these funds. Lastly, the figures quoted above show that external liabilities are small compared to net financial assets, or net wealth. American securities are far from being depleted – by 2004 they comprised 50 percent of the stock of world assets, and amounted to $33.4 trillion.[53] By 2007, they had declined to just below $30 trillion and accounted for roughly 37 percent of the world share.[54] Portfolio constraints are only an indirect

---

[51] Cline 2005, 157–61.   [52] Cline 2005, 164; Lewis 1999.
[53] Levey and Brown 2005; Mann 2003.   [54] IMF 2008b.

way of knowing if the United States will be able to service debt. The proper way of evaluating the United States' debt servicing capacity is to look at the balance of income on current account – whether what it pays creditors exceeds what it receives in investment income from abroad. So far investment income has remained positive.

While the United States' net international investment position reached 29 percent of GDP in 2008, a figure which lies below the "40 percent of GDP" threshold often cited as hazardous, its current account deficit exceeded 6 percent of GDP in 2006, which is well above the 4 to 5 percent share of GDP considered dangerous.[55] As a second limiting factor, the sizeable current account deficit may endanger the United States' external position. To sustain deficits, the United States must sell more and more assets to foreigners; in other words, increase external liabilities. Amassing external liabilities is potentially dangerous because, anticipating a dollar correction to adjust trade imbalances, investors are likely to precipitate a dollar slide, and the Federal Reserve likely to raise interest rates to prevent a sharp drop in the dollar. Before the financial crisis, this was the scenario being played out in the United States, with question marks around the magnitude of such hikes and their growth-inhibiting effect.

The meaning of a liability

All borrowing translates into investment. When a firm sells shares, the government issues bonds, or a household has a mortgage, these amount to different ways of borrowing. On the other side of this transaction, someone is undertaking an investment. There are, of course, differences between debt and equity. When debt is issued, lenders expect to receive fixed payment of interest, in addition to the initial loan, whereas with equity, investors do not have a claim to recuperating principal but share in the company's profit, and are (depending on the amount of shares bought) able to gain a certain degree of control of the company. At bottom, these are, however, different ways of raising capital. Whenever borrowing occurs, liabilities increase. But not all liabilities lead to net debtor status, since the value of liabilities may increase at a slower rate than claims and since not all liabilities are technically debt.

[55] Cline 2005, 154; BEA 2008a, 2009a, 2009b.

A household analogy is useful in distinguishing between different countries' ability to borrow, and the consequences, bringing home the point that increasing liabilities beyond claims sometimes spells trouble and at other times is wealth-enhancing. Wealthy investors frequently borrow for investment purposes. They use debt as a financial tool to increase returns on investments. If the investment pays off, they augment their resource base. If not, they face loss, not necessarily dire straits. In normal times, affluent investors have money to burn. Private bankers call this practice "strategic debt." Of course, even big investors can be caught on the wrong side of a bet, as the current financial crisis has shown. The fact that so many banks were dumbstruck by the precipitous loss that eventually wiped some of them out, reinforces the point that they had grown accustomed to absorbing extraordinary levels of risk, and were even quite prepared to undertake risk that they did not understand – the very height of risk-taking. Trades in complex financial instruments, such as collateralized debt obligations (CDOs), would eventually come crashing down, and when catastrophe loomed, the US government devised a series of packages to bail banks out, to stimulate the economy and for households to resume deposits with commercial banks, so that these could invest long-term in the economy. In contrast to these wealthy investors, the middle class is neither able nor, as a rule, probably willing, to borrow to invest in risky assets, although there are examples of people having done this, as we have seen with the current sub-prime lending crisis. If a person from the middle class were to borrow to play the stock market and the investment turned awry, they would teeter on the brink of disaster. The most common form of middle-class borrowing is a mortgage. Buying a house is usually seen as a wise investment, a rational use of debt, and an example of the ways in which the capacity to acquire debt is itself a sign of power and a reinforcement of power. Normally, it is much more difficult for poor people to borrow because they cannot point to a future income stream that will allow them to service debt. Therefore they cannot acquire assets in the way that the middle class can. When lower income people were nonetheless granted loans to buy property, the consequences were disastrous when the credit instruments financing the loans collapsed. Many people were forced out of their homes through foreclosures. In cases where the size of the loans rose above the value of their homes, people mailed back the keys to the property in an attempt to walk away from the debt, a practice known as "jingle mail."

Although banks and other lending institutions were also hit by the wave of sub-prime defaults, those deemed "too big to fail" were offered deals to prevent systemic drift. In March 2008, the Federal Reserve provided emergency funding to Bear Stearns after a steep fall in its stock price. After this proved insufficient to support the investment bank, it brokered the sale of Bear Stearns to JP Morgan and agreed to fund $29 billion worth of the illiquid assets inherited from Bear Stearns. In November 2008, Citigroup was bailed out, and the Federal Reserve agreed to cushion $249 billion of its losses, without changing management. Citigroup became increasingly strained after its take-over of Wachovia in September, even though the Federal Reserve agreed to take on $270 billion of Wachovia's ($312 billion) losses on mortgage and property securities. In January 2009, the Treasury and the Federal Deposit and Insurance Corporation (FDIC) agreed to absorb $10 billion worth of Bank of America's illiquid assets and the Federal Reserve to provide loans in order to cover a further $88 billion in potential losses. Bank of America's difficulties are in large part a hangover from the acquisition of the investment bank, Merrill Lynch. Out of the $250 billion set aside by the Treasury to provide relief to ailing banks, half went to the nine largest banks in the industry, while the rest was to be shared among hundreds of smaller banks. In total, President Obama's financial rescue plan was expected to make available up to $1 trillion to soak up unsafe assets. For comparison, $75 billion was set aside to help three to four million "responsible" homeowners refinance their loans and another $200 billion funnelled to government-backed mortgage lenders Fannie Mae and Freddie Mac in order to bring mortgage rates down for another four to five million borrowers. This is not to argue that these measures were ill-advised, or that doing more to help homeowners and less to assist financial institutions would be a better way to reboot the economy. But it does show how the structure, in this case the structure of the financial system, requires us to move the goal posts for what we consider "responsible" borrowing, and to argue that how this gets recast is largely a function of size. There is much truth in the old adage – the rich get richer, the poor, poorer.

Just as large banks and financial institutions have been able to solicit the help of taxpayers in individual countries – primarily the United States, but also European countries – large countries are in a better position to assist corporate banking. Although the crisis has two immediate sources, the spread of credit risk through complex instruments and over-leveraging, the credibility of these ailing institutions has as much to do with their own performance as the ability of their government to save them, should they start to fall through the cracks. Iceland is the most potent example. All three of the banks – Glitnir Bank, Landsbanki, and Kaupthing – that went under were well capitalized and they were not exposed to illiquid assets. Their main sin was the huge asset position relative to the overall economy. Collectively, these three banks accounted for almost eight times the country's GDP. This left the central bank unwilling to fend off a speculative attack on their behalf. When the banks became insolvent and some of them nationalized, the Icelandic krona fell like a stone, raising the prospect of sovereign default (i.e., the government's inability to service debt). Iceland is an obvious outlier but several industrialized countries have upsettingly high shares of bank assets to GDP. Australia, Belgium, France, Germany, Ireland, Japan, the Netherlands, Portugal, Spain, Switzerland and the United Kingdom, all have bank assets valued at more than 200 percent of GDP. For comparison, all of the United States' bank assets are valued at barely more than 100 percent of GDP.[56] In addition, and as can be seen from figure 4.1, which shows all the individual financial companies in the world that account for more than 50 percent of GDP, several countries face significant systemic risks. Notice that Japan and the United States are not included on the chart. These banks are simply "too big to be saved."[57] For comparison, the biggest financial enterprise in the United States, JP Morgan, has assets valued at 15 percent of GDP.

What is particularly worrying is that many European banks are highly leveraged. Apart from the main trend towards de-leveraging – to bring the underlying equity in line with the assets on bank's balance sheet – to meet adequate capitalization requirements, these companies are not in a good position to recapitalize to deal with (toxic) asset write-downs, which hits equity disproportionately. According to the Federal Reserve of St. Louis, 4 percent, i.e., a leverage factor of 25, is adequate capitalization. A rough estimate of the de-leveraging required for major banks in Belgium, Denmark, France, Germany, Ireland, Japan, Spain, Sweden, Switzerland, the United Kingdom and the United States to attain adequate capitalization is more than $10 trillion. As shown in figure 4.2, this de-leveraging process is a significant share of many countries' GDP, but only a minor share of the GDP of Spain or the United States.

Although, at the time of writing, the crisis is in full swing in the United States, the long-term effects may very well be more difficult to

[56] Allianz 2008.   [57] *Financial Times*, September 3, 2008.

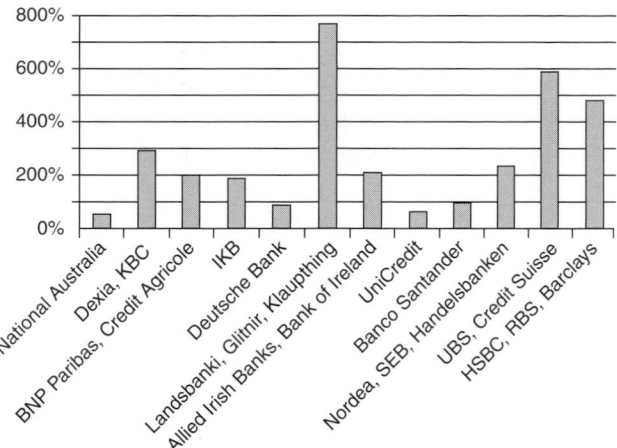

Figure 4.1 Bank assets as share of GDP, 2008
Source: Author's calculations based on *Financial Times* data.

bear in Europe, mainly because American banks are for the most part much bigger than their European counterparts but smaller as a share of the overall economy.

As home to the most advanced capital markets in the world, the United States has had an especially easy time borrowing from other countries, and has, despite its net liability position, not faced challenges comparable to other countries' with large external liabilities. Of course, part of the reason for this is that the United States attracts a lot of investment by offering equity in return. Even setting aside equity as a special form of borrowing, it is important to highlight that not all forms of borrowing are used in the same way, or speak equally to the perils of debt. As is the case for individuals, there is strategic and hazardous debt at both the government and country level.

Apart from acquiring assets (as in the above example), debt often arises because an actor, or agent, buys more goods and services than it sells. If, for instance, a household spends more than it earns, it is essentially running a deficit. Households that spend more than they earn have to find some way to cover surplus expenses, for instance by selling stocks, bonds, or property, or by borrowing against some collateral – a house, for example. As the household sells assets – i.e., borrows – to fill the spending gap, it is running down its net asset position. The household is getting mired in debt. By the same token,

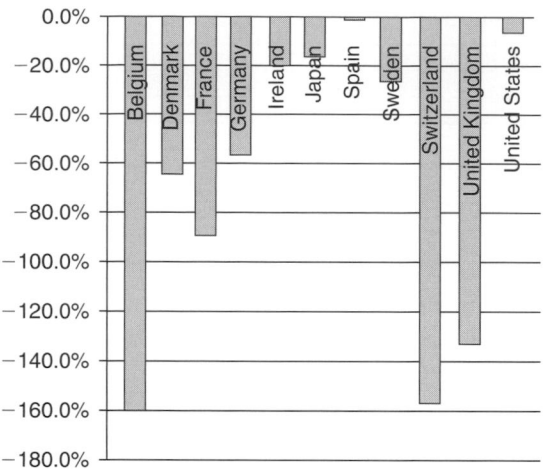

Figure 4.2 De-leveraging as share of GDP, 2008
Source: Author's calculations based on balance sheet data from IMF 2009a, 2009b and ECB 2009.

a government that overspends runs a fiscal deficit, which it finances by selling assets. The government equivalent of mortgage financing is to issue bonds. And as in the case of a household, a government that sells securities is running down its net asset position. If the household or government is running down assets to invest productively in, for example, education, there is an underlying bet that the current short-fall will pay off in the future. If they are selling assets for immediate consumption, they are selling themselves short.

A country's external relations are governed by these same funda-mental principles. As we saw earlier, a basic macro-economic law sug-gests that the current account and the financial account sum to zero on the balance of payments. If a country spends more on imports than it earns from exports it runs a trade deficit and, as in the examples above, this deficit has already been financed by selling assets to for-eigners. The immediate counterpart to a trade deficit is a surplus on the financial account, and a concomitant increase in external liabil-ities. But firms and households cannot purchase imports in excess of the total level of savings in the economy, wherever those savings come from. In other words, the danger with the deficit is not that the United States will be unable to pay for goods that have already been imported, but that foreign investments will dry up and that imports cannot be sustained in excess of exports.

As in the case of a household or government, the real test for the
sustainability of the deficit is what foreigners make of the role of
imported goods in the economy. Are imports predominantly intermediate inputs used to lay the foundations for future productivity
gains and investment opportunities, or have imports been feeding
current consumption? The ultimate paradox is that while much
American borrowing has been used for productive investment, much
has also been used to finance consumption gluts, behavior which the
market normally punishes in the harshest way.

American households have had access to easy cash because banks
and other credit institutions have benefited from foreigners' need for
liquid dollar assets.[58] By lending to households on soft terms, the banking sector is effectively recycling foreign capital but not necessarily in
a way that is good for America. There is a definite limit on how far
American households can go in exploiting lax borrowing constraints.
Whereas it is theoretically possible for corporate America to raise
capital without raising the debt-to-equity ratio (given their ability to
sell equity, bonds, or other instruments to foreigners), households can
only raise capital by borrowing on credit or via a mortgage. So, easy
money must increase household debt.[59] The imploding financial crisis
is a function of easy money passed on to households and the repack-
aging of such loans into complex financial instruments to spread the
underlying risk. No one looking at the scale of calamity in financial
markets can argue that the current turbulence in financial markets
is a boon to America. But a curious feature of the financial mayhem
the world is currently wading through is that the United States has
fared comparatively well. It has reasserted itself as the world's ref-
uge currency, and can borrow to finance stimulus and rescue plans
at a cheaper rate than any other country and, as a consequence, is
expected to contract at a lower rate and for a shorter period than
Japan or the euro-zone, its main competitors.

Different kinds of liabilities

A country's net international investment position (NIIP), or net foreign asset position (NFA), is the difference between the value of the
country's assets held abroad and the value of foreign assets held in the

[58] McKinnon 2001a.   [59] Mckinnon 2001a.

home country. Here, I reserve the term "debt" for borrowing that is not an attempt to acquire cash in exchange for equity. The United States moved into a net external liability position in 1986 and has not moved out of that position since then. By 2002, net external liabilities, the gap between what the rest of the world owes America and what Americans owe the rest of the world amounted to $2.4 trillion, approximately 23 percent of GDP, and by 2008 to 29 percent of GDP.[60]

Contrary to something like the national debt, which is a country's total stock of public debt, net external liabilities only refer to a country's transactions with the rest of the world.[61] In contrast to the public debt, external liabilities comprise the stock of assets held by both private and official investors.[62] The composition of creditors has important consequences for a country's ability to honor external liabilities. Whereas private actors are motivated by risk-adjusted returns, official investors often have political motives, such as sustaining export growth, repaying dollar denominated debt, or buttressing an important ally.

Harmful liabilities

Being in liability is manageable when the cost of borrowing is lower than the returns on the investment financed by the loan. The nature of the liabilities also matters in assessing their viability. When the investment takes the form of portfolio investment (non-FDI equity, bonds, and other liquid forms of capital such as bank loans), capital will usually flow in the direction of the lending country, since the borrowing country must pay back principal along with interest. Although there is no guarantee that whoever is lending will recuperate the amount of the investment if money is placed in stocks, there is otherwise an expectation that an even greater amount than the initial investment will in due course accrue to whoever is lending. Otherwise, the investment

---

[60] BEA 2008a, 2009a, 2009b.
[61] The national debt does include one such external liability – government debt owed to foreigners (whether to private or public investors), which is an external liability. Public sector borrowing gives rise to public debt through issuances of government securities, whereas borrowing in the private sector gives rise to liabilities in the private sector through issuances of equity, corporate securities, or other financial instruments.
[62] Private assets are those held by individuals or companies. Public, or official, assets are those held by governments.

would not have occurred in the first place. The lamentation of the Nigerian president, Olusegun Obasanjo, is illuminating: "All that we had borrowed up to 1985 or 1986 was around $5 billion and we have paid about $16 billion yet we are still being told that we owe about $28 billion ... If you ask me what is the worst thing in the world, I will say it is compound interest."[63] By 2004, the external debt of all developing countries amounted to $2.2 trillion, and between 1995 and 2004 they had paid back $2.8 trillion in interest and amortization.[64] The only way for the borrower to ensure that the loan does not become a constraint is to invest the borrowed funds productively so that a surplus remains after the debt has been paid back. Unless wise investment choices are made, the borrower will end up with less capital than at the time of borrowing. If, on the other hand, the loan is invested in such a way that returns on the investment exceed whatever is owed to the lending entity, both the borrower and the lender are better off than they were before the financial transaction took place. The standard account of the debt crisis is that developing countries borrowed at high cost, made poor investment choices, and frittered away their borrowed funds on current consumption. One way to escape this trap is to attract foreign direct investment (FDI), in which case the initial investment is likely to stay in the host country as long as the subsidiary company benefits.

The United States has not faced challenges comparable to developing countries because it has for the most part invested borrowed funds wisely, getting higher returns than the costs of borrowing. But not all of the funds that Americans have borrowed have been used productively. Some have been squandered on consumption. Surprisingly, FDI in the United States is a relatively small share of total liabilities. In the last twenty years, 1987–2006, the share of FDI in the United States as a portion of total liabilities was 15 percent; by 2006 it had declined to 11 percent.[65] Because of the size of the American market, it still attracts the largest number of multi-national firms in the world (the United Kingdom ranks second).[66] Both the United States and the United Kingdom (where FDI is c. 11 percent of total liabilities) have

[63] www.jubileeresearch.org/jubilee2000/news/london180800.html, August 19, 2006.
[64] IMF 2003b, 69.   [65] BEA 2007b.
[66] UNCTAD 2006.

had relatively low levels of FDI and sustained high levels of debt as a portion of total liabilities as compared to other industrialized net debtor countries. Both Australia and Canada had much higher penetration of stable foreign investment (i.e., FDI).[67]

The United States and the United Kingdom stand out among other industrialized countries with significant net external liabilities. In both cases, FDI comprises a small share of total liabilities, and both have profited handsomely from external liabilities through a positive income balance and exceptionally high capital and exchange rate gains on the NFA (in the case of the United States).[68] Out of the two, however, the United States' *net debt* is higher as a share of GDP, and its benefits are higher as well (see chapter 5 for a full discussion).

A surprising feature of our world economy is the high external debt sustained by industrialized countries. In measuring external debt, I have kept with the IMF's definition of external debt, which includes all components of liabilities in the NIIP except for equity securities, FDI (although it does include "other capital" i.e., "inter-company lending"), and financial derivatives.[69] In the last two decades, the United States' external debt averaged 70 percent as a share of total liabilities, and the United Kingdom's 85 percent, whereas Australia's average share was 61 percent for the same period. Canada's share averaged 60 percent between 2002 and 2006, and Switzerland's 59 percent between 1997 and 2006.[70]

These figures provide an interesting backdrop for comparison with developing countries. A rough comparison, constrained by the paucity of data on developing countries' external indicators, suggests that the United States has been increasing the fraction of its external debt at a time when FDI in the United States has decelerated, whereas developing countries on the whole have been doing the exact opposite – reducing external debt while raising the stock of FDI at home. In the decade spanning 1990 and 2000, the debt to GDP ratio rose from 31 to 50 percent in the United States whereas it shrank from 39

---

[67] ABS 2006b, Statistics-Canada 2007. FDI averaged 30 percent of total liabilities between 1988 and 2006 in Australia, whereas it averaged 30 percent between 1997 and 2006 in Canada.
[68] The meaning and significance of capital and exchange rate gains (i.e., valuation adjustments) on the NFA is explained in chapter5.
[69] IMF 2003a, 27–32.
[70] *National-Statistics 2006b*; SNB June 2007, *Statistics-Canada 2007*.

to 37 percent in the developing world. We should expect FDI to be a much smaller share of the American economy than of a developing country economy, but the FDI share of the external debt remained constant in the United States between 1990 and 2000, whereas it increased from 51 percent to 111 percent in developing countries.[71] This is not to suggest that developing countries should emulate the American and British example, but rather to point to the ability of the United States and to a certain extent the United Kingdom to attract capital even though they do not conform to expectations about the kind of capital to attract. Since developing countries cannot borrow low-cost as the United States and, to some extent, the United Kingdom have done, they should continue to welcome foreign direct investment, which is steadier than liquid portfolio investment.

Amassing liabilities has different consequences for different countries. The inability to pay is harmful when the creditor is in a position to impose specific conditions. Not all creditors are well placed to impose such conditions. If the creditor is a commercial bank, it can only demand interest and principal. Official creditors, however, can claim other forms of compensation. A domestic analogy is again appropriate. Government agencies, for instance, make student grants and loans contingent upon academic performance. New grants and loans will not be forthcoming unless the student in question passes a series of exams. The same principle underpins the relation between a government agency, or multilateral institution, and a debtor government. If the debtor cannot pay, the creditor will demand some other form of recompense. The debtor is typically asked to pursue a course of action that suits the creditor. Without the means to pay, the debtor must accept the creditor's conditions. Under the Roman Empire, peasants defaulting on the land tax were enslaved or in some cases could agree to compensatory services until the debt was cleared (so-called nexum).[72] Less extreme consequences can still be unpleasant. A developing country may for instance be asked to undergo reform (a "structural adjustment program," or SAP). Whether such reform is inherently desirable is for the purposes of this analysis moot. While the IMF is currently not in a good position to preach laissez-faire capitalism, there are plenty of examples when the prescriptions of financial institutions set a country on a steady course to ruin, as well

---

[71] BEA 2007b, 2007c; UNCTAD 2003.   [72] Jupp 2000, 28–9.

as examples of reform having improved growth and living standards. From a political economy perspective, however, the essential point is the loss of policy autonomy. All states want to maximize policy independence. But in quite a few cases, the creditor – in this case the IMF or the World Bank – is in a position to demand policy change, and the debtor has little choice but to agree. The reason why the conditions imposed by financial institutions are accepted is the debtor country's inability to pay back old loans, and by the same token receive new ones. Needless to say, the debtor would never have agreed to the reform package had it not been in a structurally weaker position. If it thought the imposed policy change desirable, policy change would already have been underway.

What happens if the debtor does not accept the conditions imposed? Creditors usually have ways of enforcing payments. A government can confiscate property or, in the last resort, incarcerate recalcitrant individuals. Citizens, or firms, can ask their government to enforce contracts on their behalf. In certain sub-cultures, the mafia or street gangs use violent extra-legal means to enforce payment. Force can also be and has been used to collect debt from refractory governments. As recently as the twentieth century, the United States gave the British, Germans, and the Italians a green light to blockade Venezuela's ports for this purpose. Just a few years following this incident, the United States intervened in the Dominican Republic to collect debt. In the present systemic context, where the world's largest "debtor" is the world's foremost military power, armed enforcement of debt is unthinkable (more on this in chapter 6).

The reward of ongoing trade deficits

The United States has pursued a deficit policy since the breakdown of the Bretton Woods system of flexible exchange rates. In the decades immediately after the Second World War, the United States could not have pursued a similar policy because Europe and Asia relied heavily on American products and capital to rebuild their war-torn economies. During this time, the United States strengthened its manufacturing industry through large-scale exports. Through FDI, it extended its commercial network, buying up foreign companies and establishing subsidiaries abroad. Once a worldwide commercial system was in place, and other countries had built up their industrial base, the direction of net outflows was reversed, as goods and capital started to flow in the direction of the United States.

For thirty-one of the thirty-eight years from 1970 to 2008, the United States has had a current account deficit. A deficit policy has been beneficial in three ways. First, it has provided American individuals with a larger cheaper menu of choice, which is the textbook definition of bliss in economics. By sustaining trade deficits, the United States has raised consumption beyond what is produced in the United States. The point of all trade is, of course, to raise consumption beyond the production possibility frontier. But the United States has gone one step further. It has systematically consumed beyond the export possibility frontier. Through trade, the United States has, for prolonged periods of time, enjoyed more goods than it has produced. From a trading point of view, this is the better side of the bargain, since maximizing imports over exports allows a country to raise consumption above what it must offer in exchange.

Second, easy access to intermediate inputs is productivity-enhancing. Although some imports have been squandered through current consumption, a substantial share of imports is used as intermediate inputs. In 2003, 65 percent of all imports consisted of – capital goods, industrial supplies, and other – materials vital for raising investment and productivity.[73] By sourcing from the most efficient producer, the United States has made effective use of a global division of labor. At times this has meant importing from foreign companies; but often the United States has imported goods from its own firms dispersed across the globe.

Third, offering a large market where countries can offload imports is a source of bargaining power. Maintaining a sizeable open market is politically expedient, since the government can threaten closure to get better commercial deals for American firms. The United States derives considerable bargaining leverage from its integrated, consumer-oriented, market. The strategic aspect of high import demand is a central feature of America's commercial expansion. By making access to the American market conditional on trade liberalization in other countries, the government has opened up foreign markets on behalf of its firms. To some extent, however, the outward extension of corporate America is a boon enjoyed in stealth, given that sales of foreign affiliates do not appear on the trade balance.

---

[73] *Global Economic Forum*, April 5, 2004.

In the subsequent section, I examine how MNC activity on foreign soil has helped American firms take advantage of scale economies and production synergies to create a territorially unbounded commercial network and to what extent this has been beneficial for Americans in general. In the following section, I show, in concrete terms, how import expansion has been a source of bargaining power, and how, under different size ratios, this leverage has given rise to the disproportionate gains discussed in chapter 3.

Commercial diffusion: real and invisible exports

No other country imports as much as the United States. Between 1948 and 2008, America's share of world imports hovered between 10 and 20 percent. In 2008, the United States' share of world imports was the same as it was in 1948, whereas its share of world exports was 14 percent lower than it was in 1948. While this could be mistaken for commercial decline, it says more about the reorganization of the world economy and even reflects commercial prowess. The United States remains a commercial pace-setter despite sustained trade deficits. To appreciate America's mercantile footprint fully one must look at the trade that takes place between the home base and foreign countries, as well as the trade that American firms conduct from foreign locations. American commercial expansion transcends traditional ways of conceiving trade, as firms themselves have done by separating production and sales from the home base. It is well known that *production* is increasingly fragmented, and that it is hard to decipher where goods are "made", when firms rely on importing intermediate inputs and use distant locations for assembly operations. It is less well known how the international diffusion of sales benefits the home economy.

A proper assessment of the United States' commercial performance depends on what we make of the fact that sales through foreign affiliates are more than three times the size of American exports. Multinational companies prefer to sell to the host market where they are located and often use foreign soil as a platform for exports. But sales of foreign affiliates do not appear in official trade statistics. Figure 4.3 reports the value added, the net income and the number of American majority-owned foreign affiliates between 1999 and 2007. Notice that I have not included all American foreign direct investment, only foreign affiliates that are majority owned, in other words, those that the United States "controls." In addition, I use value added instead of "sales," since this represents the production uniquely determined by the foreign affiliate, as opposed to the production of other companies furnishing them with intermediate inputs, and thus reflects what the company contributes to American GDP.[74] As can be seen, from figure 4.3, there has been a steady rise in all three measures – in the value added, net income, and number of foreign affiliates. In 2007, the value added of foreign affiliates was more than $1 trillion and net income $765 billion. With truly global reach, almost 25,000 American-controlled companies are dispersed around the world, strategically placed to see what the competition has to offer and what consumers want.[75]

As is visible from figures 4.4 and 4.5, no other country is home to as many large firms as the United States. It has nearly half of the top twenty-five firms, and approximately half of the sales and profits of the twenty-five largest firms in the world. This is three times as many firms and sales, and as much profit, as the closest competitor, the United Kingdom. The United States commands 30 percent of the 2,000 biggest firms in the world, 34 percent of their sales, and 29 percent of their profits. For comparison, its closest peers have 13 percent of the largest firms (Japan), 12 percent of their sales (Japan), and 9 percent of their profits (United Kingdom). Notice that China does not even make it on to the first figure and is at the very bottom of the second one.

The United States' liberalizing frenzy, which started with the creation of the GATT in 1948, has now touched every continent and benefited American firms and consumers alike. Predictions of a secular decline in American commercial preeminence are as misplaced as they were in the 1980s. Dispersing production around the world is not only good for business but for Americans in their consumer and investment capacity. Operating on a broad scale, large firms producing differentiated products can raise profits significantly by meeting customer needs and confronting rivals head-on. This strategy of openness benefits the American people, who not only gain in the form of low-cost product variety but from the income generated by

---

[74] Mataloni 2008. Note that I have not presented "real" trade figures and therefore do not use real value added.
[75] Quinlan and Chandler 2001.

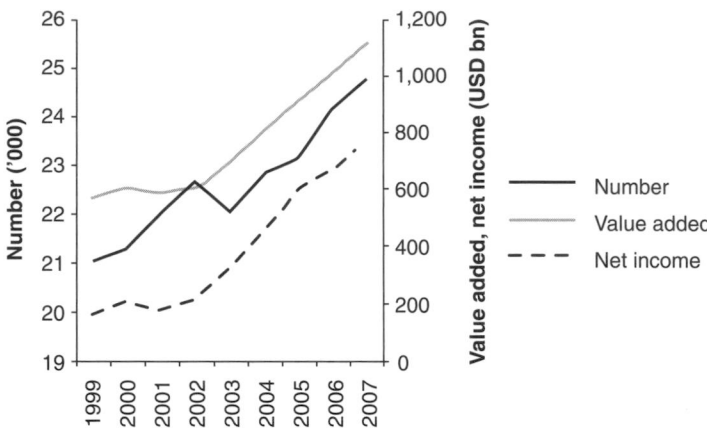

Figure 4.3 Value added, net income, and number of american majority-owned foreign affiliates
Notes: Number of foreign affiliates is measured on the primary y-axis. Value added and net income is measured on the secondary y-axis.
Source: Author's calculations based on data from BEA 2007a.

multinational activity. The income from foreign affiliates flows back to the United States as a matter of accounting practice. It shows up on current account as income from direct investment, regardless of whether profits are repatriated to the United States or not. American households, which hold between 80 to 90 percent of US equities, are the principle beneficiaries of the profits generated through the worldwide diffusion and integration of production.[76] *Imports* from foreign direct investment are more visible than *income* from foreign direct investment, since FDI-driven imports (c. 60 percent of total imports) appear on the trade portion of the current account at their sale price, whereas income under the receipts portion of the current account is listed as profits on sales.[77] This asymmetry contributes to the tendency to underestimate the benefits to the United States from spreading production worldwide. Although producing and selling from foreign destinations could have a negative impact on American employment, its potential repercussions on the American labor market are not unambiguously negative. The impact essentially depends on whether such FDI is primarily market-seeking or efficiency-seeking. As long as "market-seeking" foreign investment is expanding faster

[76] Farrell 2004, 14.   [77] Farrell 2004, 15.

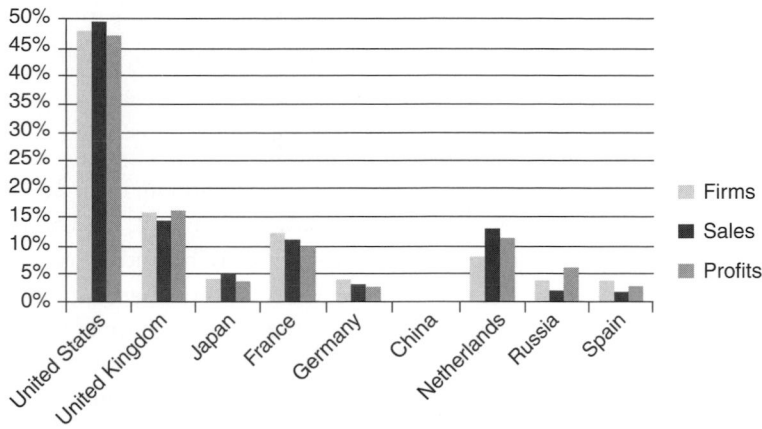

Figure 4.4 Country share of top 25 firms in the world (in terms of numbers, sales, profits, assets, and market value), 2008
Source: Forbes 2008.

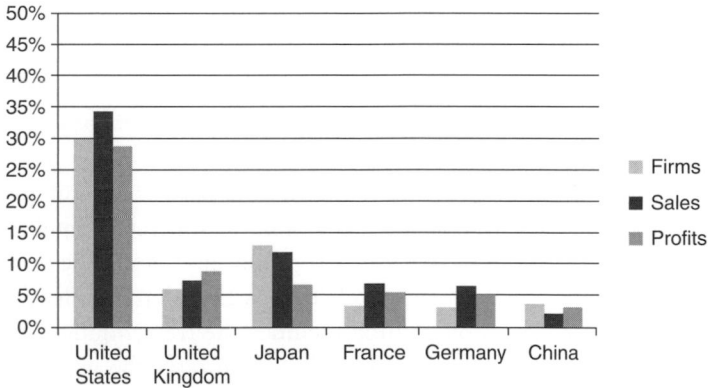

Figure 4.5 Country share of top 2,000 firms in the world (in terms of numbers, sales, profits, assets, and market value), 2008
Source: Forbes 2008.

than (production-shifting) "efficiency-seeking" investment, employment in the United States might actually expand as new personnel is needed to supervise expansion in overseas markets.[78]

However, in pointing to this favorable dynamic between import and commercial expansion, I do not mean to suggest that the trade deficit

[78] Mataloni 2004, 55.

does not exist or that its size is insignificant. The subsequent section outlines how the United States has made strategic use of its import pull.

Buying power as a source of bargaining power

The United States was the largest exporter in the world up until 2003, when Germany overtook America. As we saw in chapter 2, the United States is today the world's third largest exporter, behind Germany and China. Every year since 1948, the United States has imported more goods than any other country. The United States' share of world merchandise exports and imports between 1948 and 2008 is on display in figure 4.6. As mentioned in chapter 2, some caution is warranted in looking back at the United States' share of world trade in the immediate postwar years when Europe and Japan lay in shambles. The graph nevertheless makes plain the secular decline in the share of world exports and the long-term increase in the share of world imports. Notice the coincidence with the growth in America's world import shares in the early 1970s when flexible exchange rates were introduced. Since then, the American share of world imports has systematically been much larger than its share of world exports. A comprehensive discussion of the relationship between monetary policy and trade policy is offered in chapters 5 and 7.

This policy of domestic openness has created excellent business opportunities for American firms. The commercial benefits of import expansion cannot be assessed by simply examining the impact it has had on world export shares. Whereas this share is clearly in decline, a broader view – one which includes the tremendous dispersion of American production worldwide – calibrates the assessment of American commercial performance. Furthermore, while the deficit has not raised America's share of world merchandise exports, America's share of world service exports has grown considerably. Here, data is only available between 1980 and 2008.[79] During this period, America's share of world service exports has always been higher than its share of service imports. In addition, in this interval both the United States' share of world service exports and its share of world service imports increased by 3.4 percent. Whereas trade in services used to be a rather small share of overall trade, this share

---

[79] All trade data based on author's calculations using WTO 2009a, 2009b.

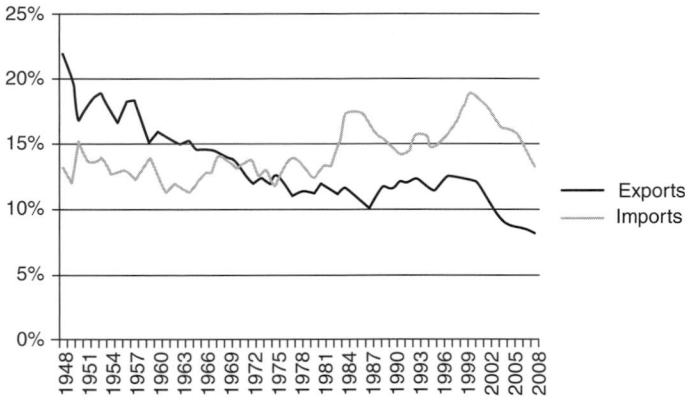

Figure 4.6 America's share of world merchandise trade
Note: The vertical axis measures the percentage of world trade.
Source: Author's calculations based on WTO 2009a.

has become increasingly important. The share of American service exports in its overall exports doubled between 1980 (14 percent) and 2008 (29 percent). American service imports as a share of all of its imports was 10 percent in 1980 and increased to 14 percent in 2008. Moreover, world trade in services is growing more rapidly than trade in goods. In 1980, the fraction of world exports in services was 10 percent (7 percent for imports) and by 2007 it had risen to 14 percent (11 percent for imports).

The United States gets a lot of mileage out of other countries' desire to access its product market. The dependence on the American market as export outlet provides the United States with an important instrument with which it can cajole other nations. The deficit is strategic, in the sense that it raises the credibility of the protectionist threat, making it possible to extract concessions in trade negotiations. As the world's favourite export destination, the United States derives considerable bargaining leverage from using its sizeable consumer-oriented market as bait. By making access to the American market conditional on trade liberalization in other countries, the government has prised open foreign markets, creating export opportunities and extending the global reach of its firms.

Equipped with a large internal market, the United States can afford to bargain coercively. It can adopt risky tactics, since the consequences of failed negotiations are less dramatic than for a small country highly dependent on trade. Despite the consensus rule guiding trade negotiations, the United States, along with other large traders such as the EU and Japan, has by virtue of its size had a disproportionate influence on negotiated outcomes. Whether negotiating in the context of GATT rounds or WTO ministerial meetings, consensus has been reached by first forging agreement within a group of core states. Because small countries are typically less patient than large ones, they have settled for limited concessions.[80] The United States and the EC were the major players before the Uruguay Round. Since then, the Quadrilateral (Quad) group, which also includes Japan and Canada, has functioned as an informal steering committee in international trade negotiations.[81] The United States' ability to offer access to a large consumer-oriented market has given it greater say than other members of the Quad group. In the following section, I explore further how buying power produces bargaining power in the context of the trade regime.

How the United States controls the global equilibrium through the trade regime

American dominance has often seemed benign because of the way it is exercised. The United States does not control states directly but manages them through international institutions. The GATT, for instance, was set up in the postwar era as a framework agreement of rules and principles to govern international trade relations, and ever since its inception, the United States has shaped its evolution. By providing rules of engagement, the United States has used the trade regime to set the terms for trade cooperation and has practiced rule bending as well as rule enforcement.

The first aim of this section is to point to the high consistency between American trade legislation and the agreements contained in the GATT/WTO, and to demonstrate how this coherence has allowed the United States to practice "conditional" free trade. If the United States were strictly committed to free trade, it would not be able to credibly threaten protectionism. Without the threat of market closure, it could not use market access as a bargaining tool after liberalizing trade in a particular sector. Second, I examine how trade statutes

---

[80] Drahos 2003, 81.   [81] Blackhurst 1998, 41–3, 47.

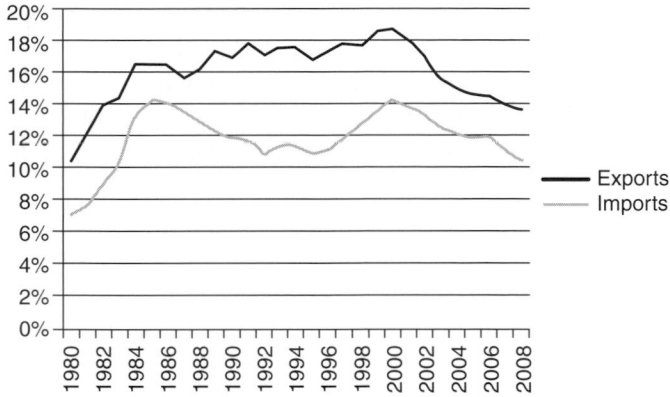

Figure 4.7 America's share of world trade in services
Note: The vertical axis measures the percentage of world trade.
Source: Author's calculations based WTO 2009a.

have been used to threaten and implement protectionist policies in order to induce others to open their markets. Third, I review how a high capacity and readiness to raise imports has been used to expand American commercial interests during GATT rounds and WTO ministerial meetings. Specifically, I show how, during the course of the Tokyo and Uruguay Rounds and the five WTO ministerial meetings that have been held to date, American influence has waxed and waned with the relative power gap in relation to other states as well as with variations in relative power among other states. In analyzing these negotiations, I will highlight what the United States wanted that conflicted with what other states wanted, who got what, and how the United States was able to use and reinforce its size advantage.

Agenda-setting, rule-bending, and rule enforcement

The United States' role in creating the GATT gave it major advantages by allowing it to model the institution on its own domestic trade law. In so doing, it permanently built in a number of safety valves through which the letter and spirit of negotiated trade agreements could be circumvented. While all states have an interest in such opt-out measures, the tight fit between American and international trade law allows the United States to maintain an open market on a revolving door basis. By setting the rules of the game, the United States has stayed one step ahead of its trade partners and controlled the global equilibrium to which others have had to adjust. This political framework has allowed the United States to turn its import market into a bargaining chip, threatening market closure by maintaining sufficiently large loopholes to wriggle out of trade commitments.

American trade laws

The United States has two statutes that deal with the effects of increased import penetration – the escape clause and trade adjustment assistance – and two that address unfair trade practices – the statutes on anti-dumping and countervailing duties.[82] When they have needed to do so, American firms have had a relatively easy time insulating themselves from import competition because provisions in the GATT and WTO for anti-dumping (AD) and countervailing duties (CVD) were directly imputed from the United States' own legal framework. Although there has been some movement to reform the WTO code on anti-dumping, the administration continues to use its AD laws as a protectionist device rather than as an instrument to counter below-cost pricing by foreign firms in the United States. American trade laws also include unfair trade statutes, such as section 337 to protect patent law and antitrust violations, and section 301 to oppose foreigners' "unfair" trade barriers. These trade laws are the necessary background prerequisites of the United States' commitment to an open market with high import penetration and have contributed to its success in liberalizing trade through successive GATT rounds and WTO ministerial meetings. Were it not for the existence of these statutes, which offer import-competing interests a way out in times of distress, the United States would not be able to offer broad-based market access to gain concessions from trade partners. Were it not for statutes, such as section 301, through which American firms can petition the United States Trade Representative (USTR) to remove trade barriers in foreign markets, protection at home could easily provoke retaliation abroad.

The GATT specifies a number of exceptions that countries can invoke when they are temporarily unable to meet the demands of free

---

[82] Goldstein 1986. Anti-dumping duties are levied on products that are sold at a lower price abroad than in the home market. Countervailing duties offset the use of export subsidies.

trade and for domestic reasons need to protect certain industries from international competition. Article 19, for instance, provides emergency protection against imports threatening serious domestic injury. But since Article 19 is cumbersome to use, the United States has relied on GATT provisions for AD and CVD under Article 6.[83] Although amendments to the 1979 Trade Act made it necessary to administer CVD complaints in conformity with GATT, the GATT codes for CVD and AD measures were modeled on the United States' trade statutes in the first place.[84] Instead of using GATT's article 19, American firms have thus been able to fall back on the more expedient AD and CVD statutes. The greater the compatibility between domestic and international trade laws, the lower the costs of adjusting trade practices to conform to those laid down in the international trade regime. This conformity, and the fact that dumping and subsidy complaints are administered at the domestic rather than at the international level, has been an advantage in preparing and winning such cases.

Although anti-dumping and countervailing provisions were designed to prevent exporters from using aggressive pricing strategies to gain monopoly control over markets, the United States has changed the very meaning of what constitutes dumping and turned these laws into a protectionist device. American AD laws are fraught with biases that inflate dumping margins, and unfortunately the AD code of the Tokyo Round accepted the idea that the normal value – the price of the product, or a similar product, charged in the exporter's home market – could be "constructed" by estimating production costs, overhead, and profits.[85] Moreover, to determine whether the domestic industry is materially injured as a result of dumping, the International Trade Commission (ITC) cumulates imports from different countries, a practice that overstates the injury caused by any single exporter and that presumes that foreign companies are colluding against American firms.[86] Some biases – such as averaging methods that bring prices below "normal value," and the practice of subtracting sales costs from the export price but not the home market price – have been corrected through the WTO Anti-dumping Agreement, but not

---

[83] Jackson 1997.   [84] Hoekman and Kostecki 2001, 306.
[85] Finger and Dhar 1994, 203–5. The dumping margin is the difference between the price of the export product and the normal value divided by the export price.
[86] Palmeter 1993, 188–9.

the practice of "cumulation," or the complicated reporting requirements that work against exporters.[87] American firms not only benefit from the indirect way AD complaints are administered, they also
gain, much more controversially, from collecting AD dues. Under the
"Continued Dumping and Subsidy Offset Act of 2000" (CDSOA),
also known as the Byrd Amendment, the United States distributes the
proceeds of AD duties to injured firms, a practice denounced by the
WTO in September 2002 (confirmed in the appellate body's January
2003 decision).[88]

AD measures were especially effective in the 1980s, since many
of the complaints were either approved or led to other forms of protection. Out of the 480 AD and 345 CVD investigations initiated by
the Commerce Department between 1980 and 1989, approximately
50 percent of the petitions that came up for review were accepted,
and almost invariably the government negotiated voluntary export
restraints (VERs) to console firms that had been denied relief.[89]
Through such VERs, countries imposed voluntary and fixed quantitative limitations on exports to the United States. Sometimes the
United States would also seek to increase its market share in the foreign country by a pre-specified quantity (voluntary import expansions). In many cases – 82 percent of the cases in 1988 – the United
States would strategically link AD investigations to VERs, promis-
ing to retract dumping allegations if the exporting country agreed
to limit sales to the American market.[90] For instance, the United
States negotiated VERs in color televisions with Japan, South Korea,
and Taiwan, as well as in cars with Japan.[91] The United States also
persuaded Japan to voluntarily expand imports in semiconductors.
Under the 1986 semiconductor agreement, Japan agreed to desig-
nate 20 percent of its market to foreign suppliers, an agreement that
American companies claim successfully countered "keiretsu," i.e.,
horizontal networks of firms.[92] In economic terms, VERs have been
more damaging than voluntary import expansions but they have been
politically more expedient.[93] Broader market opening commitments

[87] Niels 2000, 479–80.
[88] The United States appealed the first decision in October 2002.
[89] Destler 1995, 154.   [90] Hindley and Messerlin 1993.
[91] Aggarwal and Ravenhill 2001, 3–4.   [92] Tyson 1993, 257, 265.
[93] VERs are more price-distorting than VIEs; export limitations encourage
both domestic and foreign producers to raise prices.

have rather been achieved by threatening and implementing export restraints than by directly persuading countries to expand imports. The size of the American market explains why target countries were willing to accept voluntary measures of this sort. Temporary export restrictions were deemed more desirable than a general closing of the American market. Another large trader, the EC, was also able to negotiate VERs, before these were outlawed under the WTO, although not as frequently as the United States.

The United States has also negotiated more lasting forms of protection in specific areas. It has endorsed generalized forms of protection in sectors characterized by low entry and high exit barriers where temporary restraints such as VERs or VIEs would be of little use.[94] Whereas VERs have been an appropriate way of dealing with competition in industries characterized by scale economies – i.e., among countries producing similar goods, such as steel and automobiles – more general forms of protection have been negotiated with countries producing less sophisticated goods such as footwear and televisions, while institutionalized protection has been the best way of managing competition in areas with even lower entry barriers, such as in textiles and apparel.[95] This pattern of protection, the temporary protection among rich industrialized countries, the semi-permanent protection against intermediate traders, and the permanent forms of protection towards developing countries, could already be detected in the early 1980s.[96] The United States has supported liberalization in areas where its firms can compete and resisted liberalization in areas where domestic producers cannot compete with low-cost suppliers in developing countries.

The United States started to use anti-dumping and unfair trade allegations more and more strategically with the burgeoning deficits of the 1980s. Leaning on section 301 to target foreign obstacles to trade, it has unique trade policy powers with which to correct the deficit. Large-scale firms dealing in semiconductors, commercial aircraft, and telecommunications equipment became conditional free traders that threatened and at times took action under unfair trade statutes to counter rivals in Japan and Europe.[97] American trade law

---

[94] Aggarwal, Keohane, and Yoffie 1987.
[95] Aggarwal, Keohane, and Yoffie 1987.
[96] Lipson 1982, 428–33.   [97] Milner and Yoffie 1989.

became a tool with which the United States' Trade Representative (USTR) and the President would identify, threaten and retaliate against "unjustifiable" and "unreasonable" trade barriers in order to expand foreign market shares. Section 301 of the Trade and Tariff Act of 1984 gave the USTR authority to initiate investigations into such "unfair" trade practices, extending the President's authority to strike against "unjustifiable" and "unreasonable" barriers under the Trade Acts of 1974 and 1979 in services, intellectual property, and foreign direct investment.[98] As a new innovation in the 1974 Trade Act, private firms could petition the USTR to investigate unfair trade practices. Here, one can note that while European firms have (since 1996) had recourse to a similar procedure known as the Trade Barrier Regulation (TBR), there was increased pressure after 1995 (and the introduction of the WTO) to use trade policy powers in ways consistent with the Dispute Settlement Body, which served as a constraint on its discretionary nature.[99] The precursor to the 1996 TBR, the New Commercial Policy Instrument (NCPI), could only be triggered on an industry basis, not by individual firms.

The United States has maintained an open market but it has reserved the right to protect firms' interests both at home and abroad. Administrative agencies and trade statutes have been on standby to intervene on behalf of American firms. When business interests have been threatened at home, the United States has responded with anti-dumping and countervailing duties. When American firms have had a hard time competing in foreign markets, the United States has used its trade policy powers to enforce trade "rights". Interventions of this kind have allowed the United States to reap the benefits of open markets without fully internalizing their constraints. The ability to negotiate loopholes in various sectors has provided the flexibility to ascertain when and what goods are traded freely, enhancing domestic support for liberalization. Because of these flexibility measures, the United States has been better equipped than other countries to adopt import-reducing policies in order to adjust trade deficits that have grown too large. While other countries have resisted free trade

---

[98] Bayard and Elliott 1993, 24–5. The 1974 Trade Act was itself an elaboration of the 1962 Trade Expansion Act (section 252) which authorized the President to retaliate against "unjustifiable" practices in agriculture, as well as some other fields.

[99] Van Eeckhaute 1999, 199–201.

as well, they have not been able to flout GATT/WTO principles, in GATT or WTO-consistent ways, as the United States has done. The United States' influence on the trade regime has ensured a high degree of conformity with the provisions of the trade regime and American trade laws.

Bargaining rounds and ministerial meetings

From the Tokyo to the Uruguay round and through WTO ministerial meetings, the United States has used foreigners' eagerness to access the American market tactically. At times threatening to exercise its exit option with one of its trade partners (e.g., with the European Union in the Uruguay Round), and at other times forming provisional coalitions with trade partners, the United States has tried – and for the most part succeeded – in extracting concessions in multilateral negotiations. Throughout GATT rounds, the United States and Europe have dominated discrete phases of the negotiating process, from the stage of initiating and developing proposals, to discussing and drafting texts, to merging different schemes into a final act.[100] As predicted by the model presented in chapter 3, the ability of the United States to devise trade agreements that reflect its own interests, to a greater extent than its partners', varies with the distribution of power in non-linear ways.

The Tokyo Round

The United States was generally understood to be in relative decline during the time of the Tokyo Round negotiations, which lasted from 1973 to 1979. With two oil price shocks as well as the ensuing inflation, eyes turned away from the United States and towards her nearest competitors, the European Community (EC) and Japan. The EC, which then comprised the six founding members – Germany, France, Italy, the Netherlands, Belgium, and Luxembourg – underwent an important phase of enlargement, as Denmark, Ireland, and the United Kingdom joined in 1973. The first seeds of the euro had also been planted at this time, with the introduction of the European Exchange Rate Mechanism (ERM) in 1972. In the east, Japan was

---

[100] Steinberg 2002, 354–55.

rising, implementing reforms to navigate the world economic shocks, which would turn out to be the foundation of the miracle years in the 1980s. In terms of the model presented in chapter 3, the distribution of power during this period and halfway through the Uruguay Round can loosely be described as 6:3:3.

Given this configuration of power, the United States was less able to influence the terms of agreement than during the period after 1948, when it was more dominant. Not surprisingly, and as the model in chapter 3 predicts, the EC prevailed in tariff negotiations. However, the United States managed to reform rules on certain non-tariff barriers (NTB), while scuttling reform in areas where it had an interest in maintaining grey-zone rules. Over the longer term, American objectives were well served, since NTB protection had become more pervasive and allowed for greater discretion and flexibility.

By the time of the Tokyo Round, cooperation within the EC had accelerated significantly and Europe emerged as a major force in international trade. The first wave of European enlargement in 1973 when the United Kingdom, Denmark, and Ireland joined the EEC, left its imprint on the Tokyo Round talks. The EC prevailed in negotiations on how to reduce tariffs. A method close to the EC's tariff-cutting preference, the "Swiss formula," was used to harmonize tariff dispersions, bringing them down by an average of 30 percent. The benefits tied to this method, however, were counterbalanced by a series of victories the United States enjoyed in negotiating non-tariff codes.[101] By the mid 1970s, non-tariff barriers were increasingly used to block imports in the industrialized world. The United States itself had become keen on using administrative trade laws to restrict imports, and wanted non-tariff barriers such as orderly marketing arrangements (OMAs) to persist in textiles, clothing, and footwear. The extensive use of subsidies in Europe, and Japan's defiant attitude towards government procurement, were especially vexing to the US government. In the end, the United States accomplished some of its negotiating objectives by winning reforms on certain non-tariff barriers – customs valuation, government procurement, import

---

[101] Hoekman and Kostecki 2001; Whalley 1982, 60, 346. The United States preferred the linear across the board formula used in the Kennedy Round due to the relatively high escalation in its tariff structure. The Swiss formula brought tariffs down in the following manner: $T_2 = rT_1/(r+T_1)$ with r ranging between 14 and 16 percent.

licensing, and product standards – while blocking the elimination of non-tariff barriers (NTBs) in other sectors – in agriculture, food, textiles and apparel, footwear, iron and steel, consumer electronics, and shipbuilding.[102]

The United States accepted revisions to the AD and CVD codes. These codes were modified by incorporating a clause that any injury suffered must be "material." Yet the term "material" was never properly defined; the Commerce department and the USTR thus retained wide latitude in determining what injury should count as "material."[103] The United States also started playing around with the MFN principle – a cornerstone of the non-discrimination principle upon which GATT is founded – by proposing that the Tokyo Round codes only apply to signatories.[104] The codes covered a slew of issues ranging from countervailing duties and subsidies, anti-dumping, technical barriers to trade (standards), import licensing, government procurement, customs valuation, bovine meat, dairy products, and civil aircraft. To the United States' dismay, developing countries insisted that the anti-dumping and subsidies codes were interpretations of GATT obligations and should therefore apply on a non-discriminatory basis.[105] This legalistic approach did not go down well with American trade negotiators who threatened to walk away from the regime and set up an alternative preferential regime.[106] Developing countries were not denied their treaty-based rights, but they did have to accept non-tariff barriers (NTBs) to trade in labor-intensive goods.

The Uruguay Round

At the beginning of the Uruguay Round, which began in 1986, the American economy had experienced rapid sustained growth for several years but Japan too was booming, and European consolidation was well on its way with the signing of the Single European Act (SEA) in 1987 to establish a single market by 1992. By the beginning of the 1990s, problems were starting to appear in Japan, whereas the Maastricht Treaty, establishing the European Union, was signed in 1993. After long-protracted negotiations, the United States and the

---

[102] Deardorff and Stern 1983, 609.   [103] Krasner 1979, 517.
[104] Krasner 1979, 515.   [105] Steinberg 2002, 357.
[106] Steinberg 2002, 357–60.

EC became the hub of the Uruguay Round talks, which lasted from 1986 to 1994. Towards the end of negotiations, the distribution of power started to look a lot like the size ratio 6:4:2 (in the language of chapter 3). This phase would last from 1992 to 2002 and include the onset of the euro, which was formally introduced in 1999. This growth in European power, which occurred at the expense of Japan's position, gave the United States renewed clout.

The United States had a strong preference for extending trade to new areas such as intellectual property, services, and investment, and also wanted to strengthen the GATT's dysfunctional dispute settlement mechanism. The EC had similar preferences. The EC's preferences were, however, less intense when it came to liberalizing trade in services, and it had no desire to subject textiles or agriculture to GATT discipline.[107] The United States also wanted to liberalize trade in farm grains, which the EC eventually agreed to do. Due to the higher escalation in the United States' tariff structure, it insisted on an offer-for-offer approach, instead of the harmonizing approach proposed by the EC, and introduced the concept of "open sectoralism" with "zero-for-zero" tariffs.[108] Taking such a sectoral approach allowed the United States to achieve a great deal of liberalization in key sectors without significantly touching protectionist strongholds in textiles and agriculture. By "cherry-picking" sectors where the United States had a comparative advantage it was able to avoid liberalization in areas where import-competing industries sought protection. This approach is beneficial for countries who trade in goods similar to the United States but not for developing countries who trade in different, complementary, goods.[109] A sectoral approach favors countries whose firms compete in intra-industry trade, and damages countries whose trade is based on the traditional comparative advantages underscored by classical and neo-classical theorists.

As home to the world's largest corporations, the United States and the EC have also been able to benefit from superior access to information through "networks of commercial intelligence" that connect administrative agencies, business organizations, and private corporations.[110] The United States in particular has been very forward in

---

[107] Cline 1995, 2.   [108] Cline 1995, 2.6.
[109] Aggarwal and Ravenhill 2001; Krueger 1999, 916–17; Stiglitz 2000, 443.
[110] Drahos 2003, 83–4.

this regard, as when it created the Advisory Committee for Trade Policy and Negotiation in 1974, an association that has informed policy-makers on how to link trade, intellectual property rights, and investment.[111] In 1986, the USTR invited a handful of large American companies to highlight the importance of intellectual property in key industries.[112] The inclusion of these three new areas – intellectual property, services, and investment – promised high rewards. Other countries' gradual convergence on American standards for intellectual property protection would allow the United States to appropriate considerable rents, and leave other countries with the burden of adjustment in exchange for improved access to the American market.[113]

Extending the trade regime's coverage to include intellectual property rights, services, and investment was one of the American government's top priorities at the time of the Uruguay Round negotiations. The EC and Japan finally came around but developing countries fiercely resisted their inclusion. When recalcitrant states finally acquiesced to bring intellectual property rights protection under the WTO's umbrella, this was in large part due to the deterrent threat at the interface of American trade law and the "single-undertaking" approach. In order to force countries to accept the Final Act in its entirety, the United States and the EC retired from the GATT and its obligation to grant unconditional MFN.[114] As predicted in chapter 3, the prospective bilateral coalition between the United States and the European Union would have been a very expensive proposition for the United States, who had much to lose from a general closing of borders, had it been concretized without a follow-up multilateral accord. The United States' opportunity cost of not getting its many demands – in dispute settlement, agriculture, services, intellectual property, and telecommunications – signed into international agreement was extremely high. Fortunately for the United States, other states were able to see the danger in an exclusive arrangement between these two mammoth-sized traders, without testing them with exceedingly high demands (i.e., requests for side-payments). Their threat became a first step in constructing a multilateral text rather than the end phase of negotiations. The efficacy of this threat lay in the fact that once the "single-undertaking" approach was sealed, a refusal to sign up to the

[111] Drahos 2003, 83–4.   [112] Stegemann 2000, 1242.
[113] Stegemann 2000, 1241–2.   [114] Steinberg 2002, 357–60.

agreement on trade in intellectual property rights (TRIPs), or any other of the Uruguay agreements, meant being denied entry to the WTO. More than that, it meant losing access to the American and European markets, since both the United States and the European Union had promised to rescind GATT 1947. Rejecting TRIPs was to dispense with major export outlets and to accept increased exposure to unilateral action under super 301 – which asked the USTR to establish an annual "hit-list" of countries and practices deemed particularly "unfair" – without recourse to WTO arbitration.[115] The United States ultimately succeeded in liberalizing trade in telecommunications and financial services as well, although these agreements were not concluded until 1997. In both cases, the United States prevailed in negotiations by persuading developing countries, especially in Asia, that a failure to reform telecommunications and financial services would deter foreign direct investment.[116]

The Uruguay Round also brought on changes in the regulatory framework consistent with American trade policy preferences. Most importantly, the Uruguay Round enhanced the enforcement powers of the dispute settlement system. With trade deficits looming larger in the 1980s, there had been specific attempts to target countries that had large bilateral trade surpluses with the United States. This was the aim of the infamous Gephardt amendment, which never came to pass. Instead, section 301 of the 1988 Omnibus Trade and Competitiveness Act was amended to include "special 301" – to defend intellectual property rights – as well as the aforementioned super 301.[117] These measures were never intended to close off the American market to foreign goods but as a means to pry open foreign markets without obliging the United States to offer concessions in return. The mere threat of retaliation, which these instruments evoked, was sometimes enough to induce market-opening measures. Trade sanctions were only imposed in fifteen out of the ninety-eight cases launched between 1974 and 1995.[118] The Uruguay Round was negotiated under the shadow of this threat. According to a letter from President Clinton to the Speaker of the US House of Representatives Thomas Foley written on December 15, 1993, the top priority of the Uruguay round was to enhance the effectiveness of GATT dispute settlement

---

[115] Stegemann 2000, 1243.   [116] Crystal 2003.
[117] Bayard and Elliott 1993, 24, 32.   [118] Puckett and Reynolds 1996, 689.

and to ensure that American rights were enforced.[119] Faced with the choice between unilateral or multilateral enforcement of trade agreements, other countries were easily persuaded to revamp the GATT's dispute settlement procedure. The United States' use of "aggressive unilateralism" to reduce trade barriers in foreign markets through section 301 legislation produced tangible results. It helped broaden GATT coverage to include new areas such as services, intellectual property rights, and foreign investment, and to conclude separate liberalizing agreements with Brazil, Japan, South Korea, and Taiwan.[120] Super 301 led to sectoral agreements in cellular telephones and third-party radios in 1989, supercomputers in 1990, and lurked in the background when the United States negotiated the structural impediments initiative in 1989, as well as the market-oriented sector-specific talks with Japan between 1985 and 1986, and the 1992 agreement on trade in commercial aircraft with the EC.[121]

Under GATT, there was very little else that countries could do to counter the enforcement of trade rights. Although the GATT detailed the specific circumstances under which markets could be closed off, and provided a dispute settlement system to adjudicate trade conflicts, it lacked the authority to enforce panel rulings, and so could not reign in American unilateralism. The problem with the GATT's dispute settlement mechanism was that members had to agree unanimously to adopt panel rulings. With the introduction of the WTO's Dispute Settlement Understanding (DSU) in 1995, panel rulings have to be adopted unless there is unanimous agreement to reject the decision, which effectively makes panel decisions binding. Since the United States is bound to use dispute settlement procedures whenever a WTO agreement is called into question, these enhanced enforcement powers toned down the unilateral streak in American trade policy.[122] While strengthened procedures for settling disputes has constrained the United States' ability to pursue its interests unchecked, other countries must still fear a closing of the American market and how this will affect their export interests. Moreover, although section 301 has been used in ways consistent with the DSU, the United States has shown no signs of relinquishing its statutory powers. Section 301

---

[119] Puckett and Reynolds 1996, 688.
[120] Bayard and Elliott 1993, 39, 41–2, 53, 64.   [121] Tyson 1993, 256–8.
[122] Schoenbaum 1996, 171–4.

remains a coercive instrument that the United States can use to pry open foreign markets and take on trade partners bilaterally. Out of twenty-seven section 301 cases initiated between January 1995 and August 2002, the WTO arbitrated seventeen cases while ten were resolved bilaterally outside WTO purview.[123] As one might expect, retaliatory threats have been particularly effective when used against countries that are heavily dependent on the American market.[124]

Five ministerial meetings: from Singapore to Hong Kong

The WTO came into force in early 1995, after the conclusion of the Uruguay Round in 1994 at Marrakech. Since then, five ministerial meetings have been held on a biannual basis, with mixed results. The "built-in-agenda" agreed upon at Singapore in 1996 launched the ninth Geneva Round in 1998, produced a failed meeting at Seattle in 1999, the Doha Round (2001), another mishap at Cancun in 2003, and the Hong Kong ministerial meeting of 2005.[125] At the beginning of this period, the distribution of power was largely what it was at the end of the Uruguay Round negotiations. During the Doha Round, however, and especially after the 9/11 attacks and China rising, the United States has often been characterized as being in decline, with the distribution of power approximating the size ratio 5:4:3. The year 2002 was also the last in which the United States was the world's largest exporter.

Confrontation between the United States and developing countries produced deadlock at both Seattle and Cancun. At the time of the Seattle ministerial meeting, American proposals for harmonizing labor and environmental standards were high on the agenda. Bringing these issues into the trade realm was fiercely resisted by developing countries. They saw this as an attempt to erode their comparative advantage in labor- and resource-intensive goods. A series of moves on the part of the US administration brought the conflict to a head. Just before the Seattle meeting, President Clinton declared that market access should be made conditional on high labor standards, and in the run-up to Cancun, President Bush approved steel tariffs and the US Farm Bill, while the USTR Robert Zoellick backpedaled on the American offer to slash agricultural subsidies in the midst of negotiations at Cancun.[126]

---

[123] Iida 2004, 216.   [124] Bayard and Elliott 1993.
[125] Wolfe 2004, 575–6.   [126] Bhagwati 2004.

Spearheaded by Brazil, India, and China, the G-21 was extremely critical of attempts to limit reductions in export subsidies to "products of particular interest to developing countries" and America's attempt to legitimize its own Farm Bill by sneaking in a new class of "less trade-distorting domestic support."[127] The real bone of contention, however, was the item dubbed "Singapore issues" – competition policy, investment, trade facilitation, and transparency in government procurement – especially the former two. With a dominant position in imperfectly competitive markets, the United States was less adamant than the European Union, Japan, and South Korea about bringing competition policy under the WTO's wing. Negotiations proved cumbersome, with little movement in countries' negotiating positions. Eventually, the chair, Mexico's foreign minister Luis Ernesto Derbez, brought the negotiations to an abrupt halt, a move endorsed by Zoellick, who wanted to signal that the United States was prepared to go it alone and deal with "will-do" nations on a bilateral basis.[128]

The Doha Round talks were put on ice in the summer of 2008. Halfway through the talks, China seemed to accept the American offer on farm subsidies and industrial tariffs but, as time lapsed, China moved away from this position (and toward India's position). With the demise of the US–China coalition, both parties lost a potential bargaining chip. Given the lack of common ground between the European Union and Japan/China, or the European Union and the United States, no party has, for the time being, been able to impose its preferred solution. Instead, these heavyweights are expected to continue negotiating bilateral agreements with medium-sized and smaller states. Despite the inauguration of a new administration, there is still no sign of resolving the impasse between key players. The breakdown in the talks can be blamed on American intransigence. The United States has not been able to build a grand coalition around its policy preferences because its demands are too costly for the other players. The eminent trade economist, Jagdish Bhagwati, calls the United States a "selfish hegemon."[129] The more self-serving demands include America's request to retain farm subsidies, as well as the insistence that emerging markets completely eliminate or drastically cut tariffs in industrial sectors (e.g., chemicals including pharmaceuticals,

---

[127] Cho 2004, 228.   [128] Bhagwati 2004.
[129] Bhagwati 2008.

electronics, and industrial machinery). The call to retain subsidies has raised the ire of developing countries, especially super-developing countries such as China and India, because their interest to protect small farmers from import surges of more than 10 percent through the "special safeguard mechanism" has not been heard (the United States recommends a trigger at 40 percent). As Bhagwati points out, the Doha Round, which after all was launched as a development round, initially exempted developing countries from agricultural concessions. More broadly, however, asking countries to commit to opening up entire sectors does not leave them with much negotiation space to bargain liberalization in areas where they have a comparative advantage.

The Doha Round was log-jammed before the financial crisis swept over the world but currently the specter of the devastating Smoot-Hawley tariff, introduced in the wake of the Great Depression, does not seem to haunt policy-makers enough to unblock the stalemate. Although it will be difficult to forge a trade deal in the current climate, everyone realizes that a global deal is preferable to the fragmentation of the world trade system into bilateral and regional blocs, so this phase should be transient. Ironically, the United States is in a good position to reap extraordinary gains from this round but has not made the right moves. A more effective, less egregious approach would be to give in on the 10 percent trigger for the special safeguards provision. If it did that, it could probably achieve a dispensation to dole out farm subsidies at current levels in exchange for a commitment to phase out farm support, and even get emerging countries to take another look at the sectoral approach. They could be encouraged to open up their markets to American products to a greater extent than before because not doing so carries greater risks in the current world climate. American protectionism is predictable unless the country is able to export itself out of the crisis or absorb less of the world's exports (i.e., world trade contracts) over a sustained period. Saving the world economy without aggravating its current problems entails stimulating demand in big emerging markets, and building a stable coalition to avert bilateralism and a general slide into protectionism – everybody's worst-case scenario. As suggested in the first part of this chapter, the ability of American markets to absorb foreign savings is a precursor to the trade deficit, so creating investment opportunities – whether in the form of equity, debt, deposits, or real estate – in countries with large surplus savings (of which emerging countries comprise a large share) is vital to correcting the American deficit.[130] Opening up the manufacturing base to competition in super-developing countries could take care of two flies in one go. It would protect against shrinking trade and encourage domestic savings to stay home while attracting foreign investment. Both these developments would reinforce each other and go some way towards correcting global imbalances, but not replace the need for improved capital markets in emerging markets through which lenders and borrowers can meet.

Conclusion

Traditional theories (the classical and neoclassical approaches) construct free trade as a public good, from which everyone benefits. According to the theory, the gains from trade are non-rival so it makes no sense to exclude states from trade benefits. Only under very special circumstances are states able to benefit at the expense of trade partners. A leading state can, for instance, shift gains in its favor by imposing an optimal tariff on smaller states. New trade theories point to ways in which firms and states can exclude each other from trade benefits. They complement traditional theories by pointing to rivalry over trade, and emphasizing that firms under certain market conditions behave in ways which, at least temporarily, lock competitors out of a particular market segment. They explain the extensive trade that takes place among similar, industrialized, countries. To grasp current trade patterns fully and understand how trade affects the distribution of income among countries, one needs to look beyond classical and neoclassical approaches. New trade theories are better suited – indeed, were designed – to address questions of distribution and can help us understand why American firms have projected themselves into other parts of the world, established foreign production sites, and adopted "make where you sell" tactics.

American trade laws have helped the United States maintain an open market in ways that benefit American consumers and internationally oriented firms. The United States' share of world imports started to increase in the mid-1960s and began to exceed its share of

[130] Martin Wolf has an excellent article on the need to stimulate private borrowing in surplus countries in order to adjust global imbalances and promote free trade: see Wolf 2008.

world exports in 1976. Many view this trend as worrying and a sign of weakness. Yet the world's dependence on American import expansion is what underpins American wealth and power. The import pull has not only raised American living standards but provided the administration with an effective bargaining tool capable of furthering American commercial interests regardless of where they are located. By threatening to exclude parties from trade benefits – both by threatening to restrict access to the American market, and by threatening exclusion from trade arrangements – the United States has been in a good position to negotiate favorable trade agreements. However, gains shifting is more difficult to achieve when smaller Great Powers are equally sized, as was the case in the Tokyo Round.

A permanent policy of maximizing imports over exports would of course be unsustainable. After a long wave of import expansion, the dollar and the deficit have typically declined over a five- to seven-year period. Foreigners' reliance on the American market during good times has made them more inclined to facilitate adjustment during bad times, partly because other alternatives do not seem viable or desirable. An account of how this mechanism works, and the benefits tied to it, are the subject of the next chapter.

5 | *Interactive effects between monetary and commercial power*

The specific focus of this chapter is how monetary privilege interacts with commercial dominance and, in particular, how the United States' special position in the monetary domain has produced commercial advantages, and how commercial power has enhanced monetary gains. While the extent of these gains varies over different periods, the political and economic benefits over the last quarter-century have, on the whole, been extraordinary and arguably greater than what any other state has been able to achieve.

Chapter 2 raised concerns about how to quantify benefits from international economic cooperation and suggested possible measures. In this chapter, I will show that the United States benefits disproportionately in the trade and monetary realm. Over the twenty-five-year period under consideration, more goods have come to the United States than have been shipped out to foreign destinations. By implication, more capital has also flowed into the United States than out of the United States (see chapter 4). More significantly, aggregate yields on the smaller capital outflow (or, more precisely, stock of foreign assets) have been higher than on the larger capital inflow (i.e., stock of foreign liabilities). Due to its financial hegemony, the United States has also experienced significant capital and exchange rate gains on the value of its foreign assets and liabilities. Even when scaled to economic size, i.e., as a share of GDP, these gains are higher than the gains experienced by any other state. As I will also show, the United States is able to pursue and benefit from policies that would be disastrous for other countries, and so also gains politically in terms of policy autonomy. Although it is not entirely free from the constraints of the market, it has more degrees of freedom and is not as easily disciplined as other actors in the system.

First, I point to the benefits of monetary hegemony and the way in which monetary hegemony can ease commercial expansion.

How monetary privilege facilitates commercial expansion

There are several ways in which the dollar's role in liquidity creation produces commercial benefits. In the previous chapter I argued that the ability to stretch imports over exports for sustained periods has generated production and consumption benefits, as well as bargaining advantages within the trade regime, some of which have helped maintain the necessary flexibility to adjust trade deficits. In this section, I show that the United States' special position in monetary affairs, its role as financial intermediary, and the continued role of the dollar in the world economy, have facilitated commercial expansion and sustained trade deficits for unusually long periods.

The structure of international lending

The United States derives unique economic benefits because it is the key currency country and home to the world's single largest market for goods and capital. The overarching rationale for a key currency is to achieve efficiency and stability in international transactions. In a world of nearly 200 countries, trading goods and assets would be very costly if the currency of each partner country had to be accepted (or acquired) at each sale (or purchase). Dealing in one currency drastically reduces transaction costs. A key currency is needed for "efficient management of information and the minimization of search costs [as well as] efficient management of risk [fostering] diversification."[1]

A key currency effectively has to perform three main roles. It must serve as (1) a medium of exchange; (2) a unit of account; and (3) a store of value. The key currency must play these roles in private and public international economic transactions, though for somewhat different reasons. All three functions generate demand for the key currency (see table 5.1).

As a *medium of exchange*, private actors use the key currency, as an intermediary currency, instead of their respective currencies, to buy goods, services, and assets. In other words, the key currency functions as a means of payment. Thus, the key currency will be the most frequently traded currency in foreign exchange markets. Governments

[1] Kenen 2002.

Table 5.1 *Key currency functions*

Role	Private use	Official use
Medium of exchange	Vehicle	Intervention
Unit of account	Invoice/quotation	Peg/reference
Store of value	Banking/investment	Reserve

Source: Krugman 1991a.[2]

too will use the key currency as a means of intervening in foreign exchange markets, if they wish to defend the value of their own (or another) currency. The key currency also serves as a *unit of account*, with the price of goods, services, and assets quoted in the currency. Officially, governments track the value of the key currency in order to determine the price of their own currency, either by fixing their exchange rate against the key currency, by pegging to it, or more loosely by considering its value when delineating monetary policy. As a *store of value*, the key currency is used by private actors to hold their investments because they believe the value of their investments will increase, not erode, over time. A currency that is a good store of value is also an attractive reserve currency for official investors. This is a comprehensive list of the structural demand for the key currency.

What this suggests is that, as world income grows, the demand for dollar assets also grows, and that, as the world's largest capital market, the United States is able to meet this demand by providing a wide range of liquid assets – cash, bank deposits, and public and private bonds.[3] As we will see, this ability to satisfy world demand for an array of liquid dollar assets also implies that the time constraint on American debt is very fluid. The United States has long been regarded as a financial intermediary, providing long-term loans through direct investment and purchases of other risky foreign securities while satisfying foreigners' demand for liquidity by offering them low but "safe" returns on short-term securities held in the United States.[4] Because of foreigners' need for safe and liquid capital markets, America's international investment position is longer in assets than in liabilities. The international investment position (IIP) or foreign asset position (FAP)

[2] Krugman modifies the framework elaborated by Cohen 1971.
[3] McKinnon 2001a, 4.
[4] Despres, Kindleberger, and Salant 1966.

is a balance sheet over the value of the country's foreign assets and foreign liabilities. Despres, Kindleberger, and Salant saw the United States' role as financial intermediary as beneficial for the United States but also for other countries, who now had access to long-term financial flows.[5]

When undertaken by banks, the practice of borrowing short – in effect selling low-yield securities to buy high-yield securities – is called "gapping." Recycling low-cost foreign capital by lending to households on soft terms, banks act as intermediaries between the international and home markets. This view of the United States as "banker to the world" has been taken to another level in the characterization of the United States as a "world venture capitalist." Over time, the foreign asset position has become increasingly leveraged; the share of risky assets rose from 50 percent in 1973 to 60 percent in 2004.[6] Like a venture capitalist, the United States has a leveraged portfolio, purchasing risky assets through low-cost borrowing.

Banks' capacity to borrow on soft terms, because of the demand for liquid dollar assets in the world economy, is reinforced by unparalleled military might and a tradition of strong property rights protection, which combine to diminish the risks and therefore the costs of attracting funds. Capitalizing on the ability to secure its home base both militarily and legally, through property rights protection, the United States has collected a huge security premium (see chapter 6 for more on these security aspects). As will be discussed later in this chapter, foreign demand for dollar assets is also a function of foreign governments' own policy objectives. For instance, official investors accumulate reserves by investing in American government bonds (Treasury bills) as part of an export-promoting strategy. Between 2000 and 2008, foreign official assets held in the United States were on average 16 percent of overall liabilities, similar to the levels in the mid-1980s.[7]

While motives for placing capital in the United States will vary, there is clearly no shortage of incentives. The capital that flows to the United States is then reprocessed through the banking sector in part to households, in part through the corporate sector, and in part through the public sector.[8] Before we have a look at the benefits tied to

---

[5] Despres, Kindleberger, and Salant 1966.
[6] Gourinchas and Rey 2005a, 15–16.   [7] BEA 2007a.
[8] McKinnon 2001b, 4.

the structure of America's investment relationships with other countries, we need to ask: what precisely is the extent of the capital surge into the United States?

As can be seen from figure 5.1, the United States has attracted an enormous share of world capital. The figure shows the American share of world current account deficits (or, surplus for the years 1980 and 1981) and so the share of world capital flowing to the United States, and the evolution of the United States' share of world external liabilities as a result of capital inflows. Although, the world's current account deficits should, in theory, equal the world's current account surpluses (and by definition, world capital inflows), there is a discrepancy, not least because all countries do not report to the IMF and because some countries only do so for select years. I have chosen 1977 as starting point, since this is when Japan first started to submit data to the IMF and because that year brought the total number of reporting countries up to 144 (as compared to only eighty-six the year before and twenty in 1971). During twenty-five years of this thirty-two-year period, the United States absorbed more than 20 percent of world savings, and for thirteen years it absorbed more than half of world savings, at times swallowing more than 70 percent of world savings (e.g., 2002 and 2003). Measured in real numbers, the surplus capital flowing out of the United States was between 1977 and 2008 roughly $7 billion whereas the surplus capital flowing into the United States amounted to more than $7 trillion ($7.5 trillion). Even if one allows for the need to adjust net capital outflows for inflation (given that the surplus is confined to 1980), no plausible inflation rate can make these figures seem ordinary. Is it good for a country to draw in large amounts of foreign capital? The following section explores benefits, before looking at potential downsides.

The specific benefit of seignorage has been known for a long time and the United States is not the first to enjoy it. The word seignorage comes from Medieval French ("droit du seigneur") and means lord's right, i.e., the prerogative of the lord to claim something. Here, it refers to the privilege of creating money, coining, or printing money; or, today, increasing credit on the Federal Reserve's balance sheet, and the profit made by creating money. There are two components to seignorage. On the one hand, the United States receives an interest-free loan when people all over the world hold dollars. Dollars travel to other countries because Americans have bought something from

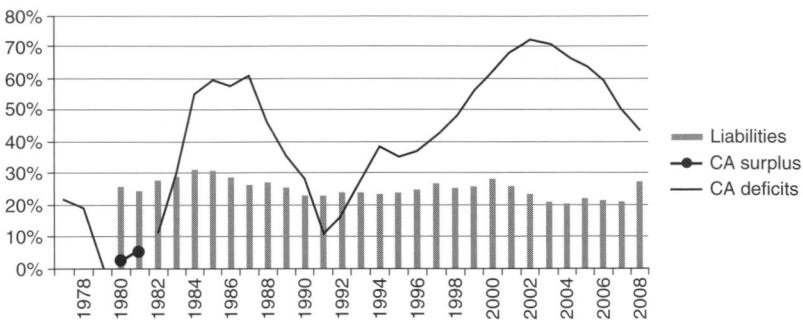

Figure 5.1 America's share of world capital flows and liabilities
Source: Author's calculations based on IMF 2009b, 2009d.

other countries: merchandise, a service, or securities. As long as the dollars stay abroad – and do not come back in search of goods, services, or assets – foreigners holding dollars are extending an interest-free loan to the United States, or the Federal Reserve, or the Treasury to be more precise. The dollars abroad are nothing but paper IOUs – i.e., claims on the United States – but, as long as they stay abroad, nothing is being claimed, and the funds can be recycled through the banking sector. The second aspect of seignorage is related to the first. The more dollars in circulation, the more the United States is able to borrow interest-free from foreigners. The United States therefore has an interest in extending dollar use, and may be tempted to increase the supply of its currency. Excess supply amounts to an inflation tax and reduces the value of the dollars held abroad and therefore the value of what the United States has to pay back in the form of goods, services, or assets. Aside from seignorage, the United States also gains in terms of policy autonomy through its ability to transfer the cost of economic adjustment onto other countries. These gains were highlighted by Benjamin Cohen, who was skeptical of the United States' commitment to price stability and argued against a dollar standard in the late 1970s.[9] A larger interpretation of seignorage includes not only the ability to borrow interest-free but to borrow at preferential rates.

By recycling easy money to small innovative enterprises, the American financial system could be described as a public good from which all states benefit. Developing countries gain access to long-term capital that they cannot raise through their own financial markets

[9] Cohen 1977.

and American investors enjoy high returns from supplying them with long-term loans. The structure of this investment relationship is mutually beneficial. But is it equally beneficial, and is it beneficial for other industrialized countries as well? One need not be inherently suspicious of markets to see that the generous returns enjoyed by American investors are a function of weak capital markets in developing countries. If either were given the opportunity to be in the other's shoes, developing countries would want well-functioning capital markets and an overall ability to borrow short and lend long (as reflected by their IIP), whereas American investors would not trade their more advanced capital market for less advanced ones, nor their ability to turn short-term borrowing from foreigners into long-term lending to foreigners. Since there is no generic "American investor," but a multitude of investors with different needs, there will, of course, exist plenty of opportunities for Americans to borrow long from foreigners and to provide them with short-term credit, so the point is not that investors within the same borders have the same interest or that markets are not properly mediating interests. The point is that the structure of international lending allows American banks to attract low-cost capital and that this benefits Americans in general by keeping interest rates down. Different Americans will make different uses of easy access to credit. They may use the money to increase consumption, to invest in property, or to purchase domestic or foreign assets. Indeed, any domestic financial system is built on the principle that the average citizen will have shorter assets than liabilities because of their simultaneous demand for liquidity and for advances on large item purchases such as a house. It is in this sense that the United States acts as "banker to the world," creating liquidity internationally in ways similar to how banks create liquidity domestically; and just as banks profit from the different rates at which they borrow and lend, the United States also benefits from providing this service. As we have seen with the credit crunch, everyone has an interest in a healthy banking sector, and reluctantly see their interest in subsidizing it when trouble appears. As we will see, the same case can be made for the United States in its investment relationships with the rest of the world.

The bottom line is that all countries share the same interest – to access a stable flow of as much capital as possible at the lowest possible cost – and the United States has an exceptional ability to meet this interest because of the dollar's role in the world economy. The

included countries for which there is data during twenty-four or more of the years between 1982 and 2006.[14]

I split the data between developed and developing economies. The World Bank reports exports and imports of goods and services as a share of GDP for twenty-seven of the thirty economies classified as developed. Data is available for the full twenty-five years for most developed countries.[15] When only developed economies are considered, the median number of years that countries run deficits is six years.[16] When it comes to the size of advanced countries' trade position, large surpluses are more common than large deficits. The average trade balance is 0.95 percent of GDP for the period, whereas the median trade balance is 0.55 percent of GDP. As one would expect, developing countries as a group run larger trade deficits than developed ones, and also tend to sustain them for longer periods. The median number of years that ninety-two developing countries run trade deficits is twenty-three, and the median size of their trade deficits is 6.15 percent of GDP, slightly below the average, which is 6.57 percent.

Thirteen developed countries have higher than median trade deficits, as measured by their duration and size. These are Australia, France, Germany, Greece, Iceland, Israel, Malta, New Zealand, Portugal, Spain, Turkey, the United Kingdom, and the United States. Among them, France, Germany, Malta, the United Kingdom, and the United States have a positive income balance on a cumulative basis. But France, Germany, and Malta have a positive NFA, so we should expect them to experience greater income receipts on their assets than the income payments they make on their liabilities. However, the fact that these countries have a positive NFA does not necessarily preclude a positive return differential since all that is required for such a differential to exist is for the overall rate of return on assets to exceed the rate of returns paid on liabilities.

A "back of the envelope" measure of the return differential, for any given year, can be obtained by dividing income receipts by the stock of

[14] Whenever possible, I have supplemented the World Bank data with IMF statistics for "missing" years.

[15] The average and median number of years for which data is available is 24.96 and 25 years, respectively.

[16] The average number of years countries are in deficit is 10.37, so when countries run deficits in excess of the median number of years, it is more common for them to run deficits for many years than it is for them to run deficits for a few years.

assets and subtracting this amount from the amount obtained by dividing income payments by the stock of liabilities. A positive difference indicates a positive return differential. A country's average return differential gives us some idea of whether the country has been able to sustain a positive return differential over time (as can be seen in the last column of table 5.2). We should expect deficit countries to have a negative return differential, especially if ongoing trade deficits have significantly weakened the NFA. Taking the average NFA for the years between 1982 and 2008 (or for whatever years are available) can tell us something about the size of each country's NFA (fourth column of table 5.2).

Table 5.2 reports the average NFA, in increasing order, starting with the United States, which has the highest net liabilities. Surprisingly, the United States also has the highest average return differential. In fact, the United States is the only country that has been able to consistently sustain a positive return differential over the entire twenty-seven-year period, and this despite a persistently negative NFA since 1986. Other outliers (highlighted in bold) are the United Kingdom and Iceland. They have also experienced positive return differentials on the income balance despite averaging negative NFAs, albeit to a lesser extent than the United States and at much lower levels of net liabilities. It is interesting to note that during the current financial meltdown – which arose because of financial products that reflected excessive leveraging – the leveraging of these three countries' balance sheets has played out so differently. Whereas capital fled to the United States in the midst of the crisis, capital fled from the United Kingdom and Iceland. Whereas the United Kingdom and Iceland were brutally reminded that borrowing cheap to invest profitably is potentially very costly, the US government is currently enjoying historically low borrowing costs; in November 2008 the three-month Treasury bill offered a yield of 4 basis points and even turned negative for a brief moment in December 2008. Whereas the pound and the Icelandic kroner have fallen hard, the dollar has risen considerably. The turmoil in financial markets is obviously not a positive for the United States but it does seem to be able to weather the storm quite a bit better than other countries that embarked on a similar high-risk strategy of extreme leveraging.

As can be seen in table 5.2, what is interesting is the ability to sustain a pattern of combined negative NFAs with a positive return differential (or as in the case of Germany to sustain positive NFAs with

Table 5.2 *Return differentials, select economies*

	Period	*Years*	*Average NFA, $mn*	*Average return differential*
United States	1982–2008	27	–874,352	1.22%
Australia	1986–2008	23	–238,439	–1.50%
Turkey	2000–2008	9	–155,208	–0.17%
Greece	1999–2008	10	–151,310	–0.24%
United Kingdom	1982–2008	27	–96,227	0.09%
Spain	1982–2008	27	–61,915	–0.69%
New Zealand	1989–2008	20	–57,098	–2.81%
Iceland	1986–2008	23	–8,149	0.42%
Malta	1994–2008	15	1,258	–0.92%
France	1989–2008	20	1,298	0.20%
Germany	1982–2008	27	249,766	–0.10%

Note: Return differentials are no longer calculated on the basis of FDI at market value because such data is not generally available for countries other than the United States. The column "years" refers to the number of years for which data is available.
Source: Author's calculations based on IMF 2009b, 2009d.

a negative return differential). I will leave aside the case of Germany, since I am interested in a country's capacity for positive return differentials. Again, the most remarkable feature on display in table 5.2 is the ability of the United States to combine the highest average NFA with the highest average return differential.

Within the group of forty-five developing countries that have higher than median trade deficits, income balance data is substantially or totally missing for seventeen countries. This leaves twenty-eight countries, of which one – Swaziland – has a positive income balance on a cumulative basis.

However, while the United States, the United Kingdom, Iceland, and Swaziland are all unique in combining a positive income balance with serial deficits, Swaziland does not have a positive investment relationship with the rest of the world whereas the United States, the United Kingdom and Iceland do. We should expect deficit countries to have a negative return differential, especially if ongoing trade deficits have significantly weakened the net foreign asset position.

Capital and exchange rate gains are another indication of an underlying return differential. Capital and exchange rate gains are also referred to as valuation adjustments, because they refer to changes in a country's international investment position as a result of fluctuations in asset and currency prices. When the net international investment position increases, as a result of changes in asset or currency prices, a country experiences a positive valuation adjustment. When the net international investment position decreases, due to changes in asset or currency prices, it experiences a negative valuation adjustment. Other things being equal, a positive valuation adjustment is desirable because it indicates that the value of a country's foreign assets is rising faster than the value of its foreign liabilities, and a negative valuation adjustment is undesirable because it suggests stronger growth in the value of its foreign liabilities than its foreign assets. Of course, there may be circumstances in which states pursue policies that they know will lead to negative valuation adjustments because the overall effects of these policies are more advantageous than the losses created by negative valuation adjustments. Another caveat applies in thinking about valuation adjustments, and requires us to think in terms of absolute (not just relative) value gains. To see this, imagine greater increase in the value of home's foreign assets than foreigners' assets in the home country. Then investors in the home country with assets abroad are better off than foreign investors in the home country. However, if the value of foreigners' assets in the home country are declining at a rapid rate and the home country's foreign assets are also declining but at a slower rate, then investors in the home country with assets abroad are still better off than foreign investors in the home country, but one would hardly infer that the home country is well positioned in the international economy. For my purposes here, the important point to see is that a positive valuation adjustment is a benefit and a negative valuation adjustment is a cost from any state's perspective.

Taken alone, higher capital and exchange rate gains on assets than on liabilities is not necessarily evidence of a return differential. By adjusting for the amount of capital outflow and inflow, however, we can find out whether such a return differential exists, or, more precisely, by scaling capital and exchange rate gains to every dollar invested both abroad and at home.

By putting the value of American assets and liabilities in relation to capital outflows and inflows, one can see whether the value of foreigners' assets held in the United States increases at a slower pace than the value of American assets held abroad. Apart from the structure of international lending (examined above), this can occur as a result of a favorable return differential or exchange rate differential. Either the American market is offering lower returns than foreign markets or dollar depreciation is increasing the dollar value of American foreign assets held in foreign currency while keeping dollar denominated liabilities constant.[17] Note that dollar depreciation would have the exact opposite effect if American foreign assets were predominantly denominated in dollars while foreign assets in the United States were mostly denominated in foreign currency. But this is not the case, American foreign assets are mostly in foreign currency, whereas American liabilities are mostly dollar denominated. Conversely, capital and exchange rate *losses* will arise (again apart from the structure of international lending) when the American market offers higher returns than foreign markets or as a result of dollar appreciation, which would tend to reduce the dollar value of American foreign assets while the value of dollar denominated liabilities would again remain constant. In either case, the size of the valuation adjustments will depend on the net effect of the underlying return and exchange rate differential, and it is of course possible that these combine in different ways, for instance, a positive return differential and a negative exchange rate differential or vice versa.

Assuming relative stability in the structure of the American investment position over time, positive valuation adjustments will tend to occur when the American market is offering lower returns than foreign markets and when the dollar is depreciating. Positive valuation adjustments can therefore be seen as a hedge against decline and represent a built-in advantage vis-à-vis other countries. As can be seen from figure 5.3, capital and exchange rate gains are higher between 1982 and 1990 when the United States declines relative to Europe and Japan (what I have characterized as the size ratio 6:3:3) than between 1992 and 2002 when Europe grows relative to Japan (roughly corresponding to the size ratio 6:4:2). Then between 2002 and 2006, capital and exchange rate gains explode when the United States declines relative to a third smaller Great Power, China (i.e., 5:4:3). As is also

---

[17] The value of American liabilities on the international investment position is constant but not from the perspective of foreigners who see the value of their assets decrease once converted into their home currency.

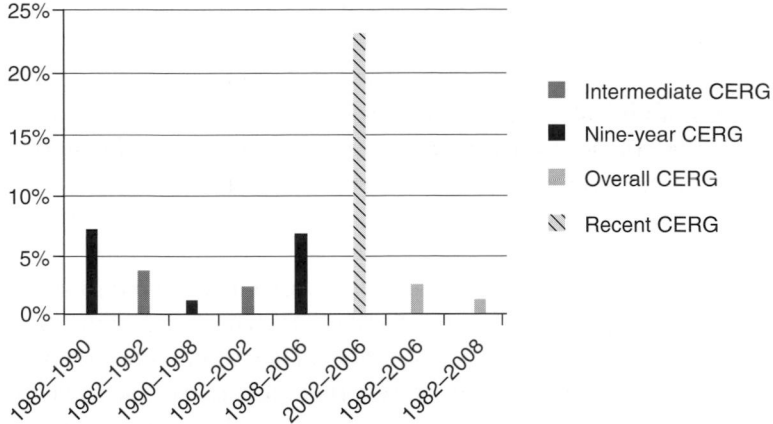

Figure 5.3 Capital and exchange rate gains for the United States
Notes: CERG refers to capital and exchange rate gains. Assets include FDI at market value and financial derivatives.
Source: Author's calculations based on BEA 2009c, 2009e.

displayed in figure 5.3, there is generally some variability in capital and exchange rate gains, as one might expect. Looking at capital and exchange rate gains in three segments of equal nine-year intervals between 1982 and 2008 basically confirms the trend associated with my earlier classification of American decline, recovery, and further relative weakening. One point that emerges from this discussion of the changing nature of capital and exchange rate gains is that what matters is whether overall valuation adjustments are positive not whether they are positive within a limited period. As is plain from figure 5.3, capital and exchange rate gains have been positive over a quarter of a century. Of course, these gains may at some stage reverse, but here I want to highlight that, along with a positive return differential on the income balance since 1986, possibly longer, positive valuation adjustments have persisted over time.

In the American case, cumulative net capital inflows scaled to GDP for each year amounted to 63 percent of GDP between 1982 and 2006 whereas the net foreign asset position was 7 percent of GDP in 1982 and −14 percent of GDP in 2006. In other words, over the same period, the net asset position only declined by 21 percent despite cumulated net capital inflows to the tune of 63 percent. In sheer numbers, net capital inflows amounted to $5.7 trillion, whereas the net asset position declined by $2.1 trillion. The difference, $3.6 trillion, represents gains on the NFA from valuation changes of $144 billion per year. Even if one includes the period of financial trauma that started in 2007, this windfall is more than $90 billion per year. Over time, good years and bad, this is some bonus indeed. Economists characterize the difference between cumulated net financial flows and changes in the NFA as a free ride or a transfer of wealth from the rest of the world.[18]

Although I do not have access to the data that would allow me to calculate other countries' capital and exchange rate gains in the NFA, calculations performed by economists suggest that the United States has experienced exceptionally high capital and exchange rate gains when compared to other countries. No other country has such a large spread between net foreign assets and the cumulative current account.[19] Nor is there any country that has enjoyed a positive income balance for such a long time despite recurrent sizeable current account deficits and a concomitant deterioration in its net international investment position.

Three other countries – Britain, Switzerland, and Canada – also benefit handsomely from the discrepancy between the value of the net foreign asset position and the cumulative current account.[20] Among these countries, the United States and the United Kingdom stand out. Uniquely, they have benefited from persistent current account deficits in the form of a positive income balance and valuation adjustments. Switzerland on the other hand is a net creditor. While valuation adjustments have worked in Canada's favor, its income balance has been negative for at least sixteen years, and on the whole its net liabilities are lower than the United States' when scaled to either GDP or population given its history of regular current account surpluses.[21] Australia is another case in point. Like the United States, it has run persistent current account deficits, and its net liabilities are much higher than the United States' when scaled to GDP and population but unlike the United States it has not experienced substantial gains in

[18] Cavallo, 2004; Cline 2005.
[19] Lane and Milesi-Ferretti 2006, 20.
[20] Lane and Milesi-Ferretti 2006.
[21] BEA 2007b, 2007e; Statistics Canada 2006a, 2006b; US Census Bureau 2006. When scaled to population, the United States' net external liabilities are 42 percent higher than Canada's, 15 percent higher when scaled to GDP.

the form of valuation adjustments or benefited from a positive income transfer on current account.[22] In particular, the change in net liabilities was actually lower than the cumulated current account balance for the period 1972–2004 and the income balance was negative for the entire duration of this period.[23] So while the United Kingdom and Canada have experienced substantial capital and exchange rate gains on the net international investment position, Australia has not. And, while the United Kingdom, like the United States, benefits from positive net income flows, Canada and Australia do not.

The United States and the United Kingdom are the only two countries that have enjoyed a positive balance of income on current account despite large current account deficits. Only they have experienced substantially positive capital and exchange rate gains notwithstanding net liabilities that are a sizeable share of GDP. Out of the two, the United States has enjoyed higher capital and exchange rate gains despite higher net liabilities. When scaled to population, the United States' NIIP is 321 percent higher than the United Kingdom's, 218 percent higher when scaled to GDP.[24] As a common feature, the structure of the United States' and the United Kingdom's investment position is optimal; both countries are long in foreign equity and short in foreign debt.[25] There is nothing fortuitous about this composition effect. The United States is the undisputed hegemon of our time and the vestiges of the British Empire still reverberate economically and politically.

Size matters in considering valuation effects.[26] With the American market devouring $16 trillion in foreign investment, and overseas investments amounting to around $14 trillion (approximately 40 percent of which are held in foreign currency), a 35 percent depreciation of the dollar improves the US asset position by $2 trillion. If the difference between American claims and liabilities stay at $2 trillion, but the United States instead manages to attract $20 trillion in foreign investment while holding $18 trillion in overseas investment, the net international investment position improves by $2.5 trillion. This

---

[22] ABS 2005, 2006a, 2006b. Australia's net liabilities are much higher than the United States' when scaled to population (236 percent) or GDP (225 percent).

[23] Foreign Affairs and International Trade Canada 2006; Lane and Milesi-Ferretti 2006, 31.

[24] National Statistics 2006a, 35, 2006b, 100; US Census Bureau 2006.

[25] Gourinchas and Rey 2005b.   [26] Tille 2003.

windfall contributes significantly to external adjustment and dwarfs "seignorage," the conventional measure of the key currency country's privilege.

How significant are capital and exchange rate gains more generally? There is a great deal of controversy surrounding this question. Gourinchas and Rey show that a positive return differential within each investment category accounts for approximately three-quarters of overall gains.[27] Their results are controversial. The most trenchant critique comes from inside the Federal Reserve Board and applies to any attempt to deduce valuation adjustments by comparing cumulative changes in asset and liability values (i.e., positions) with cumulative capital outflows and inflows using official data. Critics charge that this incorporates an upward bias in valuation gains because the Bureau of Economic Analysis (from where the data is drawn) revises asset positions but not capital outflows.[28] For Gourinchas and Rey, these revisions reflect valuation gains whereas for Curcuru *et al.*, they reflect unrecorded capital flows, implying that the current account deficit is smaller than official estimates suggest.[29] Curcuru *et al.* do not dispute the existence of a return differential but dispute its size, which Gourinchas and Rey estimate at more than 3 percent and they estimate at 1 percent.[30] Using monthly data on bilateral positions instead of the revised positions available through the Bureau of Economic Analysis, they find that a significant portion of the overall return differential is due to the superior ability of American investors to synchronize shifts between different types of foreign holdings with market developments as compared to foreign investors in the United States.[31] Apart from valuation gains or unrecorded capital flows, the "other changes" or "residual adjustments" used to update initial positions can also reflect a mis-measured stock position, which Lane and Milesi-Ferretti show is the case for past FDI holdings, which seem to have been underestimated.[32] In the case of FDI, residual adjustments

---

[27] Gourinchas and Rey 2005a, 2005b.
[28] Curcuru, Dvorak, and Warnock 2008a.
[29] Personal communication with Pierre-Olivier Gourinchas.
[30] Curcuru, Dvorak, and Warnock 2008a; Gourinchas and Rey 2005a, 2005b.
[31] Curcuru, Dvorak, and Warnock 2008b.
[32] Lane and Milesi-Ferretti 2008. As they state, this would imply a faster deterioration in the NFA since present holdings would have been reached must faster given larger past holdings.

are likely attributable to capital gains.[33] With a bit of a hedge, however, they attribute most of the residual adjustment to unrecorded financial flows, by stating that this "leads to the emergence of a new puzzle."[34] Because measuring capital and exchange rate gains is notoriously difficult, and the verdict is not yet in on what the closest approximation is, any conclusion at this stage must be preliminary.

Disaggregating financial flows and the NFA gives us a more precise idea of where the American advantage lies. Curiously, American private investors have been better at coordinating their foreign investment with changes in asset price than private foreign investors in the United States. Their greater adeptness at adjusting capital outflows to changes in asset value is not the same as the "timing effect" noted by Curcuru *et al.*, which refers to reallocations between different investment categories. Rather, an increase in American private investment overseas has to a greater extent coincided with an increase in the value of American private assets overseas than greater private foreign investment in the United States has coincided with an increase in the value of foreign-held private assets in the United States. Similarly, a decrease in American private investment overseas has to a greater extent coincided with a fall in the value of American private assets overseas than lower private foreign investment in the United States has coincided with a drop in the value of foreign-held private assets in the United States.

Unpacking financial flows and the NFA also shows that private capital on the order of 88 percent of GDP left the United States between 1982 and 2006. During the same period, foreign private investment in the United States amounted to 129 percent of GDP. Yet despite the much greater capital inflow, the value increase of privately held foreign assets in the United States over the period amounts to 86 percent of GDP, which is similar to the the value increase of privately held American assets abroad, which amounted to 85 percent of GDP. The difference is pronounced for FDI. Over the period, foreigners poured capital equivalent to 28 percent of GDP into FDI in the United States. Capital outflow from the United States in the form of foreign direct investment represents a similar share of GDP, roughly 27 percent. However, the value increase of FDI in the United States only amounts to 21 percent of GDP, whereas the value increase in American FDI amounts to 26 percent of GDP.

---

[33] Lane and Milesi-Ferretti 2008, 16.   [34] Lane and Milesi-Ferretti 2008, 19.

There is wide agreement on the role of American foreign direct investment in producing a return differential relative to foreign investment in the United States.[35] In the span of twenty-five years, returns on American FDI have consistently been higher than returns on FDI in the United States. Whereas returns on portfolio investments have been fairly similar, American foreign direct investment has on average outstripped foreigners' returns on direct investment in the United States by 6 percent; only US official investment abroad, which is rather negligible, has received lower returns than official investment in the United States.[36]

The higher returns on American FDI than on FDI in the United States is not particularly surprising. Over the long term, we should expect returns on American FDI to be higher than FDI in the United States, as long as some American FDI is going to developing countries where returns will be higher to cover political risks. While this explanation for a positive discrepancy between outbound and inbound foreign direct investment could be applied to all industrialized countries, the return differential on foreign direct investment is especially high for the United States. A possible explanation for the variability in FDI returns is that American business operates under the biggest government umbrella in the world and so is in a particularly good position to both absorb and specialize in risky investments. Government assistance comes in two forms. American military might has been used to defend property rights abroad and it is well known that the American government has used its influence to pressure foreign governments to secure American investments abroad. But there are other reasons for the excess return on American foreign direct investment than the propensity to venture into more risky areas. Having undertaken foreign direct investment well before other countries began establishing subsidiaries in the United States, American foreign affiliates enjoy certain incumbency advantages in the form of expertise and amortized startup costs.[37] Return differentials on FDI are also reinforced by the larger share of FDI on the asset side of the international investment position; so attributable to a structural advantage.

[35] Higgins, Klitgaard, and Tille 2006; Lane and Milesi-Ferretti 2008; Kouparitsas 2005.
[36] Kouparitsas 2005, 2.
[37] CBO 2005.

Large-scale capital imports have allowed the United States to invest and consume in ways that have been extremely advantageous. Attracting foreign capital at low cost, the United States has invested the funds profitably elsewhere, and benefited from the differential. Capital inflows have raised domestic investment and productivity, led to an expansion of overseas investment, broadened consumption possibilities and increased personal wealth. By transforming incoming capital into lucrative investment opportunities, the United States has extended itself economically and politically.

Exhausting the advantage

By 2002, foreign claims on Americans exceeded American claims on foreigners by 23 percent of GDP, but despite large persistent deficits between 2002 and 2007, the share declined to 11 percent in 2007.[38] Since 2000, the current account deficit has always been above 4 percent of GDP, and oscillated between 5 and 7 percent after 2002. In 2007, the deficit was approximately 5 percent of GDP. The hollowing out of the NFA despite sizeable and recurrent deficits is due to the asymmetrical structure in the American NFA as well as the favorable return differential, discussed above. When external liabilities peaked at 23 percent of GDP in 2002, there was a great deal of concern that record-breaking deficits were perilously wearing down America's assets and credentials, leaving the country unable to emerge from external liabilities unscathed.[39] But the particular scenario many had in mind of a run on dollar assets and crippling interest rates, to lure capital back, has not come to pass.

Nevertheless, dependence on outside investment is potentially dangerous. As mentioned in chapter 4, there is a dual constraint. On the one hand, there is a limit on the extent to which foreigners are willing to add American assets to their portfolios, given the high share they already possess and given home bias. Second, there is a danger that the flow of funds to the United States will dry up or even reverse because of expectations of dollar depreciation. These two phenomena interact, since any limitation on the stock of liabilities implies a problem attracting capital.[40] If foreigners were suddenly to stop supplying

---

[38] These figures are at market value from BEA's release of revised year-end positions between 1976 and 2008.
[39] Gray 2004; Setser and Roubini 2005.   [40] Cline 2005.

new credit, or worse, suddenly withdrew their savings, a sinking dollar and soaring interest rates would not only choke consumption and investment but could significantly undermine American power, if the spiral unraveled in aggressive fashion. A quick recall of private investments would have especially serious consequences if official investors were to follow suit. With central banks contributing to a hostile drain on American assets, the economy would be heading for a long, hard fall.

Yet, while the United States, like any country piling on large current account deficits, must consider the risk of capital flight in anticipation of dollar weakness, or pay higher interest rates to retain and attract capital, foreigners are more likely to hold dollars than they would be prepared to hold the currency of any other country facing similar conditions. The reason they are willing to take these greater risks goes back to the dollar's status as key currency.

In theory, the principal factor determining whether an unfavorable cycle of reduced capital inflows, a falling dollar, and higher interest rates will materialize or not, is how foreigners perceive American spending. In order for capital flows to persist, foreigners must be convinced of the American economy's capacity to regenerate itself. If assets are being run down for immediate consumption without regard for prospective consumption, the growth of external liabilities is an accident waiting to happen. If used conscientiously, on the other hand, the net capital inflow, fueling the deficit, can continue to provide the United States with large rewards. If the savings extracted from other countries are channeled towards investment, enhancing productivity and export growth, current import expansion need not compromise stability in financial inflows. In other words, the deficit need not have negative repercussions as long as government policies, as well as firm and household activity, inspire confidence in the country's ability to pull in future resources. The crucial question is to what extent American borrowing has been used to raise investment and to what extent it has propelled a consumption binge.

As can be seen from figure 5.4, the decline in private savings and increase in government savings between 1975 and 1979 coincided with greater domestic private investment. Home mortgages increased and so did consumer credit during this period. The increase in private savings and the decline in government savings between 1979 and 1983 pretty much overlaps with a decline in domestic private investment.

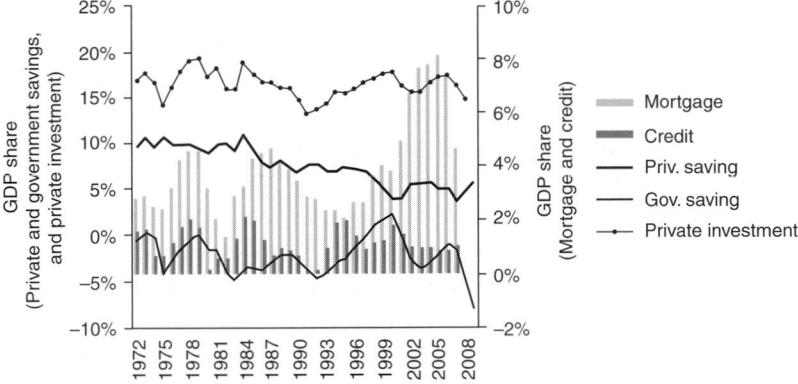

Figure 5.4 Savings dynamics
Source: Author's calculations based on data from Federal Reserve Statistical Release, Flow of Funds Accounts of the United States.

Home mortgages fell as well, as did consumer credit before picking up somewhat. The drop in private savings and increase in government savings between 1983 and 1989 was associated with a steep rise in domestic private investment in the first year, followed by decline. The general picture is an upward push in home mortgages and a decline in consumer credit (except for a spike between 1983 and 1984). Private savings increase minimally between 1989 and 1992, government savings fall, and domestic private investments drop significantly. Home mortgages and consumer credit are both reduced. The precipitous drop in private savings between 1992 and 2000, which reached an all-time low in 2000 (3.9 percent of GDP), and the sharp rise in government savings, which reached an all-time high in 2000 (2.3 percent of GDP), is associated with a steep rise in domestic private investment. Home mortgages and consumer credit also increase somewhat. A moderate increase in private savings accompanied the 6 percent decline in government savings, the highest ever, between 2000 and 2003, and domestic private investment declined substantially. Home mortgages increased considerably during this period but consumer credit shrank. Private savings declined marginally between 2003 and 2006, whereas government savings increased and domestic private investment climbed. Home mortgages increased up to 2005, while consumer credit stayed fairly constant. Private savings plunged between 2006 and 2007, recovering moderately in 2008, while government savings remained on a continued downward slope. Domestic private invest-ment plummeted during this period and attained levels comparable to the low-point reached in 1975 (15 percent of GDP) surpassed only by the 13 percent mark touched upon in 1991. Home mortgages declined to an unprecedented −0.14 percent of GDP and by 2008 consumer credit had decreased significantly.

Figure 5.4 suggests that foreigners have been willing to invest in the American market even when productive investment has not been prioritized. For instance, between 1984 and 1989, domestic private investment declined and home mortgages increased, but foreign invest-ment in the United States remained high between 1984 and 1987. A similar but starker pattern can be discerned for the years between 2005 and 2007, when foreign investment increased 50 percent despite a weakening of domestic private investment.

Nevertheless, there are risks involved with continuous deficits, which the United States, just as any other country in similar condi-tions, faces. One such risk is greater dependence on foreign creditors, especially in so far as they are governments. Another risk is rapid withdrawal of capital from the United States – a danger that has increased over time simply because the United States attracts a lower share of stable FDI than it used to. Financial fragility is another risk with a lax borrowing constraint (one of the drivers of the deficit) which the United States enjoys.[41] The financial sector is vulnerable to the escalating household debt that comes with easy money. When American banks have easy access to foreign capital, they pass on soft loans to American households, who can only raise capital by bor-rowing on credit or via a mortgage. As a result, easy money increases household debt.[42] In principle, the soft terms transmitted to American firms need not raise their debt-to-equity ratio, given their ability to sell equity to foreigners.[43] In reality, parts of the bank sector used the favorable interest rate environment to acquire assets without raising equity, contributing to the current financial mess (see chapter 4).

As manifested by the credit crisis that came to a head in early August 2007, over-leveraged investors, whether households with large mort-gages, or banks with lean capitalization, pose a risk to the financial system. Today's turbulence is rooted in the ease with which American

[41] McKinnon 2001b.   [42] McKinnon 2001b.
[43] McKinnon 2001b.

banks have been able to borrow on international markets, and their eagerness to pass easy money on to households with dubious credit profiles. Because banks were willing to lend to households with weak credit histories (the so-called sub-prime market for loans), and because banks repackaged the loans and passed on the risk to investors by selling them securities with exposure to the sub-prime market, defaults on home mortgages hurt investors worldwide. Both factors combined to create the credit crunch. A major reason for the financial upheaval we have seen as of late is that banks bundled sub-prime loans into new instruments, spreading risk in mysterious ways, thus fostering a climate of uncertainty. Investors harmed by the defaults, especially large-scale institutional investors, started to sell equity in order to cover their losses and provide the collateral banks asked. As a result, the crisis spilled over into the market for equities. To make matters worse, the computer models used by certain hedge funds were badly equipped for the crisis.

The US government has taken a number of steps to meet these challenges and restore confidence in financial markets. A stimulus package of $168 billion was approved in February 2008, and another $825 billion in February 2009. Congress also passed the troubled asset relief package (TARP), a financial bailout in October 2008, amounting to $700 billion. A financial cleansing program was also set in motion rather quickly, starting with the Term Asset-Backed Securities Loan Facility (TALF) in November 2008. Through this vehicle, the Federal Reserve will make available $200 billion to lower the cost of lending for investors holding securities backed by assets such as cars, student, and small business loans, as well as credit cards. The Federal Reserve committed an additional $800 billion to this loan facility in February 2009, and financing was extended to cover commercial and residential mortgages. A new initiative, in addition to the TARP and the TALF, is also designed to deal with bad loans and assets – the Public Private Investment Program. The scheme will use $100 billion of TARP capital, and also provide capital from the Federal Reserve, the Treasury, and the FDIC to give private investors the incentives and leverage to buy troubled loans and assets. This formula is expected to raise up to $1 trillion to soak up the toxicity clogging banks. By removing bad loans and assets from banks' balance sheets, the program is intended to make them healthy again and encourage them to pump credit into the rest of the economy. The final piece in the government salvo to tackle the crisis is $75 billion worth of assistance, in the form of reduced loans, to homeowners risking foreclosure. The low interest rates currently prevailing in the United States, the crisis notwithstanding, help finance these measures. By contrast, members of the euro-zone agreed on a $270 billion stimulus package in December 2008, but there is no coordination between governments on how the money is to be spent and some countries have been reluctant to implement fiscal measures.

It is of course noteworthy that although the problems originated in the United States, the credit crunch reverberated worldwide. In the immediate aftermath of the crisis, forty-six companies in the world incurred heavy losses, twenty of which could be found in the United States, eighteen in Europe, another eight in Asia. To balance the negative repercussions, nine companies gained significantly by taking a short position on low-rated mortgage bonds, and by devouring companies adversely affected by their subprime exposure. None of these "winners" can, however, be found outside the United States. If there had not been an international contagion effect, the fact that some firms in the United States lost while others gained would simply imply a domestic redistribution of income. But because of the international dimension of the crisis, there is a sense in which the costs of low-cost borrowing are shared internationally but not the benefits. Of course, in the medium to long term, how individual countries cope with the economy-wide repercussions of the credit crisis will be much more important for gauging competitiveness.

Although the financial disorder which started in 2007 can be traced back to American external imbalances, one of the supreme ironies is that the consequences of the shakeout are widely shared and not in any way restricted to the United States. The very fact that the United States has been able to sustain large current account deficits for such a long time without punitive interest rates is a benefit and an indication of hegemonic power. The ability to attract large amounts of merchandise and low-cost capital is not only good for households in their consumer and borrowing capacity but for firms seeking access to easy finance to expand their business worldwide. These benefits also carry risks, although the unraveling of those risks creates an environment of uncertainty, which is favorable to the United States, because it is perceived as the country most capable of securing investments. In the next section, we will see who bears the cost of America's low-cost borrowing and, more generally, why countries have had an interest in sustaining American buying power and why, when the time has come, they have contributed to orderly adjustment.

How commercial strength reinforces monetary privilege

America's ability to attract large amounts of capital is related to its ability to absorb large amounts of imports. If the United States were not able to sell a wide range of assets in exchange for capital, it would not be able to import as much, and if it were not capable of taking in as many imported products, a substantial portion of the funds, specifically those invested by central banks, would not make their way to the United States to the same extent. The large dollar reserves created in central banks propping up American buying power have also turned the central banks into stake-holders in a reasonable dollar value, providing them with incentives to smooth eventual adjustment. The ability to sustain long waves of import expansion and capital intake followed by orderly dollar adjustment has reinforced capital and exchange rate gains on America's external balance sheet. The United States' commercial position is key to understanding its ability to play dollar cycles, and these cycles have been extremely beneficial from an economic point of view. America's commercial position can in these various ways be said to have produced monetary benefits.

Deficit financing through import deterrence[44]

In 2000, the United States accounted for 19 percent of world imports, a share that was down to 13 percent in 2008. This import expansion would not have been possible unless foreigners had been willing to invest in the United States, both in the private and official sector.

In the 1970s, the French economist Jacques Rueff scoffed at the relationship between the United States and its creditors under the Bretton Woods system of fixed exchange rates by calling it a "deficit without tears":

If I had an agreement with my tailor, that whatever money I pay him returns to me the very same day as a loan, I would have no objections at all to ordering more suits from him.[45]

At that time, capital was flowing in from western Europe and Japan. Later in the 1970s, OPEC countries started exporting savings on a

[44] The phrase "import deterrence" is due to *International Herald Tribune*, February 27, 2002, Editorials and Commentary.
[45] Rueff 1972.

massive scale, with industrialized countries eventually following suit. Today, American buying power is propped up by East Asian countries. In an arrangement known as "Bretton Woods II," these countries siphon off the dollars they receive in export earnings and invest them in American Treasury bills in order to prevent their currencies from appreciating.[46] Such interventions have ensured relatively stable exchange rates toward the dollar, and are reminiscent of the Bretton Woods system of fixed exchange rates.

As can be seen in figure 5.5, the dollar has appreciated against China's renminbi, the Hong Kong dollar, and Malaysia's ringgit since 1980. China, Hong Kong, and Malaysia each abandoned managed floats and basket-determined rates in favor of an official link to the dollar. Hong Kong did this in 1983, China in 1994, and Malaysia in 1998. While China switched from fixed to flexible rates on July 21, 2005, there has been little movement in the renminbi.

In addition, the dollar appreciated very considerably against Indonesia's rupiah and South Korea's won (see figure 5.6). While the rupiah was never fixed against the dollar, the won was, before the link to the dollar was severed in 1980. From the mid-1980s to the mid 1990s, however, the dollar depreciated quite significantly against the yen and the Taiwanese dollar. Japan moved away from a fixed exchange rate as Bretton Woods collapsed in 1971 and, since 1978, Taiwan has also turned away from fixed rates. The dollar appreciated against South Korea's won and Indonesia's rupiah during this same period. From the middle of the 1990s until the beginning of the third millennium, the dollar appreciated against the yen, the Taiwanese dollar, the rupiah, South Korea's won, and the euro. After that, the dollar depreciated against all currencies except for the Indonesian rupiah, which behaved erratically after the Asian financial crisis of 1997.

Despite the dollar's decline towards the yen, the Taiwanese dollar, and the Chinese remninbi as of late, most of the adjustment has been borne by the euro, which has appreciated more than 15 percent against the dollar since 2001 (see figure 5.6). There are two possible interpretations for the tendency of East Asian countries to intervene in exchange rate markets to keep the dollar high; their actions can either be read as a market access story or as a problem of undeveloped capital markets.[47] These interpretations are not necessarily incompatible.

---

[46] Dooley, Folkerts-Landau, and Garber, 2003.
[47] Dooley, Folkerts-Landau, and Garber 2003; McKinnon and Schnabl 2004a.

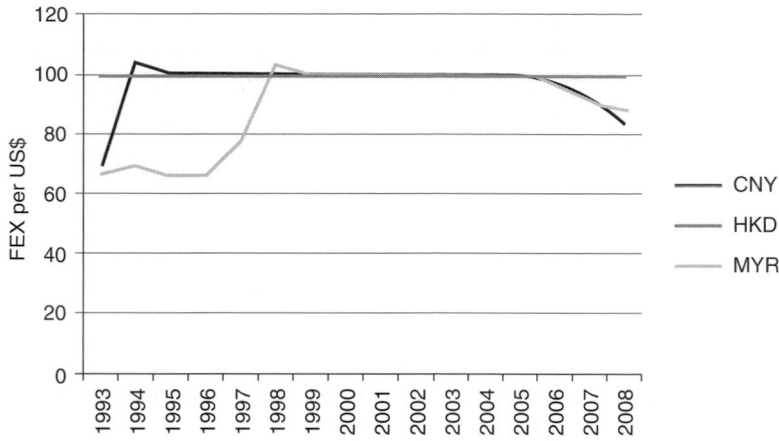

Figure 5.5 Chinese yuan, Hong Kong dollar, and Malaysian ringgit per US$

Note: 2000 = 100.

Source: Author's calculations based on data from Econstats.

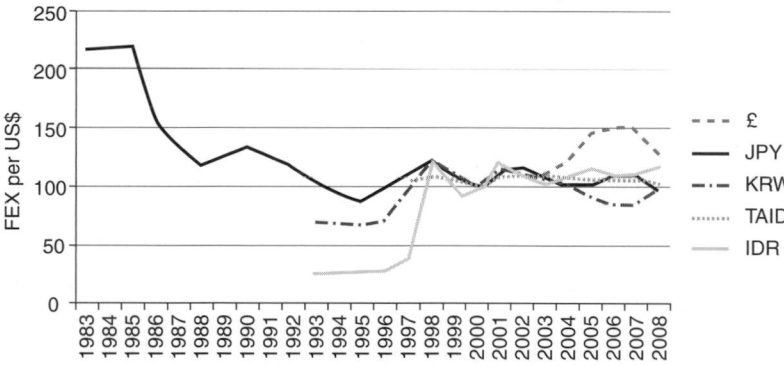

Figure 5.6 Euro, Japanese yen, South Korean won, Taiwanese dollar, and Indonesian rupiah per US$

Note: 2000 = 100.

Source: Author's calculations based on data from Econstats, ECB.

East Asia's dependence on the American market is on evident display in table 5.3. China, Indonesia, Japan, Malaysia, and South Korea all rely heavily on the US market to absorb their export products, although they all sold a lower share of their overall exports to the United States in 2008 than they did in 1991. Reliance on the American market, which on average has absorbed 15 to 35 percent of total exports, is still high and, as will be argued in chapter 7, this dependence is likely to continue.

Table 5.3 *Share of East Asian countries' exports to the United States*

	1989	1990	1991	1992	1993	1994	1995	1996	1997
China	23%	25%	26%	30%	34%	32%	31%	34%	34%
Hong Kong	13%	12%	9%	8%	7%	6%	6%	5%	5%
Indonesia	16%	13%	11%	13%	15%	16%	16%	17%	16%
Japan	34%	31%	29%	29%	30%	30%	28%	28%	29%
South Korea	32%	28%	24%	22%	21%	20%	19%	17%	17%
Malaysia	19%	18%	18%	20%	22%	24%	24%	23%	23%
Taiwan	37%	34%	30%	30%	29%	28%	26%	25%	26%

Source: Author's calculations based on data from the WTO and Department of Commerce, TradeStats Express.

The close tracking of the dollar makes the market access story seem plausible. Frail capital markets also explain the close connection to the dollar. Before the Asian financial crisis in 1997/98, countries with weak financial markets, such as South Korea and Malaysia, not only had most of their trade invoiced in dollars, they also took up loans in dollars, which provided them with yet another incentive to adopt a soft dollar peg.[48] Countries with bad inflation and depreciation records along with fragile capital markets tend to use dollars.[49] Foreigners will not extend loans in local currency to countries that have had problems curbing inflation or depreciation because they risk getting less back than the value of the original loan. Nor can the borrowing country use forward markets to hedge loans if capital markets are deficient. Borrowing in foreign currency therefore leaves the borrowing country exposed to rising borrowing costs (should the foreign currency in which the loan is denominated appreciate). This inability to use capital markets to mitigate problems associated with a history of bad inflation or depreciation is known as "original sin." If capital markets were developed, borrowing countries could hedge against the risk of an appreciating dollar by selling an amount of local currency equivalent to the dollar loan at the current exchange rate in the futures market. But since financial markets are weak, they bear the full exchange rate risk when borrowing in foreign currency and have to face the prospect of giving up more of their own currency to settle debt. Countries that cannot hedge against exchange rate risk are said

[48] McKinnon and Schnabl 2004a.   [49] Eichengreen and Hausmann 1999.

1998	1999	2000	2001	2002	2003	2004	2005	2006	2007	2008
39%	42%	40%	38%	38%	35%	33%	32%	30%	26%	24%
6%	6%	6%	5%	5%	4%	4%	3%	2%	2%	2%
19%	19%	16%	18%	16%	15%	15%	14%	13%	12%	11%
31%	31%	31%	31%	29%	25%	23%	23%	23%	20%	8%
18%	22%	23%	23%	22%	19%	18%	15%	14%	13%	11%
26%	25%	26%	25%	26%	24%	22%	24%	23%	19%	15%
29%	28%	27%	27%	24%	21%	19%	18%	17%	16%	14%

to have "fear of floating," which they try to overcome by stabilizing exchange rates through frequent interventions.[50] A soft dollar peg has, in other words, provided a way out of this conundrum. This is wholly rational for East Asian countries who *borrow* in foreign currency but is less explicable for countries such as South Korea and Malaysia, who have been exporting savings ever since the Asian financial crisis, and for countries such as China, Taiwan, and Singapore, who were exporting savings long before the crisis.[51]

As it turns out, *creditors* in East Asia face a similar problem. The widespread use of the dollar for commercial and financial transactions, the region's poorly developed capital markets, and the United States' own preference for borrowing in dollars has encouraged dollar lending, resulting in a dilemma known as "conflicted virtue."[52] East Asian governments are virtuous because they scramble to save and export surplus savings to other countries. However, large-scale lending places them in a quandary. If dollar claims are repatriated, the currency appreciates, deflationary pressures ensue and they lose competitiveness. If, on the other hand, they stack reserves in American Treasury bills, they face complaints about exchange rate manipulation. Between a rock and a hard place, "rigging" the exchange rate has seemed the lesser of evils.

These two explanations – the market access and weak capital market interpretation – for the relatively stable exchange rates towards

[50] McKinnon and Schnabl 2004a; Calvo and Reinhart 2002.
[51] McKinnon and Schnabl 2004b.
[52] McKinnon and Schnabl 2004b, 181, 85–6.

the dollar are perfectly compatible. Stabilizing the exchange rate is export-promoting. For at least another decade, East Asia will try to preserve America's import pull. China will be especially eager to cooperate, looking as she is for a way to integrate 3 million workers per year in the export sector.[53] Exchange rate stabilization also prevents investors with mixed portfolios, holding both dollar claims and local liabilities, from incurring large-scale losses.[54] For both trade and investment purposes therefore, East Asian governments have a keen interest in preventing a sharp decline in the dollar.

Dollar compellence: orderly dollar adjustment

One of the unique features of America's external imbalance is that others have an interest in maintaining America's deficits on current account, whether intentionally, through a series of strategic policy decisions, or inadvertently by simply holding dollar assets. When that is no longer possible, they have an interest in assisting the United States to close the imbalance in such a way that as little damage as possible is inflicted on the American economy and, as a consequence, on their own countries. The United States gains in policy autonomy as a result. Cohen's distinction between the "power to delay" and the "power to deflect" is useful in thinking about this benefit in policy autonomy.[55] The power to delay is simply the power to defer adjustment and absorb real resources in the process. The power to deflect is the power to assume as little of the cost of adjustment as possible, and the United States has more latitude than any other country in terms of both these indicators.

As we saw earlier in this chapter, the United States has for a sustained period managed to attract a large share of world capital and goods at low cost and to invest some of that capital in higher-yielding assets abroad, partly in FDI, thus facilitating the country's commercial expansion. But if the United States is gaining more from its overseas investments than foreigners are gaining in the American market, how is the high opportunity cost of investment in the American market distributed across countries? Who are the major investors in the

---

[53] Dooley, Folkerts-Landau, and Garber 2003.
[54] McKinnon and Schnabl 2004b, 187–8.
[55] Cohen 2005.

United States, and how stable have their investments been? Whose investments have lost value in the United States and where has the United States gained the most? In this section, I will also show that other governments do not have the resources to force the United States to adjust economic imbalances. Because collective action is needed to unseat the United States from its status as the single most significant economic power in the world, countries have preferred to pull their punches and even take some hits than to confront the United States head on. The United States has therefore been able to ask other countries to adjust their policies to the imbalances it creates. This happened in the 1980s, as American current account deficits became the world's problem, and it is happening again. Although some countries are starting to question the resilience of a system so heavily dependent on one entity, China and Russia, who have been outspoken against the dollar's continued role as reserve currency, will, I think, find it difficult to impose another standard. For a discussion of where key currency changes are first likely to appear, see chapter 7. Despite changes in the economic and geopolitical context in the last quarter-century, the parallels between the handling of the imbalances in the mid-1980s and the imbalances of the last decade are more salient than one might expect.

Who bears the cost?

The US Treasury Department provides information about who invests in the United States but the data has a number of limitations.[56] Historical survey data are only available for select years and the breakdown of the data is uneven.[57] A full breakdown of American securities into short- and long-term lending is only available between 2002 and 2006 on the liability side, and from 2003 to 2005 on the asset side.

---

[56] A methodological note released by the Treasury and a discussion paper by Bertaut and Tryon (2007) for the Board of Governors of the Federal System helps clarify some of these complexities. The discussion below is based on that information and personal communication with Carol C. Bertaut, a senior economist with the Division of International Finance, for the Board of Governors of the Federal Reserve System.

[57] Data covering US liabilities is available for the years 1974, 1978, 1984, 1994, 2000, and from 2002 to 2006, whereas data covering US foreign assets is available for the years 1994, 1997, 2001, and 2003–05.

While the Treasury's Office of International Affairs publishes monthly transactions data in addition to the survey data, the former contain a number of distortions and therefore differ markedly from the latter. "Financial center" bias and absence of information from which to deduce valuation changes in the monthly transactions data are the two most important reasons for the discrepancy.[58] While the survey data gives us a better idea of who is investing in the United States and where the United States is investing, it has a number of drawbacks. First, as already stated, the data does not cover a complete run of years. Second, while it eliminates the "financial center" bias, it does not remove errors that arise from "custodial bias." Financial center bias occurs because cross-border transactions on behalf of third parties tend to occur within financial centers such as the United Kingdom and the Caribbean financial centers. Custodial bias refers to countries specializing in financial safe-keeping on behalf of third parties, such as Belgium, the Cayman Islands, Luxembourg, and Switzerland, who do not report the nationality of the owner holding the asset.[59] The reported liability positions of these countries therefore overstate the positions actually held by them. Unless these depository centers start reporting their positions according to the owner's country of residence, this particular distortion will persist. With these caveats in mind, the data is nonetheless able to give us an idea of who holds what in the United States and where the United States invests.

The long view

What is the profile of American long-term lending to other countries, and how does it compare with long-term lending in the United States? A rather comprehensive analysis of long-term lending is possible thanks to the data set made available by two senior economists at the Federal Reserve Board of Governors. Bertaut and Tryon develop a procedure for constructing survey estimates based on monthly transactions data.[60] Their constructed estimates match "known" survey estimates with remarkable precision. The data cover the period 1985–2005 for foreign long-term securities in the United States, and

---

[58] The Caribbean financial centers are the Bahamas, Bermuda, the British Virgin Islands, the Cayman Islands, the Netherlands Antilles, and Panama.
[59] This distortion is considerable; together these countries accounted for 21 percent of all foreign investment in the United States in 2006.
[60] Bertaut and Tryon 2007

1995–2005 for American long-term securities held abroad; positions do not include FDI.

What does an analysis of the data show? The United Kingdom was the number one investor in the United States in 1985 and accounted for 17 percent of overall long-term investment in the United States. Together the United Kingdom and Japan were the two largest investors, accounting for 30 percent of overall investment. The top three (the United Kingdom, Japan, and Germany) accounted for 39 percent; the top four (the United Kingdom, Japan, Germany, and Canada) for 47 percent; the top five, which included the Netherlands, accounted for 50 percent of overall investments in the United States. This list was basically unchanged a decade later, except for the fact that Japan became a larger investor than the United Kingdom, and Singapore replaced the Netherlands in the group of top five investors. The overall shares also increased across the board, with the top five investors accounting for 54 percent of overall long-term investment in the United States. A decade on (in 2005), China replaced Germany as the third biggest investor in the United States, and the Netherlands reclaimed its spot (from Singapore) as the fifth largest investor. The "major investor" share of overall investment was significantly reduced across all categories; as the top five investors accounted for 44 percent of overall investment in 2005. As a general observation, however, one cannot help but notice the continuity in the profile of major investors in the United States.

Where does the United States invest? In 1995, the largest single share of America's long-term investment went to Japan (16 percent). Together, the two largest outlets for American long-term investment (Japan and the United Kingdom) received 28 percent of America's long-term investment, whereas the three largest destinations (Japan, the United Kingdom, and Canada) received 40 percent, the four biggest destinations (Japan, the United Kingdom, Canada, and Germany) 46 percent, and the top five destinations (Japan, the United Kingdom, Canada, Germany, and the Netherlands) 53 percent. In 2005, the top five investment locations were, in descending order of importance, the United Kingdom, Canada, China, France, and Germany, which together accounted for 45 percent of overall American long-term investment. Here too, there is remarkable stability in American foreign investment, although there is a higher incidence of change. By 2005, China replaced Japan as the top destination for American investment, and France became a more important outlet than the Netherlands. From the United States' perspective, however, it is more important to ensure a stable pattern of investment at home than abroad. Indeed, given the time and risk elements at the core of the asymmetrical structure of the American investment position, we should expect at least some diversification of American assets to areas in need of high-risk capital, such as China. (A similar role was played by Japan in the 1980s and 1990s.)

There is also significant overlap between major American investors and major targets for American investment. Only France receives a high share of American long-term investment without making the top five list of major American investors; that being said, France is the tenth largest investor in the United States. France is also one of the countries where the United States has experienced the highest valuation adjustments since 1995.

The United Kingdom, Canada, France, Germany, and Japan account for 44 percent of America's *valuation gains* on long-term investments since 1995.[61] The data for foreigners' valuation gains on American long-term investments permit us to go back a bit further. Since 1985, all of the above countries, except for France, including the Netherlands, account for the highest individual shares of overall valuation gains in the United States; together they account for 50 percent of overall valuation gains in the United States. America's valuation losses on long-term investment, on the other hand, are more dispersed: only 10 percent are concentrated across the biggest losing destinations, Argentina, Malaysia, Pakistan, the Philippines, and Syria. Most of this loss is due to American long-term lending to Argentina having gone awry; 8.6 percent of the 9.9 percent share of the top five losing destinations' overall valuation loss is concentrated in Argentina. While Americans seem to have gained in the same countries that have gained in the United States, and in similar proportions (i.e., share of overall gains), this similarity does not extend to the loss domain.

Valuation losses in the United States are fairly concentrated. China accounts for 65 percent of the overall loss since 1985; together China and South Korea account for 80 percent of the losses, while South Africa, Turkey, and the Czech Republic jointly account for the remaining 9 percent. In total, this amounts to 89 percent of the valuation loss in the United States spread over five countries. At first, it

---

[61] These valuation estimates are based on the dataset provided by Bertaut and Tryon 2007.

seems surprising that Japan does not figure within this group. Since 1985, China (36 percent) together with Japan (65 percent), Korea (76 percent), Brazil (80 percent), and the United Kingdom (83 percent), shouldered the bulk of overall losses on long-term American Treasury securities. However, while Japan, Brazil, and the United Kingdom all experienced *valuation losses* on American Treasury bills and corporate bonds, they all experienced countervailing *valuation gains* on the American stock market and long-term agency bonds.

The short view

A few countries – Japan, Russia, and Ireland – have very high shares of short-term investments in the United States. Between 2001 and 2006, Japan's average share of short-term investment in the United States was 20 percent, while Russia and Ireland each invested 8 percent of the total.[62] Japan's high share of the outstanding value of foreign-owned short-term securities in the United States suggests that Japan subsidized America during this period. In fact, it would not be surprising to learn that Japan has been subsidizing America for the twenty-five-year period under consideration. Although we do not know whether Japan made large-scale investments in other short-term securities in the United States for the *entire* twenty-five-year period, we do know that Japan has been one of the world's major reserve holders since 1982, and the world's largest buyer of American Treasury securities (see below). Despite the absence of a complete dataset over trade in short-term securities, the evidence, suggesting that Japan bears much of the cost, is quite compelling.[63]

Which countries beside Japan, Russia, and Ireland have large values of short-term investment in the United States, or, more precisely, more than 1 percent of the overall share? In order of importance, they are: Belgium and Luxembourg, the Cayman Islands, Mexico, Hong Kong, China, the United Kingdom, Bermuda, France, Canada, Switzerland, South Korea, India, Germany, Australia, Barbados, Turkey, Indonesia, the Netherlands, and Israel. All of them (except perhaps for China, Turkey, and Indonesia) are strong American allies.

---

[62] Author's calculations based on IMF 2008.

[63] Especially since more than 10 percent of American long-term lending goes to Japan, and about 15 percent of America's long-term borrowing comes from Japan. As mentioned before, US foreign direct investment in other countries tends to earn higher returns than FDI in the United States, so there are several reasons to believe that the United States–Japan investment relationship tells us something about the United States' positive valuation effects.

Although we cannot know who the ultimate buyers of short-term securities are for three of the investing countries (because of custodial bias), their combined share is only 11 percent. Consequently, 50 percent of American short-term securities are spread over relatively few actors, i.e., nineteen investing countries.

The preceding analysis puts a new spin on the familiar public goods logic of International Relations. A common assertion in that literature is that hegemonic powers pay a disproportionate cost because small states can get away with a free ride when contributions are scattered across a wide range of actors. This may well be true for very small actors but not for medium-sized states who share the high opportunity cost of low-yield investment (in the United States).

Why are these countries investing in the United States? What makes the United States an attractive investment venue for private actors is the demand for liquid dollar assets, the ability to choose from a broad range of investment vehicles, and the perception that the American market is safe. Governments, on the other hand, have had a whole set of reasons for investing in American assets. Motivations range from safe investment solutions, to "too big to fail" concerns, export-led growth strategies, and reimbursement of dollar denominated debt.

In the years between 1983 and 1986, oil-exporting countries' reserves averaged 16 percent of the world total, most of which was held in dollar-denominated assets in the United States (see table 5.4).[64] During this time, G-7 countries held 37 percent of overall reserves, a share that would increase to 40 percent over the next half decade.[65] G-7 countries, especially Japan and the United Kingdom, and to some extent Germany and France were indispensable in engineering a soft landing of the American economy. While the recycling of petro-dollars made it possible for the United States to keep buying oil, providing investors with secure assets in exchange, G-7 countries went quite a bit further in extending the American credit line. They helped battle an unwieldy deficit by coordinating interventions to push the dollar down, and by signing onto macro-economic policy adjustments enunciated in the 1985 Plaza Agreement. Governments also set aside an $18 billion dollar "war chest" to cruise control the fall in the dollar through coordinated interventions.[66] This turned out to be a whole

[64] Author's calculations based on IMF 2007a.
[65] Author's calculations based on IMF 2007a.   [66] Funabashi 1988, 23.

Table 5.4 *Major reserve holders*

	1983–1987	1988–1992	1993–1997	1998–2002	2003–2007
G-7	39%	38%	30%	29%	25%
ME oil exporters	7%	3%	2%	2%	2%
Japan	8%	9%	11%	16%	19%
China	3%	3%	5%	9%	19%
Hong Kong	...	4%	6%	7%	4%
South Korea	1%	2%	2%	4%	5%
Taiwan	6%	8%	9%	9%	9%
Top five Asian reserve holders	*18%*	*26%*	*33%*	*46%*	*56%*
Brazil	2%	1%	3%	2%	2%

Note: Data for Hong Kong from 1990 onwards.
Source: Author's calculations based on IMF 2009f.

lot more than the $10.2 billion needed to pull off the 10 to 12 percent realignment participating countries had agreed upon. Plaza was a milestone in macro-economic history. Whereas governments had not sought to coordinate exchange rates prior to the agreement, they undertook frequent interventions in its wake.[67]

The 1986 Baker-Miyazawa deal – negotiated by the United States' Secretary of Treasury James A. Baker III and Japan's Finance Minister Kiichi Miyazawa – is another example of the United States' ability to shift the burden of adjustment onto other countries. Not only was Japan persuaded to cut interest rates and stimulate demand through fiscal packages, but the United States used the settlement reached with Miyazawa to extract macro-economic concessions from a recalcitrant Germany.[68] Leaning on foreign governments helped bring the dollar down. If anything, the concerted actions taken at Plaza were too effective. Towards the end of 1986, the dollar would not stop falling. By the end of 1986 it was down 18 percent against major currencies, and plunged another 13 percent by the end of 1987.

[67] Klein, Mizrach, and Murphy 1991.
[68] Destler and Henning 1989, 58.

The precipitous fall in the dollar led to the 1987 Louvre Accord, negotiated in February. Similarly, at Louvre in 1987, the United States was able to persuade Japan and Germany to take specific policy measures to traverse the American economy onto safer ground. Japan lowered its discount rate and agreed to fiscal actions to stimulate domestic demand; Germany agreed to greater tax cuts than it had budgeted; and the United States itself promised to respect the 1985 Gramm-Rudman Act, which imposed specific and yearly commitments to lower the deficit (although it did not honor the commitment).[69] Together, the coordinated interventions and macroeconomic policy adjustments agreed upon at Louvre stabilized the dollar somewhat. By the end of 1988, the dollar had increased by 5 percent. Although recurrent deficits had become a policy constraint by the mid-1980s, the very fact that other governments were ready to undertake adjustments in order to safe-land the economy is unusual. Allied support had to be negotiated and was not always forthcoming, but there was a coordinated response and it was driven by fear of an American recession.

The ability to persuade other countries to share the burden of adjustment, often by asking them to intervene in their own economies, has allowed the United States to avoid growth-throttling interest rate hikes that would be necessary to encourage private capital flows. The United States' current policy towards China is almost a mirror image of the way it dealt with Japan in the 1980s. The American government started pressuring the Chinese authorities to float the renminbi in 2003, but the Chinese did not immediately heed American calls for currency appreciation. The standoff would last until July 2005, when the People's Bank of China raised the value of the renminbi by 2 percent, and announced that it would in future peg the value of the renminbi to a "secret" currency basket with day-to-day movements capped at 30 basis points. Since then, US Treasury Secretary, John Snow, his successor Paul Hanson, and now Timothy Geithner, have proposed that the Chinese help ease global imbalances through financial reform, tax reform, consumer credit breaks, and social security reform. Numerous official declarations suggest that the American view of the problem is not that Americans save too little and spend too much but that the rest of the world saves too much and spends too little.

[69] Funabashi 1988, 55, 60.

When the deficit reached alarming proportions in the 1980s, many observers feared a "hard landing," world recession, and the imminent decline of American power. Contrary to expectations, the United States succeeded in staging a "soft landing" by persuading other countries to revalue and stimulate domestic demand. The string of deficits experienced throughout the 1990s and into the second millennium, however, exceeds those of the 1980s. What is the likelihood that concerted action by major powers could cushion a freefalling dollar? To answer this question one must look at the composition of American liabilities.

Comparing the seven-year period between 1982 and 1988, when the deficit peaked at 3.4 percent of GDP, with the one between 2000 and the year 2006 when the deficit reached an all-time high of 6 percent of GDP, reveals important differences but also striking similarities.[70] The first difference is the remarkable increase in the GDP share of capital inflows, which is due to the increased integration of the world economy. In 1982, capital inflows amounted to approximately 3 percent of GDP whereas they amounted to roughly 15 percent of GDP in 2007.[71] But even more significant is the changing nature of the capital inflow. Between 1982 and 1988, *private* inflows averaged 91 percent of overall inflows, whereas they only averaged 82 percent between 2000 and 2007. Not only have *official* inflows increased as a share of overall inflows, but the foreign interests financing the deficit have also changed.

Central banks are unlikely to dump American securities on a large scale because it is not in their interest to do so. Any serious attempt to diversify out of dollars risks sparking off a run on the dollar, exacerbating the effect of the dollar's slide on the value of reserves. On the whole, foreign official investment has only been negative in three of the thirty-six years that have lapsed between 1971 and 2006 – in 1979, 1985, and 1998 – and, as we just saw, the 1985 dollar recall was an intentional coordinated drive to bring the dollar down at the United States' behest.[72] As long as investors can decode central bank

---

[70] A far as the composition of capital inflows is concerned, there are marginal differences in choosing 2000–06, as opposed to 1992–2006 (which captures the long-term build-up in the deficit), as the comparator group.

[71] Between 1982 and 1988, average capital inflows were approximately 4 percent of GDP whereas they amounted to 10 percent of GDP between 2000 and 2006. Author's calculations of capital inflows in this section are based on BEA 2007c.

[72] BEA 2007c.

incentives to mitigate a dollar cascade, private actors will pick up American assets in anticipation of a rebound. The dollar has been extremely resilient in the past, with investors willing to buy it at a discount on the expectation that it will rise again. This expectation has been rational given the power of the United States to coerce trade partners to help stem a deep dollar dive, as they did in persuading allies to sign on to the 1987 Louvre Accord. Belief in a future dollar rally has been all the more rational since, until recently, there was no credible alternative to a de facto dollar standard, and both private and official actors eventually need dollars as their income and opportunities expand. In the last half decade, however, the euro has emerged as a potent rival currency. Yet, although the gradual drift to the euro has capped the United States' ability to use its currency to advantage, the dollar still retains a special position in the international system. (For a full treatment of the euro as rival currency, see chapter 7.)

The composition of the stock of foreign assets in the United States is also of importance. The average share of FDI in the American economy in the last decade was 4 percent lower than in the two decades between 1976 and 1996.[73] The higher portion of private assets held in the United States as portfolio investment (stocks, bonds, and other liquid forms of capital such as bank loans) leaves the economy vulnerable to rapid change.[74] Portfolio investments can more easily be liquidated, and there is consequently greater chance of triggering a large-scale pull out by unwinding even small positions. Although a large part of the portfolio investment is in the form of low-return debt, representing a benefit to the American economy, the United States is also subject to some of the caveats that apply to other countries. On the other hand, if a run on the dollar were to occur, governments are as well placed today as in 1985, when the precipitous fall in the dollar was neutralized through the Louvre Accord, since foreign official assets now account for 18 percent of all foreign assets in the United States, as compared to 17 percent in 1985.[75]

What are the prospects of an orderly adjustment in the current round? When the dollar started falling from peak levels in 2001, the decline was mild. It fell by 1 percent in the first year against major

[73] BEA 2007d.   [74] Gray 2004; Obstfeld and Rogoff 2005.
[75] BEA 2007d.

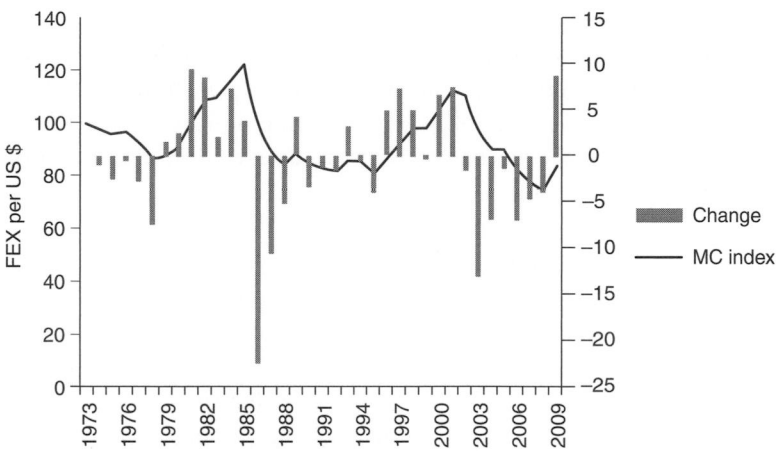

Figure 5.7 Dollar against major currencies
Notes: March 1973 = 100. Major currency (MC) per US$ is measured from the primary y-axis and yearly changes in the value of major currencies per US$ measured from the secondary y-axis.
Source: Author's calculations based on data from Federal Reserve Flow of Funds.

currencies, another 20 percent by 2004, amounting to a 24 percent drop by late 2005, and an overall decline of 30 percent by late 2008 when the dollar rallied (see figure 5.7). Notwithstanding the monstrous deficit, the adjustment now taking place is at least off to a more benign start than the steep fall that began in 1985, which the Louvre Accord was designed to stem. Continued dependence on American product markets makes it very likely that central banks will smooth-sail the dollar, just as they did at Plaza and Louvre. By 1990, the currency alignment that began in 1985 weakened the dollar by 37 percent. Although the dollar will intermittently rise and fall over the course of the next decade, it is likely that it will come down at least another 10 percent from 2005 levels.

Thus far, the dollar has held its ground fairly well and even withstood reports that central banks want to slow purchases of American securities. The dollar tumbled when South Korea's central bank presented its 2005 reserve strategy in a briefing paper submitted to a parliamentary committee. Yet while the dollar fell against major currencies as the central bank hinted at increasing its non-dollar based portion of foreign currency reserves, the fall was not as dramatic as expected. Similarly, when China slowed purchases of American securities in March 2005, Britain and a few Caribbean countries quickly stepped in to eliminate the excess bond supply. Moreover, the long-awaited July decision to float the renminbi, and the concomitant rise in its value against the dollar, only raised long-term interest rates by 2 percent. At the time of writing, the dollar's safe haven status in the midst of the financial crisis has kept it at levels comparable to those in 2005 wiping out the interim depreciation.

Global currency reserves stood at $1.6 trillion in 1996, $2.5 trillion in 2001, and $6.5 trillion in 2007. As can be seen in table 5.4, there has been a steady decline in the G-7 share of total reserves and a corresponding increase in the five major Asian reserve countries' share, especially in the shares of Japan, China, South Korea, and Taiwan. Since 1992, five countries in East Asia (Japan, China, Hong Kong, Taiwan, and South Korea) have together had 25 percent or more of the world's reserves – just slightly lower than the current G-7 share. In the last half of the decade, they held almost 50 percent of world reserves.

As we saw earlier, in table 5.3, exports to the United States are a high (albeit declining) share of overall exports. As also mentioned earlier, in this arrangement, known as "Bretton Woods II," countries siphon off the dollars they receive in export earnings and invest them in American Treasury bills in order to prevent their currencies from appreciating.[76] Intervention of this sort has ensured relatively stable exchange rates against the dollar, and is reminiscent of the Bretton Woods system of fixed exchange rates.

One can use the information about declining export shares to argue that these countries will in future be less eager to finance the deficit. Alternatively, they might be more inclined to extend credit to gain better access to the American market. Table 5.5 suggests the latter. The decline in export shares seems to have prompted governments to keep their currencies steady against the dollar. The table clearly shows a tendency for greater purchases of American Treasury securities in the last decade, although there has been a retrenchment as of late. Of course, there is a possibility that this is just a coincidence, since we do not know whether these are official or private purchases, and the American Treasury does not publish, and will not release, a breakdown of the underlying country detail between official and private holders of American securities. Other motives, as well, are at

[76] Dooley, Folkerts-Landau, and Garber 2003.

Table 5.5 *Major foreign holders of Treasury securities*

	1994	2000	2002	2003	2004	2005	2006	2008
Japan	28%	25%	31%	33%	38%	35%	31%	26%
China	4%	8%	8%	11%	11%	16%	19%	24%
Hong Kong	2%	4%	4%	3%	3%	2%	2%	3%
Taiwan	6%	5%	3%	3%	4%	4%	3%	3%
South Korea	1%	3%	3%	4%	3%	3%	3%	2%
Top five Asian reserve holders	*40%*	*45%*	*49%*	*54%*	*58%*	*61%*	*59%*	*57%*
ME oil exporters	4%	2%	3%	2%	2%	3%	5%	4%
Brazil	0%	1%	1%	1%	1%	1%	2%	7%

Source: Author's calculations based on Treasury 2009.

play when governments decide to invest in American Treasury bills. For instance, countries that cannot borrow in their own currency have incentives to acquire safe dollar-denominated assets to repay their loans. It is possible that this explains Brazil's recent purchasing spree of American Treasury bills, which reached 5 percent of the world total in 2007, up from 1 percent in 2002–05, and 7 percent in 2008.[77] Mexico, another major holder of American Treasury bills (2 percent of total) is in a similar predicament. There are also precautionary motives for holding Treasury bills, as demonstrated by the flight to safety in the wake of the financial crisis.

The power of the dollar

If it were not for the United States' commercial prowess, its ability to absorb imports, and the dynamism of its firms, it would not be able to play dollar cycles. Monetary privilege in the form of flexibility and an ability to benefit from external liabilities lies at the intersection of a large product market and the dollar's proliferation in the world economy.

[77] Author's calculations based on Treasury 2007.

As for its key currency status, the United States has the privilege of borrowing in its own currency, if need be. Borrowing can therefore be financed by creating dollars and, as a result, downward pressure on the dollar, not illiquidity, is the main constraint on American borrowing. Although the United States itself cannot entirely create dollars at will, since someone also has to be willing to hold them, the American market's ability to absorb large amounts of goods, services, and assets, provides foreigners with a motivation to hold dollars.

The United States was thought to have two major deterrent threats before 1971, which, if ever used, would seriously undermine confidence in the dollar: first, the ability to freeze foreign assets held in the United States; and second, the threat to unilaterally suspend dollar convertibility. But exercising this prerogative did not send destabilizing waves through the international system by eroding confidence in the dollar. Instead, despite President Nixon's 1971 announcement that dollars would no longer be redeemable in gold, a de facto dollar standard persisted. Up until the "Nixon shock," when the United States unilaterally suspended convertibility and imposed a 10 percent import surcharge, the removal of which was contingent upon foreign currency appreciation, the dollar had remained stable. But it was in the nature of the system that a country could not provide international liquidity without eventually jeopardizing external price stability. This was the central proposition of the "Triffin dilemma" and the reality of the experience under the dollar-exchange standard. The massive dollar outflow had made the United States' commitment to exchange a fixed amount of gold reserves against dollar claims increasingly less credible, culminating in the 1971 crisis. After the collapse of the fixed exchange rate regime, a de facto dollar standard under which the dollar has been anything but stable gradually came into view. The ability to run current account deficits and restore equilibrium through fluctuations in the exchange rate has magnified American power in the monetary realm and is a source of commercial power.

The "exorbitant privilege" did not come to an end under flexible rates. In fact, it grew stronger as a result of capital and exchange rate gains on the NFA. The unilateral decoupling of the dollar and gold was a manifestation of American power – a move to which other countries could not retaliate – and as such, proof that the United States had a first-move advantage under Bretton Woods. When flexible exchange rates were instituted, this first-move advantage seemed to diffuse into a system of mutual retaliatory powers with strong competition from other reserve currencies, such as the D-mark, the yen, and pound sterling. Far from being lost, this first-move advantage persists and, if anything, is greater under flexible exchange rates. In dismantling Bretton Woods, the United States called her creditors' bluff and learned that even if private and institutional investors had temporarily turned their backs on the dollar, they would eventually return for more. Far from being "dethroned," the dollar's resilience and unique position in the world economy would persist long after the demise of Bretton Woods, and only seriously be put into question with the advent of the euro in 1999.

Through long-term swings in the dollar, the United States has been able to appropriate a disproportionate share of world savings and off-load a considerable part of the burden of balance of payments adjustment onto other countries. With such a large portion of the American investment position comprising liquid dollar denominated liabilities, and American assets mostly denominated in foreign currency, there is built-in protection against depreciation. The effect of dollar depreciation is to boost the competitiveness of American export products and increase the dollar value of America's asset position. Meanwhile, the negative effect that depreciation normally has on external liabilities when borrowing occurs in local currency is neutralized. Since prolonged deficits imply depreciation, this implies that the cost of adjustment would have been higher for the United States had it not been the key currency country. Although liabilities are not reduced as a result of appreciation when borrowing occurs in dollars (as opposed to foreign currency), protecting against the cost of depreciation is especially important when a country experiences a long-term decline in the value of its currency.

It is true that investors in industrialized countries with advanced capital markets also can borrow in their own currency, at least partly, and hedge against the remaining foreign currency risk. Hedging is expensive, though – prohibitively so – for small-scale investors. Besides, to the extent that such hedging has occurred, it has not necessarily translated into exchange rate gains on the NFA. For instance, by 2005, the financial sector in Australia hedged about 85 percent of its foreign currency debt (93 percent in 2001) whereas other borrowers hedged 46 percent of their debt (38 percent in 2001), yet Australia has experienced negative valuation adjustments.[78]

---

[78] Harrison and Hawkins 2007, 70.

Oscillating between long cycles of a strong dollar policy and "managed drop" has enabled the United States to sustain decade-long current account deficits that would have spelled disaster for any other country and to turn a profit on net liabilities in the process. A strong dollar draws in goods from abroad but impacts negatively on exports. As a counterweight to the decline in American exports, there has, however, been a secular increase in American sales from foreign locations, as emphasized in chapter 4. A weak dollar is good for exports but raises the price of foreign goods, which, quite apart from the negative effect on the purchasing power of American consumers, can contribute to inflation. The risk, of course, is that higher interest rates to combat inflation will choke off investment, and spiral into a severe economic downturn. Yet foreign producers' readiness to lower prices (through classic optimal tariff reasoning) in order to continue accessing the American market has made it possible to enjoy an export boom on the wings of a lower dollar without damaging inflation. Regular swings in the dollar are necessary for long cycles of limit pricing and optimal tariff pricing.

Playing dollar cycles

There have been two major rounds of dollar appreciation. The first upward trend started at the end of the 1970s when the dollar regained strength after having fallen for almost a decade between 1971 and 1978. From 1978 to 1985, the dollar appreciated significantly against major currencies. Then, in the decade spanning the mid-1980s to the mid-1990s, the dollar parachuted again. This period was followed by a second dollar rally, which would last up until 2002. The dollar is currently in its third downward phase. This weakening is part of a regular pattern of dollar cycles. The dollar has typically come down about 40 percent against major currencies in a period of five to seven years.

The decline in the dollar from 1971 until the end of the 1970s, as well as its subsequent rise from 1979 to 1985, can be seen in figure 5.8. The first dollar skid came with the Nixon shock of 1971 and marked the end of the Bretton Woods system of fixed exchange rates. An attempt was made through the 1971 Smithsonian agreement to bring the dollar down in an orderly fashion by persuading countries with large reserves, such as West Germany, Japan, and Switzerland, to undertake a 10 percent revaluation against the dollar. In 1973, the dollar was devalued

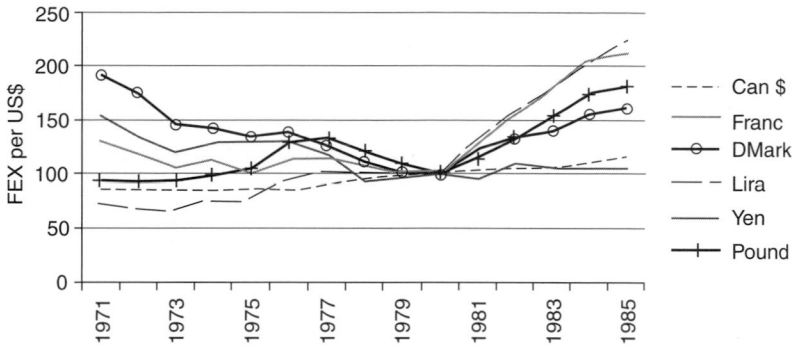

Figure 5.8 Dollar cycles, 1971–85: G-7 currency per US$
Note: 1980 = 100.
Source: Author's calculations based on data from FRBS 2009.

another 10 percent, and within a month major currencies started floating around a de facto dollar standard. From the time flexible exchange
rates were introduced in 1973 until 1978, the dollar depreciated 13
percent in real terms against major currencies. The dollar slide was not,
however, preceded by large current account deficits. Apart from the net
capital inflow experienced in 1969, dollars were instead being exported
on capital account with Americans acquiring more assets abroad than
foreigners were willing to hold in the United States.

The dollar's spectacular rise began with the seven-year ascent in
1978, when the dollar climbed 40 percent in real terms against major
currencies (see figure 5.7). High investment needs in the United States,
and the disparity between its macroeconomic policies and those pursued by other industrialized countries, were the reasons for the soaring
dollar during this period.[79] To stave off inflation in the early 1980s,
the United States cranked up interest rates, which resulted in a higher
dollar as capital flowed in. But it was not until the fiscal expansion of
1982 that import demand started to climb and nudged interest rates
and the dollar still higher.[80] Since other major industrialized countries
were accumulating budget surpluses during this time, the excess in
world savings found its way to the United States, strengthening the
dollar further. The tax cuts and increased military outlays implied by
the fiscal explosion of the 1980s could easily be filled by capital flows
from other western countries, leading to a substantial weakening of

[79] Marris 1987.   [80] Howard 1989.

the current account.[81] Within a span of six years, the 1981 surplus on current account was transformed into a deficit of 3.5 percent of GDP – a record deficit at the time.

With the dollar appreciating, foreign assets in the United States increased considerably, leading to a dramatic 82 percent drop in America's NFA between 1980 and 1985. This worsening of the NFA was so corrosive that by 1986 the United States had net external liabilities. The dollar's decline, rise, and fall in the two decades since 1985 can be seen in figures 5.7 and 5.9. In real terms, the sharp drop in the dollar that occurred between 1985 and 1995 lowered its value against major currencies by 34 percent. But the decline in the dollar did nothing to reverse the deteriorating current account position until 1988. The staid response to the fading dollar can be attributed to the so-called J-curve effect, according to which the immediate consequence of higher import prices contributes to a weakening current account position before growth in imports slow.[82]

The rise in the dollar between 1995 and 2001 was again extraordinary: at 38 percent, it was reminiscent of the appreciation experienced in the 1980s (see figure 5.9). For a brief period in the early 1990s, capital inflows covered large budget deficits, as had been the case in the mid-1980s. But this was only an interlude. After 1992, the record is one of consistent improvement of the fiscal position, resulting in surpluses from 1998 to 2001. The investment boom in 1991 lasted throughout the decade until the stock market crash in 2000. Markets were, however, quick to recover, with investments increasing by 2003. Throughout the 1990s and into the second millennium, owing to a combination of factors that in large part reflect the superior performance and stability of the American economy, foreigners have been eager to invest in it. These factors include: high productivity growth; "new economy" solutions for information and technology; the search for a safe haven in the wake of the 1997–98 Asian financial crisis; the stock market rally; and interest rates that have been sufficiently low to encourage investment yet high enough to draw in foreign funds.[83] Since 2001, the dollar has been in decline, coming down 26 percent against major currencies (35 percent between 2001 and 2008).

---

[81] Preeg 2000, 47.
[82] Howard 1989, 158.
[83] Cooper 2001; Mann 2002; Pakko 1999; Weller 2004.

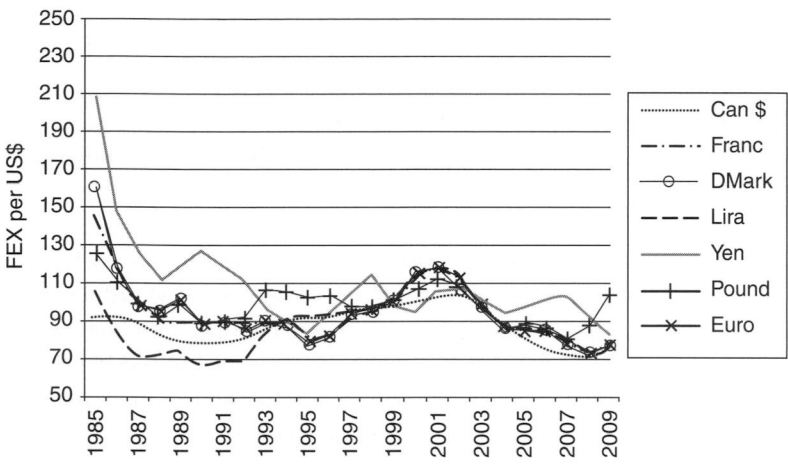

Figure 5.9 Dollar cycles, 1985–2009
Note: 1999 = 100.
Source: Author's calculations based on data from FRBS 2009.

American officials have been well aware of the benefits that flow from the stalwart dollar. In the 1980s, Secretary of the Treasury, Donald T. Regan attributed low inflation and world economic growth to the high dollar, while President Reagan frequently characterized the dollar as a magnet for investment.[84] Just a few years ago, former Secretary of the Treasury John Snow said, "it's always the same policy; our policy is the strong dollar," expressing a view reminiscent of President Reagan's mantra, "a strong dollar for a strong America."[85] The dollar has been pivotal in helping the United States stay on a high investment and consumption curve.

Conclusion

While there are plenty of signs that the United States' capacity to extract resources from the rest of the world is approaching a limit, America's ability to play cycles of limit pricing and optimal tariff pricing is more likely to continue than to change. When inquiring about the consequences of a payments crisis, it is necessary to consider what effects a collapse of the American economy and a long-term decline

[84] Destler and Henning 1989, 26.
[85] *The Globe and Mail*, January 13, 2005, Report on business.

in its military capabilities would have on the rest of the world, and the Great Powers in particular. The present situation, in which the world's engine of growth is head over heels in debt, and even bringing out the magic inflation wand (i.e., quantitative easing) to reduce external liabilities, pales in comparison with what would transpire if that engine were to break down. A massive sell-off of American assets would not only have a strongly negative effect on the United States but would also unleash a recession with consequences felt far beyond American borders. A large-scale pull-out would send the dollar plummeting, kill its reserve currency role, and have unimaginable effects on the United States and other economies. Without a viable alternative to spearhead growth, the world would be bound for depression until a new leader emerged, such as the European Union, China, or Japan, none of which is sufficiently strong to maintain economic and political liberalism. The European Union and Japan are economically strong but militarily weak; only China, not exactly a beacon in liberal thought or practice, has the potential and outright ambition to combine economic and military might. But for all Beijing's talk about a "peaceful rise," most nations prefer American dominance to Chinese hegemony. Even if China were to concretize its hegemonic aspirations, such ambitions will remain decidedly regional for the foreseeable future. Paradoxically, China's long-term bid for global dominance can only succeed if Japan does not militarize and therefore has to be planned under the cloak of America's security guarantee. This brings us around 360 degrees to the point about the hegemon's economic privilege being the wellspring of its military preeminence. The security determinants of the United States' economic position is the subject of the next chapter.

6 | *The security card*

The economic benefits of military dominance are generally denied. First-rate weapons systems are said to be expensive and the costs of coercion, including the backlash against military oppression, are often seen as outweighing benefits.

Once a technological advantage and a system of allies and bases have been achieved, however, the costs of maintaining and preserving a military edge will start to decline, and will at any rate represent a small fraction of a leading economy. The bigger challenge soon becomes how to force people to do something that they do not wish to do over the long term, but, as I will show, there are other, more subtle, ways in which military power can produce tangible economic benefits. Displays of force, and the occasional use of force, can, for instance, be used to claim control of an area and lock out competitors. Military power can also be used to secure investments domestically and abroad, producing a security premium at home and a reduction in foreign risk premiums. Lastly, extending a deterrent umbrella over other countries creates a web of allies with an interest in keeping American hegemony alive.

With these ways in which security functions can produce economic benefits in mind, I make four distinct claims about how military power is connected to American economic might. First, military means were used to keep European Great Powers out of the western hemisphere, which, by extending the domain of dollar use, allowed the United States to gather a size advantage and eventually become the key currency country. Second, investing heavily in defense through the development of sophisticated weaponry, strategic basing policies, and foreign military interventions to check challengers, the United States has, with the exception of 9/11, effectively deterred attacks on the homeland, contributing to the perception that the United States is a safe investment venue. Third, the United States has intervened militarily for economic reasons – for narrow economic purposes, in support of American business interests, and for broader economic goals in order to provide a stable political context in which economic exchange can take place, and in order to safeguard the ensuing capitalist structure from Communist encroachment. Fourth, the United States is obliged by treaty to defend roughly fifty countries (almost all of Latin America and Europe, as well as Canada, South Korea, Japan, Thailand, the Philippines, Australia, Liberia, a number of states in the Pacific, Bahrain, Egypt, Israel, Jordan, New Zealand, Kuwait, Qatar, Taiwan, and Pakistan).[1] American intervention to push back aggressors, and to defend humanitarian needs, has purchased goodwill and provided the Great Powers with an interest in preserving an American-centered world. The multi-purpose nature of American military power, including its self-appointed role as the world's cop on the beat, allows the United States to go on behaving unilaterally until the marginal benefit of these stabilizing functions falls below the marginal cost of an unstable order.

The security–dollar nexus

The central role of the dollar in the world economy is rooted in security considerations and the dynamics of gunboat diplomacy. Military power is not only necessary for *sustaining* key currency status – it actually helped *create* it by successively enlarging the scale of dollar use, starting in the Caribbean in the twentieth century.

Military power is often connected to key currency status. Since one of the key currency country's main functions is to extend loans to other countries, it must be capital-abundant, although, as is clear from the American example, it need not be a net creditor. Political economists often point out that the key currency country must be strong militarily, since it must be able to deter countries from repudiating reimbursement of the loans it extends to them.[2] But whether enforcing debt payments militarily is an effective deterrent against debt repudiation is an open question. There are those who argue that a bad reputation for not honoring debt, because of its negative effect on the future capacity to borrow, is a sufficient deterrent.[3] When one

---

[1] Tertrais 2004, 136–7.
[2] Cf. Bergsten 1975; Cohen 1977; Mundell 1998a, 1998b.
[3] Eaton and Gersovitz 1981; cited in English 1996.

considers the many ways defaults affect the cost of future borrowing, and takes a broad range of sources into account, creditors seem to be sensitive to borrowers' credit history.[4] Others argue that reputational considerations are not enough because if debts cannot be enforced, the debtor is, at some point, better off defaulting and saving (the funds, which should have gone into servicing debt) in foreign asset markets.[5] According to the historical record, force has been used to settle debt on several occasions. But the early origins of the dollar's special role in the world economy reveal that the United States was not alone in its ability to enforce debt. Many powers were capable of intervening to collect debt in the nineteenth and twentieth centuries. The ability to enforce debt payments militarily cannot, therefore, be what distinguishes the key currency country from other countries. Although it might be a necessary condition, it cannot be a sufficient one to achieve key currency status.

Today, it hardly makes sense at all to argue that military power is necessary for debt collection, since the United States has the strongest military capability as well as the largest stock of outstanding liabilities in the world. Foreigners cannot possibly expect to collect their share of outstanding liabilities through military action, and should not be lending to the United States if superior military power is crucial for redeeming loans. Nevertheless, security calculations play a role in so far as these helped the United States become the special currency country. American lending and the spread of the dollar in the Caribbean started off as a way of preventing European meddling in America's sphere of interest. Large-scale lending first began close to home in the beginning of the twentieth century because of security competition with European powers.

In the early twentieth century, British bondholders persuaded the British Foreign Office to intervene with armed force in Venezuela, culminating in the Anglo-German blockade of 1902–03.[6] The United States faced what seemed to be an intractable problem: weak, fractured Caribbean states had a propensity for repudiating debt and European lenders pushed their governments to intervene on their behalf. Not so keen on European gunboat diplomacy in their backyard, the Americans elaborated what became known as the Roosevelt

---

[4] Tomz 2007.   [5] Bulow and Rogoff 1989; cited in English 1996.
[6] Hood 1975, 55.

Corollary to the Monroe doctrine. To keep Europeans out of the Caribbean, the United States would enforce debt payments on behalf of European bondholders:

In the Western Hemisphere the adherence of the United States to the Monroe Doctrine may force the United States, however reluctantly, in flagrant cases of such wrong-doing or impotence, to the exercise of an international police power ... On the one hand, this country would certainly decline to go to war to prevent a foreign government from collecting a just debt; on the other hand, it is very inadvisable to permit any foreign power to take possession, even temporarily, of the custom houses of an American Republic in order to enforce the payment of its obligations; for such temporary occupation might turn into a permanent occupation.[7]

The United States installed an American citizen to oversee Dominican customs houses when the country defaulted in 1904; an American banker was designated collector general in Honduras in 1909 and in Nicaragua in 1911; and in 1914, the Navy was sent to Haiti to collect debt, establishing a financial protectorate over the country until 1934.[8] The United States occupied Haiti in 1915, and the Navy patrolled the wider Caribbean to protect American lives and property, as well as to preserve the Panama Canal project.[9] The Canal raised American concerns that European powers would intervene in the Caribbean to collect debt from weak states with a history of repudiating debt.[10] The Great Powers had an easier time cooperating in the Pacific. In 1923, a joint British, French, Italian, Japanese, Portuguese, and American force went to China to protect a customs house in Canton, which the Chinese were about to reclaim from foreign occupiers who maintained a presence to collect debt.[11] When sending the Navy to the Caribbean, the United States was not simply strong-arming countries in the area to refrain from debt repudiation. The primary objective was to keep the Europeans out of the Caribbean. If Americans had not stepped in to enforce debt payments, the British would have, or the French, or the Italians, who were just as eager to recover what was owed to them. According to the Monroe

[7] Cited in Perkins 1955, 229, 237–40.
[8] Perkins 1955, 237–40, 249–52, 260–6.
[9] Healy 1976.   [10] Healy 1976, 4.
[11] Cable 1994, 162.

doctrine, the United States would not tolerate such intervention in its sphere of interest. By enforcing and expanding the Monroe doctrine, successive administrations, from 1905 on, sought legitimacy for international policing rights, to substitute American for European capital in the Caribbean, and to enforce a ban on foreign acquisition of property if such purchases jeopardized American security interests.[12]

Dispatching the Navy and occupying customs houses was not the only available strategy. Another was to replace Europe as the preferred creditor in the Caribbean basin. Soon, Washington started to encourage American lending. The United States effectively preempted European intervention in the Caribbean by weakening the motivation for it. The first major extension of the dollar was, at least in part, security driven. With lending to the Caribbean, dollars were diffused on a much larger scale. This gradual expansion of the dollar's domain prepared the way for the postwar dollar standard.

The asymmetry in risk premiums

American military power affects risk premiums at home and abroad. The ability to protect the American market has lowered the price of attracting capital, and the US government's willingness to support American firms' activities abroad both politically and militarily has reduced the risk premium on foreign direct investment. As we saw in chapter 5, the US government's readiness to underwrite a system, in which American households and firms can access capital on favorable terms, and in which American firms have established a presence in risky areas, goes some way in explaining the asymmetry in the structure of American borrowing and lending. While it is generally acknowledged that security, in the form of political instability, has a decisive impact on financial flows to and from developing countries, there is not a similar sense that the outcome of military conflicts matters for industrialized countries, given the era of postwar stability enjoyed by them. As I will try to demonstrate, however, American military might has facilitated America's capital intake. Funds have more readily flowed to the United States when she has been on the winning side of a military contest and have conversely dried up when she has been on the losing side of a military contest.

---

[12] The so-called Lodge resolution: Perkins 1955, 248, 256, 266, 271–4.

The domestic security premium

One of the reasons investors are attracted to the American market is that they consider investing in it is safe. The United States has collected a huge security premium by capitalizing on the ability to secure its home base both militarily and legally through property rights protection. The United States' investment pull is not only explained by the need for dollars in the international system. The government's commitment to secure investments has also been important. The combined effect of an advanced capital market and a strong military machine to defend that market, and other safety measures such as a strong tradition of property rights protection and a reputation for honoring dues, has made it possible to attract capital with great ease. In chapter 5, we saw that three other countries – Britain, Switzerland, and Canada – have enjoyed substantial gains from the discrepancy between the value of the net foreign asset position and the cumulative current account. In common, they all have a liberal orientation grounded in property rights protection and are able to extract a substantial security premium as a result – Canada by free-riding on the United States, Switzerland by adhering to secrecy laws and unbending neutrality, and the United Kingdom (like the United States) by boasting a commitment to honoring dues and its own imperial legacy. Out of these, only the United States and Switzerland saw their currency strengthen in the wake of the financial crisis. Battered by the United States, France, and Germany, it is not clear how bruised Switzerland will emerge from suggested changes in secrecy rules and taxation agreements.

Given the size of American trade deficits and external liabilities, one would expect a lot more headwind against American-based assets and therefore the dollar. As we saw in chapter 5, however, central banks only sold more American assets than they bought in three of the thirty-six years between 1971 and 2006.[13] And only on one occasion, in 1971, did sales by private investors exceed private purchases of American assets.[14] The steady capital inflow, through good times and bad, is due to the widely held belief that the American market is safe and will rebound after a downturn. In what follows, I substantiate my claim that the United States has received a security premium

[13] BEA 2007b.   [14] BEA 2007e.

by linking increased financial flows to the United States with military successes and reduced financial flows with military defeats.

Since 1960, the first year when financial transactions between the United States and the rest of the world were reported by the Bureau of Economic Analysis (BEA), there have been approximately twenty militarized disputes involving the United States in which either party to a conflict could register a decisive "win." Although there is bound to be some ambiguity about what counts as a "decisive" win, I have tried to narrow the scope for disagreement by relying on the Correlates of War (COW) database whenever possible. The database only covers militarized disputes up until 2001, however. To gauge the success rate of the various campaigns that have taken place up until 2005, I undertook a systematic examination of American advances and retreats in Iraq as reported in the *Economist*.

The first militarized dispute reported in COW involved the Soviet Union. In November 1978, President Brezhnev asked the United States to back off in Iran; specifically, he urged the United States to reconsider the military intervention that they were contemplating in order to quell unrest in the country. By early 1979, the United States made clear its intention not to meddle in Iran. The levels of hostility surrounding this event were relatively low. Nonetheless, after yielding to the Soviet Union, capital flows into the United States fell back in 1979.

Starting in mid-February 1983, Libya attempted to steer Sudan away from its pro-western stance by supporting the Sudanese opposition against the presidency of Gaafar Nimeiry. The United States put its weight behind the Sudanese government and Libya caved in within a matter of days. Later in the fall of that year, the United States invaded Grenada, in what was called "Operation Urgent Fury," with mission accomplished by November 1, 1983. Once again, in the early spring of 1984, Libya tried to persuade Sudan to change its western orientation, this time by urging President Nimeiry's rivals to stir up trouble. When Libya went so far as to attack Sudan, and the United States stepped in and threatened to use force, Libya gave in. Between the fall of 1985 and the spring of 1986, in the midst of the Iran–Iraq war, the United States got caught up in a row with Iran in which it (along with the United Kingdom and Saudi Arabia) threatened to use force against Iran. Although hostilities continued well into 1988, Iran admitted temporary defeat. Relations with Libya continued to deteriorate in late 1985 and early 1986. After a series of terrorist attacks in Rome and Vienna (December 1985), and at the Berlin discotheque "La Belle" (April 1986), as well as a naval showdown with Libya in the Gulf of Sirte, the United States determined to send a strong signal to President Muammar Qaddafi that his support for terrorism would not be tolerated and that his maritime claims in the Gulf would not be heeded. On April 15, 1986, the United States proceeded with "Operation El Dorado Canyon" – a series of air strikes against Libyan targets. Libya attempted to strike back, but quickly gave up. Following these events – i.e., Libya's acquiescence over Sudan in 1983 and 1984, Libya's submission in 1986, Grenada's capitulation in 1984, Iran's resignation in 1986 – capital flows into the United States continued to increase, reversing the decline in flows of 1983.

The next military confrontation was in December 1989 and lasted for less than a month. "Operation Just Cause" was set in motion in order to depose Panamanian president General Manuel Noriega. Increasingly annoyed with Noriega's duplicitous role in the illicit drug trade, and wary of the domestic backlash after his failure to honor the outcome of spring elections, the United States used the slaying of an American officer as a pretext to invade the country and seize Noriega. The killing, it was argued, indicated a need to protect American lives in Panama. Broader justifications for the incursion were to defend democracy and human rights, to safeguard the Panama Canal, and to win the "war on drugs." Capital flows receded in 1990 after the Panama invasion, and constitute an exception to the pattern of increased flows following military success.

Six months later, the United States was again embroiled in a foreign military campaign. Along with Allied forces, the United States pushed back Iraq from Kuwait in the Persian Gulf War, which lasted from July 24, 1990 until March 3, 1991. Following the successful completion of the operation, capital inflows started to increase once again.

This trend of greater capital inflows continued, as the United States and coalition forces intervened in Bosnia, between 1992 and 1996, and in Haiti between 1993 and 1994. Shortly after the United States and the European Community recognized Bosnia's independence in April 1992, Serbian president Slobodan Milosevic stepped up the violence and attacked Sarajevo, unleashing a war that would last until 1995. The United States led a series of blockades – starting with "Operation Maritime Guard" in November 1992 and ending with "Operation Sharp Guard" in October 1996 – in support of the

United Nations' embargo under Security Council Resolution 787. In late August 1995, NATO launched "Operation Deliberate Force," which lasted approximately one month and amounted to repeated air strikes to protect UN-designated "safe havens" against raids by the Bosnian Serb army. The bombings put an end to the Bosnian war, and foisted the Dayton Agreement upon President Izetbegovic (Bosnia and Herzegovina), President Tudjman (Croatia), and President Milosevic (Serbia) in December 1995, thus representing a victory for the Allied forces. The United States also intervened to restore constitutional rule to Haiti, following a coup by General Raoul Cedras that ousted President Jean-Bertrand Aristide in 1991. UN-authorized economic sanctions were imposed in 1993 but proved ineffective in reinstating democracy and curbing human rights abuse. Midway through 1994, the United Nations adopted Resolution 940, which authorized the use of force in ejecting the military junta and bringing Aristide back to power. Through "Operation Uphold Democracy," which began in September 1994, an American-led multinational force, entrusted with executing the UN mandate, used coercive diplomacy and a major show of force to persuade the military junta to walk away. By October 1994, Allied forces had succeeded in bringing back democracy and Aristide to the presidency. In 1996, the United States had another rift with Libya. The fissure was over Libya's construction of a chemical plant. Presented with American threats to destroy the installation in April 1996, Libya stopped pursuing the development of the chemical site. Towards the end of 1996, the United States launched "Operation Desert Strike" to counter an Iraqi offensive against the northern, Kurdish, part of the country. With the participation of British forces, the United States proceeded with missile strikes to preempt Iraq's ability to mobilize in the south by bombing strategic parts of its air defense. Iraq backed down and the no-fly zone was extended to the 33rd parallel. Throughout this entire period of successive military successes, there were higher capital flows into the United States. This growth in foreign capital was interrupted in 1998. The break followed an incident with Iran, in October 1997. Even though the contest of wills with Iran was resolved in favor of the United States, this triumph was not sufficient to stop decelerating capital flows in the wake of the Long-Term Capital Management Crisis in 1997/1998. That the unraveling of the hedge fund overshadowed the episode with Iran is not particularly surprising, given the massive attention paid to LTCM compared with the relatively little attention paid to the US–Iranian dispute.

After the failure of the Rambouillet talks – in particular Serbia and Russia's refusal to sign the agreement, which established NATO's right to oversee Kosovo, NATO unleashed an air raid against the Federal Republic of Yugoslavia. The Kosovo war came to a close on June 10, 1999 and President Milosevic agreed foreign military surveillance of Kosovo. Allied victory was followed by increased financial flows to the United States in 2000.

Financial flows receded in 2001. Here, the September 11 attacks overshadowed other interests. In April 2000 and November 2000, allies yielded against what COW codes as Yugoslavia. It is extremely difficult to find even a sliver of information given the data provided through COW.[15] Since Al-Qaeda is not a government, however, COW does not include the 9/11 attacks in their repertoire of militarized inter-state disputes. But whether the United States yields abroad or experiences a military setback at home, the result should be the same – a decline in financial flows to the United States. With the United States as a military target, capital flows immediately reversed that year, and this reversal was sustained in the subsequent year.

The September 11 attacks, which coincided with capital reversals, completely dominated any positive impact on capital flows that the successful mission to unseat the Taliban might have had. A coalition was established in 2001 to invade Afghanistan, in order to disrupt Al-Qaeda (who were held responsible for the terror attacks on the United States), and to remove the Taliban from power, because of their unwillingness to cooperate with the US government. By mid-November 2001, the Taliban was dispersed and no longer in control of the capital, Kabul. This was a victory for the United States and other members participating in "Operation Enduring Freedom." There was, however, no positive association between the ousting of the Taliban and capital flows into the United States. The countervailing force of 9/11 and the perception of the United States as vulnerable to attack outweighed the military success in Afghanistan, which in

---

[15] The November 2000 incident may refer to Yugoslavia's threat to attack ethnic Albanians along the Kosovo border unless NATO managed to keep Albanian fighters out of the zone, although the coding seems off, given that Yugoslavia backed down on its threat to enforce the deadline.

any case was not all that much of a success, given the ultimate failure to capture Osama bin Laden.

The war in Iraq is not yet coded by the COW project. To gauge military successes and setbacks, I have therefore relied on reporting from the media, primarily *The Economist*. The first phase of the Iraq War was the invasion in March 2003, which accomplished its mission of removing Saddam Hussein from power by April 2003. One month later, the American-led Coalitional Provisional Authority (CPA) sought and acquired control over Iraq through Resolution 1483. Despite the impediments involved in stabilizing Iraq, with a car bomb that killed over twenty UN officials in late August and the steep rise in coalition deaths in November, a series of counter-insurgency operations were effective in stemming hostilities. Deprived of power and favor, the Sunnis were the principal instigators of violence. Al-Qaeda's presence in Iraq was curtailed, reduced to pockets in the north. The invasion was a success, with fewer American casualties than forecast, and the long haul of forging peaceful relations between Iraqis of different ethnicity had not yet begun. Financial flows increase quite dramatically in the year following the invasion.

Car bombs kept going off in symbolically charged places throughout 2004 (e.g., at Iskandariyah and the Ashoura festival), and a series of bloody revolts (e.g., at Fallujah and Najaf), as well as the Abu Ghraib scandal, left their imprint. The CPA left Iraq by July 2004 and sovereignty was transferred to an interim government headed by Iyad Allawi as Prime Minister and Ghazi al-Yawar as President. With progress towards a lasting solution tainted by bloody sectarian rivalry, prospects for an imminent end to the fighting seemed bleak. As confidence in a quick fix for Iraq started to dwindle, so did capital flows to the United States.

The year 2005 started out with general elections at the end of January, with the installation of a government in April. Sectarian strife between Shias and Sunnis continued to deteriorate, with Sunnis killing nearly sixty Shias and with the Shias retaliating. Despite the growing link to Al-Qaeda, the Sunni insurgency was checked by forceful offensives in October and November in which 2,500 marines and 1,000 Iraqi Security Forces participated. The incursion prevented ethnic tensions from spiraling into civil war. These developments were coupled with a significant increase in financial flows to the United States in 2006.

A wave of violence swept over Iraq in 2006. The bombing of a Shia mosque at Samarra in February triggered a series of retaliatory moves that escalated into a civil war along ethnic lines. A July report issued by the United Nations, stated that the sectarian feud was claiming 3,000 people each month, and creating an estimated total of 162,000 refugees. By May 2006, Prime Minister Nuri al-Maliki declared a state of emergency in the south, where oil competition and smuggling contributed to ratcheting up the rivalry between different sects. There were no successful raids to speak of on the part of the Americans, who started to face a two-front insurgency, and had become increasingly targeted by both Sunnis and Shias. During his confirmation hearing, Secretary of Defense Robert Gates admitted that the United States was "not winning the war" in Iraq. Around the same time, the Iraq Study Group, chaired by James Baker, presented a ringing indictment of American policy in Iraq, stating that the "situation in Iraq is grave and deteriorating. Violence is increasing in scope and lethality."[16] Financial flows receded in 2007.

The data for financial flows in 2008 were not yet available at the time of writing, but, based on developments in 2007, it would not be surprising to see an increase in capital flows to the United States in 2008; although, given the scale of the financial crisis, events tied to it should be a powerful predictor of financial flows for that year. Reporting in September 2007, General Petraeus gave a "cautiously optimistic" view of the situation in Iraq and provided evidence that the "surge" was showing signs of success, reducing inter-sectarian fighting and civilian death tolls. Through a number of raids, the Americans managed to seize Al-Qaeda's leader in Iraq, along with lower-level commanders and combatants, as well as Shia leaders gone rogue, and the deputy commander of the Iranian-backed Lebanese Hizbollah Department 2800. Both the "Sunni awakening," which turned Sunnis against Al-Qaeda, as well as the backlash against the Mahdi army for attacking Shias while praying in the holy city of Karbala, have made Americans less of a target for Sunnis and Shias.

As can be seen from table 6.1, there is a strong correlation between military successes and increased financial flows into the United States, providing support for the hypothesis that the United States has collected a security premium. A positive relationship is said to exist if

[16] Baker and Hamilton 2006.

Table 6.1 *American military successes/*
defeats and changes in financial flows

Year following military success/ defeat	Change in financial flows to the US
1979 (–)	–1.35%
1983 (+)	–0.45%
1984 (+)	0.48%
1985 (+)	0.47%
1987 (+)	0.10%
1990 (+)	–1.66%
1992 (+)	0.85%
1995 (+)	1.59%
1997 (+)	1.47%
1998 (+)	–3.67%
2000 (+)	2.57%
2001 (–)	–2.85%
2002 (+)	–0.13%
...	...
2004 (+)	5.29%
2005 (–)	–3.08%
2006 (+)	5.60%
2007 (–)	–0.74%

Source: Author's calculations based on COW
2007 and BEA 2008b.

financial flows increase/decrease the year *following* military success/
defeat. Military success (defeat) is indicated with a + (–) sign next to
the year the operation was undertaken. Specifically, we see that in
77 percent of the COW cases, military successes are positively correlated with increased financial flows, and military defeats positively
correlated with reduced financial flows. This figure is conservative
and does not include the terrorist attacks on the United States, as
explained above. Taking the attacks on the World Trade Center and
the Pentagon into account increases the correspondence between military interventions and financial flows to 85 percent. If we expand
the set of cases to include those assessed against reporting in *The
Economist* on the war on Iraq, 82 percent of the cases either depict

a positive relationship between military victory and the ability to attract capital or between military loss and the retreat of foreign capital. Again, if this figure takes the 9/11 attacks into account, the correspondence is 88 percent.

I am not, however, suggesting that the relationship between military operations and financial flows is absolute. Major developments in the economic arena, such as the financial shock of the LTCM setback, or more general macroeconomic trends, can and will often prove more consequential than hard security measures. I am simply suggesting that there are economic benefits tied to being the dominant military power, just as there are economic costs associated with that position, at least for the United States, but perhaps for other major powers such as the United Kingdom as well. This is, of course, an empirical question, although not one that I can pursue here.

As I will show in the next section, the United States has often intervened militarily in remote areas to support American firms and a capitalist structure more generally. To the extent that such foreign policies are a breeding ground for anti-Americanism, and set it up as a military target, investors will become increasingly reluctant to place their money in the American market. If policies which generate resentment continue, a long history of positive interactive effects between military and economic power could quickly recede.

The particular focus of the next section is on the immediate benefits to American firms as a result of foreign interventions.

Reducing foreign risk premiums

The US government has protected American investments in areas where property rights are not well defined, intervening on behalf of American business interests. It has also intervened on behalf of a capitalist order, which it has defended against Communist threats.

Military power has been used to enforce de facto property rights in unsafe areas and to persuade foreign governments to promote stability, thus encouraging American firms to set up production sites in foreign locations. The historical record reveals that stable governments have been favored over weak ones, and that the United States has backed a motley crew of regimes ranging from democratic to authoritarian ones. The US government has on numerous occasions intervened to protect the property of its own firms in foreign locations even though security provision in the form of military bases and naval patrols has been a public good of sorts from which other non-American firms have also benefited.

The United States started protecting American lives and property abroad in the late nineteenth century, and was for the most part successful in this enterprise. From 1865 onwards, the key task of the American Navy was to expand trade routes and protect American citizens and property as best it could. It also cooperated extensively with Europeans to protect lives and property around the China Sea.[17] Sometimes it acted in concert with other states, but often it was able to go it alone.

There is a long list of American interventions to protect property and trade privileges. The treaty of Wanghia of 1844, under which the United States obtained an inroad to the Chinese market, was negotiated at the point of a gun, and between 1848–98, the government coerced China, Japan, and Korea to extract commercial rights.[18] The United States was particularly wary of European powers lest they partition China and exclude American merchants from trade in the South China Sea.[19] The United States also intervened diplomatically to provide a framework within which trade could flourish, both in 1881 by trying to mediate a border dispute between Mexico and Guatemala, and during the War of the Pacific (1879–84), which pitted Chile against Peru and Bolivia.[20] When President McKinley decided to intervene in Cuba during the Spanish-American War of 1898, his aim was to protect American lives and property on the island.[21] As early as the middle of the nineteenth century, the United States sent marines to Nicaragua in order to protect the property of an American firm in its dealings with the government.[22] At the beginning of the twentieth century, the 1901 Platt amendment went beyond the Monroe doctrine of 1823 by requiring the Cuban government to accept American intervention in support of a government capable of securing the right to life, property and personal freedom.[23] For strategic defense reasons, and to facilitate trade, the United States forcefully acquired sovereign rights over a piece of land, which made the construction of the Panama Canal

---

[17] Hagan 1973.   [18] Graber 1959, 66, 112.
[19] Graber 1959, 110, 34.   [20] Graber 1959, 114–17.
[21] Graber 1959, 79.   [22] Graber 1959, 95.
[23] Perkins 1955, 230–2.

possible in 1901.[24] In 1909, American business interests, assisted by the American government, fomented a revolution in Nicaragua.[25] In 1919, the destroyer Thornton countered bandit attacks on a Mexican city and demanded that American property not be touched; in 1921, a naval patrol along the Yangtse river protected American lives and property; in 1923, the United States imposed an arms embargo on rebels trying to oust President Obregon, who had finally come around to enforcing American rights to property in Mexico; in 1924, marines protected American interests in Honduras; in 1926 and 1931, marines were sent to protect American lives and property in Nicaragua; in 1929, the Navy again intervened to protect American lives and property in Mexico. In 1933, US warships intervened to change government in Cuba.[26]

Military intervention to beat back Communism has been a mixed bag of success and failure. Negative long-term consequences would often outweigh short-term positive effects. Although intervention sometimes led to unintended and unwanted consequences, the meddling was part of the ideological battle in which the United States sought to eradicate Communism and cement a liberal capitalist system, an endeavor it eventually realized. The United States would often use covert operations, or proxy militaries, to secure American economic interests. A particularly popular strategy has been to recruit exiles to fight on the ground – so-called paramilitary intervention (e.g., Guatemala 1954, Cuba 1961). These tactics allowed the United States to bypass a substantial part of the cost of the war on Communism – or at least the most dreadful part: the cost in human lives.[27] Only strong military powers are generally capable of this, since full military intervention lurks in the background as a possible hedge against failure.

Efforts to safeguard the capitalist structure from Communist infringement also required extraordinary military capability. In 1945, the United States provided airlift support, and marine and naval backup to Nationalist troops in the fight against Communist China.[28] When North Korea invaded South Korea in order to force a Communist state, the United States intervened under UN auspices.[29] Major Cold War interventions to contain Communism included support for South Vietnam in the struggle against Communist forces in

[24] Graber 1959, 132–6.   [25] Graber 1959, 149.
[26] Cable 1994; Graber, 1959, 172–3, 243–5.   [27] Schraeder 1992, 131.
[28] Graber 1959, 272–3.   [29] Graber 1959, 278–9.

the north, support of the Hmong rebels against Pathet Lao in Laos 1957–74, and marine landings in Lebanon to contain the spread of Communism following the 1958 coup d'état in Iraq.[30] In 1970, the United States tried to demolish Communist bases in Cambodia. Of course, these strategies would occasionally backfire, as in the botched attempts to overthrow Castro, the Indonesian President Sukarno, and the inability to make headway in the support of Tibetan rebels against the People's Republic of China.[31]

As part of the fight against Communism, the United States frequently intervened against left-leaning regimes, sometimes by supporting subversive movements, sometimes through direct involvement in coups. In their place, they planted right-wing regimes, which often came in the form of military dictatorships. In Iran, the Soviet-friendly prime minister, Mohammad Mossaddegh, became the target of an American-sponsored coup d'état (through which the Shah, Mohammad Reza Pahlavi, was installed) after he nationalized the Anglo-Iranian oil company in 1951.[32] In Guatemala, a CIA-sponsored coup removed left-leaning President Guzman in 1954, after he embarked upon a land reform that sought to nationalize property. In Ecuador, President Jose Maria Velasco Ibarra was deposed in 1960, and an anti-Communist military junta soon installed. In Cuba, the United States tried, but failed, to topple President Fidel Castro in the 1961 "Bay of Pigs" invasion. In Brazil, the CIA sponsored a military coup to replace Joao Goulart's left-leaning government with General Castelo Branco in 1964. In Zaire, the CIA supported a military coup that installed the fiercely anti-Communist Mobutu regime in 1964. In the Dominican Republic, the United States supported the government militarily in 1965 to prevent Castro-style nationalizations and ensure that the country did not fall under Communist rule. In Greece, the CIA prompted a coup that ousted President Papandreou in 1967, and helped the United States install an anti-Communist junta led by General Papadopoulos. In Guatemala, the United States saw to it that anti-Communist leader Julio Cesar Mendez Montenegro came to power in 1966. In Bolivia, the CIA responded to President Juan Torres' nationalizations by staging a military coup in 1971, and bringing anti-Communist General Hugo Banzer to power. In

---

[30] Haass 1999, 20–5.   [31] Schraeder 1992, 133–4.
[32] Ransom 1992, 118.

Uruguay, the United States installed a military junta in 1972. Chile met a similar fate, for similar reasons, when the CIA made way for General Pinochet, after having assisted in unseating President Allende in 1973. In Angola, the United States supported the FNLA (in the mid 1970s) then UNITA (in the mid 1980s and early 1990s) against the Soviet-backed MPLA. In Nicaragua, the United States tried to counter the leftist Sandinista regime that came to power in 1979 by arming and training the Contras. In Afghanistan, the CIA supplied arms to Islamist groups (the Mujahadeen) that opposed the Soviet invasion of Afghanistan in 1979. In El Salvador, the right-wing military government of Roberto D'Aubuisson that came to power in 1980 received massive American support. In Guatemala, the United States supported General Efrain Rios Montt's grab for power in 1982. In Cambodia, the United States backed the Coalition of the Democratic Government of Kampuchea (mostly comprising Khmer Rouge rebels) against the Vietnam-backed government. In Grenada, the United States instigated a coup against Maurice Bishop's pro-Soviet regime in 1983, and replaced it with an American-friendly one. As the Cold War drew to a close, these interventions leveled off. By that time their purpose, to provide a capitalist world system within which American firms could flourish, had been achieved.

Defense commitments and humanitarian interventions

The United States has frequently intervened to protect the property of its own citizens, to overthrow anti-American governments, and install American-friendly ones, but it has also intervened to police borders and enforce agreements, and to protect human rights. When the United States intervened in the two world wars in the twentieth century, it did so as much to prevent any one power from becoming too dominant, as for moral reasons.

As Cable has shown, the Navy has been an important tool in projecting American power in distant areas and reinforcing America's role as global policeman.[33] In 1921, marines enforced a border dispute between Panama and Costa Rica. In 1925, marines quelled riots in Panama. In 1946, the United States began to deploy a naval fleet permanently in the Mediterranean. In 1947, troops were dispatched to

[33] Cable 1994.

Greek ports. In 1948, Tsingtao was reinforced. In 1950, the Seventh
Fleet deterred an invasion of Formosa. In 1952, Yugoslavia received
open support from the USS *Coral Sea*. In 1955, the Seventh Fleet evac-
uated Chinese civilians from the Tachen Islands, along with 300,000
refugees from North Vietnam. In 1956, the Navy mounted a show
of force to impress the French and British at Suez. In 1957, the Navy
threatened to intervene in Jordan unless King Hussein was reinstated;
it also promised to protect merchant ships bound for Israel. In 1970,
the Sixth Fleet was reinforced in the Mediterranean to counter Syria's
attack on Jordan. In 1973, it redeployed to support Israel. That same
year, it sailed around the southern tip of Crete to deter Soviet intervention in the Middle East. In 1974, American ships entered the Persian
Gulf to protect oil supplies. In 1987, the Navy captured and sank
Iranian gunboats to protect Kuwaiti carriers. In 1991, the Navy was
dispatched to roll back Iraq's 1990 invasion of Kuwait.[34] From 1992
to 1994, the United States led a NATO- and United Nations-endorsed
humanitarian operation in Bosnia, airlifting food and medical supplies
and enforcing a no-fly-zone.[35] A United Nations-sponsored, American-
led humanitarian operation was also carried out in Somalia in 1992,
with food and medicine deliveries.[36] Before the dust had settled over
Somalia, the United States walked into the Haiti imbroglio to avoid a
tide of immigrants on American shores, culminating in the 1994 invasion and a 1995 United Nations peacekeeping mission.[37] In 1999, the
United States led a NATO operation to push back the Yugoslav army
from Kosovo, after which it ran a peacekeeping mission under a joint
NATO and United Nations umbrella.

Unilateralism vs. multilateralism, private vs. public goods

The United States owes at least some of its ability to process debt
to allies' dependence on American security provision. As a counterpart to foreigners' economic claims, the United States is sitting on
a pile of security claims. The United States' self-proclaimed role as
global policeman is a wildcard in a hand full of economic IOUs.
Armed interventions have been routine throughout the twentieth and
twenty-first centuries, and have had both a private and public good

---

[34] Haass 1999, 33–5.   [35] Haass 1999, 37–43.
[36] Haass 1999, 43–5.   [37] Soderberg 2005, 43–53.

dimension. The security lever lurks in the background of economic relations and explains why allies are prepared to intervene to adjust economic imbalances, as they did at Plaza and at Louvre in the 1980s (see chapter 5). Under a shield of firepower, the United States can buy time and take economic risks that no other county can afford. Europe is indebted to the United States for putting an end to two world wars. But we need not go all the way back to the First and Second World Wars. There have been plenty of reminders in our own time of Europe's military subordination. The turmoil on the continent in the 1990s over-determined Europe's continued reliance on American military assistance. As a result, Europe's feeble attempt to create a credible and autonomous military force in the late 1990s and early millenia was quickly cannibalized by NATO (see chapter 7). The formal defense commitments that go out to Japan and South Korea also give two of the five largest reserve holders a powerful incentive to prevent American decline. Even China can be counted among those who have an interest in preserving American military might. As long as the relationship between China and Japan is marred by distrust, China prefers an American security guarantee to a militarized Japan. While allies' dependence on the US military for defensive purposes and global interventions will hardly make global imbalances disappear, it can buy financial assistance if external liabilities become a problem.

Since the world's leading economies are inextricably bound up with the American economy, coordinating a soft landing of the US economy has always had a clear economic rational. But central bankers also know that political stability is at the source of economic growth. The United States gets good mileage out of its willingness to protect allies and stabilize hotspots. Both economically and militarily, the United States is "too big to fail." A weakening of the economy, the fountain of the United States' military might, would be dangerous for western Europe and East Asia.

Acting unilaterally for narrow American interests will not threaten American hegemony, unless there is direct conflict between American and Great Power interests. The United States has always reserved the right to intervene to fulfill foreign policy objectives in support of its own economic and strategic interests. Non-Communist Great Powers have often turned a blind eye to American interventions because they are mostly in agreement with the liberal democratic structure as the organizing principle of politico-economic interactions and because they owe their security to extended American deterrence. Skirmishes aside, the fundamental norms and principles underlying international order have not been contested by major non-Communist Powers in the postwar era. Instead, they have converged on liberal values. While these reasons were sufficient in the Cold War era, they became less important as the Communist threat dissipated after the fall of the Soviet Union. The question preoccupying popular imagination and scholarly debate after the removal of the superpower stalemate in the Security Council has been why the United States has not, to a greater extent, intervened multilaterally for the common good within the confines of international institutions.[38]

While the United States has often avoided acting alone in the post-war era, it has not shied away from acting unilaterally when it has not been able to organize a coalition force. When it occupied Lebanon in 1958, carried out air-strikes against Libya in 1986, and invaded Panama in 1989, it acted unilaterally.[39] The 2003 intervention in Iraq is often used as evidence of increased American unilateralism but the mission was not strictly unilateral – it was yet another American-led coalition without United Nations authorization. The set of United Nations authorized Chapter VII interventions is in any case an *n* of 2: the decision to intervene on behalf of South Korea in 1950 and to "liberate" Kuwait in 1991. The United States has frequently leaned on Article 51 of the United Nations Charter, arguing that it has intervened to help an attacked state defend itself (e.g., Lebanon 1958, the Dominican Republic 1965, several times in Central America starting in 1981, and Grenada 1983); and it has used the protection of nationals as a pretext to overthrow awkward regimes (e.g., the US interventions in Lebanon 1958, in the Dominican Republic 1965, and in Grenada 1983).[40] And if what is rather meant by unilateral is a spurious connection between the intervention and international law, the second Iraq invasion is hardly unique. The United States has often violated international law when intervening militarily (e.g., Bay of Pigs 1961, Grenada 1983, Nicaragua 1981–86, and Panama 1989).[41]

Protecting citizens and property in foreign locations has both private and public aspects. The United States is, and always will be,

---

[38] See Ikenberry 2004, 2005a, 2005b.   [39] Carpenter 1992.
[40] Tanca 1993, 24, 37, 70–1, 73, 120; Carpenter 1992.
[41] Tanca 1993, 131.

more willing to intervene to promote its own objectives. Yet enforcing property rights, endorsing a capitalist order, and intervening on humanitarian grounds is a common good in so far as Great Powers share the same objectives. There is an obvious temptation to overstate the public aspect and downplay the private gain implied by any particular intervention. This is what happened recently in the debacle over Iraq. The United States insisted that enforcing regime change in Iraq was about toppling a ruthless dictator intent on wrecking the order and stability created in the postwar era by acquiring weapons of mass destruction. Opponents to the war saw the invasion as the pursuit of narrow American objectives, not the wider human rights objectives the administration claimed they were so sensitive to. The debate on Iraq is fundamentally a debate about how far the United States can push the private gains dimension of its military power without the public good properties of American security provision dropping out, and without perturbing the order such provision purports to create.

Spreading democracy, intervening on humanitarian grounds, and smoking out terrorist groups, the United States is increasingly seen as acting alone, evoking eerie parallels of how the British lost their grip on empire as they embraced unilateralism after 1865. But the problem is not that the United States is acting unilaterally in the sense of acting *alone*. The problem is that it can always find a subset of allies who are better off joining a coalition of the willing than they would be if they were not to cooperate. Note that this conclusion flows directly from the model presented in chapter 3, and is distinct from another possible interpretation of unilateralism, namely that the United States acts alone for common ends because others choose to free-ride. If the Great Powers want to remain within the inner circle of world power, they are better off joining an American-led coalition than building a Great Power coalition that excludes the United States. The international community is therefore badly positioned to ask the United States to refrain from using its military preponderance to enforce whatever cause it sees as legitimate or to pre-commit to enforce a cause it does not see as legitimate. What the international community can do is balance American power. During the Cold War, the Soviets tried to mount a challenge against American naval power but lacked the requisite resources to develop new technologies, and so never came near America's ability to deploy and maneuver battle groups worldwide. Today, any single power or conglomeration of powers is even further away from balancing the United States.

There can be no doubt that the "war on terror" – its execution and its consequences, including civil war in Iraq – is both costly and a major blow to American legitimacy. These costs are a drain on the government purse at an inconvenient time. Without belittling the problems, however, the question is whether they are problems that cannot be contained. American military spending was 4.3 percent of GDP in 2005, up from 3.6 percent in 2002, the year before the war.[42] In 2008, it was 4.5 percent of GDP. As a share of GDP, military spending was much higher when the United States was struggling with burgeoning deficits in the 1970s and in the 1980s. Up until 1991, military spending was at least 5 percent of GDP. Between 1984 and 1988, defense spending hovered between 6 percent and 6.5 percent of GDP.[43] Regarding the parallels drawn to the decline of the British Empire, the British government used about 80 percent of its revenue to cover military outlays and service interest on its national debt in the middle of the eighteenth century.[44] The military was, in other words, wearing Britain down financially more than a century before it reached its zenith under Pax Britannica in the latter half of the nineteenth century. For comparison, the "cost of war" to the United States in 2008, measured as today's commitments and past commitments – i.e., military outlays plus interest payments on bonds issued to pay for defense expenditures – amounts to 28 percent of government revenue. This share has remained fairly constant since 1969.[45] Since security was almost the only official function of the government in the eighteenth century, and revenues were primarily customs receipts, the comparison is a bit unfair. On the other hand, the essential point is that the American administration can afford to spend more than its eighteenth-century British counterpart precisely because the budget is bigger and the government has multiple sources of revenue.

During the First World War, when the lights closed on British hegemony, military spending averaged approximately 38 percent of GDP.[46] That amount far exceeds current defense expenditures by

---

[42] OMB 2007c.   [43] OMB 2007c.
[44] Brewer 1989.
[45] Author's calculations based on OMB 2007a, 2007b, 2007c.
[46] Barro 1986.

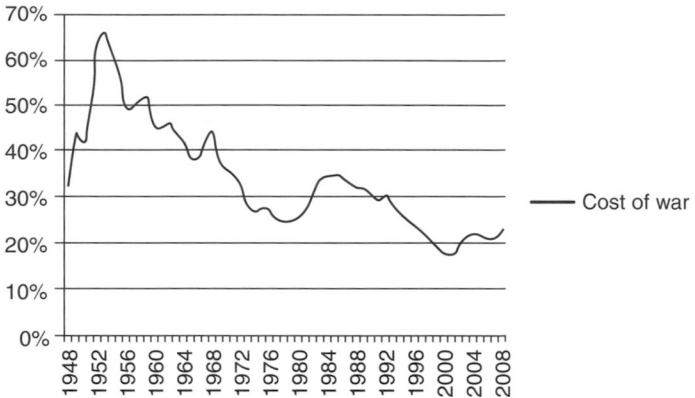

Figure 6.1 Cost of war

Note: The "cost of war" is measured as the share of defense spending and interest payments on bonds (issued to raise money for military outlays) out of government receipts. Source: Author's calculations based on data from the Office of Management and Budget (OMB 2009a, 2009b, 2009c).

the United States, which stood at 4.5 percent of GDP in 2008.[47] The economic effects of the wars currently being fought by the United States do not represent a similar burden as the First World War did on Britain, and in any case have not triggered a protectionist wave that in the end proved so damaging. As shown in figure 6.1, the cost of war is today at a historical ebb.

The cost in legitimacy may, however, dwarf the financial costs of the war. This brings us back to the question of how that legitimacy is derived. American power is not acceptable on legal grounds, or because it is morally defensible. Indeed, it has often been morally reprehensible. But if American legitimacy does not depend on the extent to which it is just or benevolent, neither is its validity restricted to its power to coerce. American power is justified in a strategic sense, and widely accepted because it is not perceived as exploitative. Hegemony is sufferable to the Great Powers, even those outside winning coalitions, as long as it provides stabilizing functions from which everyone gains. So far, the international community has judged the "public good" effects of American security policies as preferable to the way that any contender might organize the world. American hegemony

[47] OMB 2007a, 2007b, 2007c.

will survive Iraq (and Afghanistan) as it did Vietnam and a long list of interventions in Central America, Asia, and Africa unless civil war in Iraq creates a world of chaos in which the long arm of Washington becomes irrelevant for protecting allies and marshaling order.

Conclusion

Military power is connected to American economic strength in several ways. First, security considerations helped extend dollar use over a large area. Second, the United States' ability to protect investments at home and abroad has allowed Americans to borrow low-cost and invest in risky high-yielding assets abroad. Third and fourth, military interventions have not only helped promote business interests abroad and cement a capitalist structure, but to advance a particular kind of world order that other Great Powers have for the most part subscribed to, one in which aggressions and human rights have been selectively punished and enforced.

How we characterize benefits from American security provision matters. Strict public good properties are insufficient to capture the stability of American power, however, and the frustration that those who wish for another systemic context might feel. If we represent American security provision as joint and non-excludable, we mask the fact that supply has seldom been joint, and that benefits, although non-excludable, have been lopsided. This turns the problem of public good provision on its head. The problem is different from public goods provision where the difficulty is in getting as many actors as possible to contribute even though they gain whether they contribute or not. The problem is that a very high private-to-public benefit ratio can be sustained unless the hegemon is imprudent enough to ratchet up the private gain dimension at the complete expense of public gains at a time when a surrogate provider is on standby. Whether a replacement for American hegemony exists today is the subject of the next chapter.

7 | Credible threats and regional competition

Given the economic advantages enjoyed by the United States under existing arrangements, why don't other states try to initiate change to gain some of these advantages for themselves? The purpose of this chapter is to explore what sorts of developments would have to take place to challenge American hegemony and how likely it is that these will occur.

The first question to address is at which point allies will start to view American hegemony as a liability. Although the hegemon has a license to act unilaterally – refusing to sign on to international agreements such as the Kyoto Protocol, and the International Criminal Court, and even to circumvent the Security Council – a superpower that is too cavalier gathers resentment. Dissatisfaction in one area may well percolate into other areas. The further apart the United States and allies are politically, the less attractive American product and capital markets will seem. Bush era policies – the war on terror, and Guantanamo Bay, constituting the most unpopular examples – transformed the United States into a military target, and unwittingly risked severing the positive link between securing and attracting foreign investment.

The second question deserving attention is whether allies have a sufficiently strong fallback position to make withholding support of American hegemony rational. When allies turn away from American hegemony, to whom will they turn instead? In the 1980s, we had Japan and a fairly decentralized regional grouping in Europe. Today, amalgamation in East Asia and Europe is producing alternative power structures, and China shows all the signs of wanting to rule the world, though not yet having the capacity. China is the second largest exporter in the world and the world's third largest importer (see tables 2.3 and 2.4). It is the fourth largest economy, as measured in terms of GDP, and spends more on defense than any other country apart from the United States (see tables 2.1 and 2.2). China is huge and has all the drawbacks one would expect from a country with nearly 1.5 billion people, or approximately 20 percent of the world's population. It has low GDP per capita, low insularity from external shocks as a result of high dependence on outside product and capital markets, and a tight authoritarian fist to hold it all together. This is a model no one will openly say they want to emulate. In the medium term, I therefore see regionalism in East Asia and Europe as the only arrangements with the potential to jolt American hegemony.

In order to pull the plug on American hegemony, Great Powers would have to be less dependent on American markets and policies in the trade, monetary, and security sphere. There are three concrete scenarios which would make it virtually impossible for the United States to maintain its special position in the international system: the emergence of surrogate product and capital markets in East Asia; the ousting of the dollar as key currency; and autonomous security provision in East Asia and Europe. First, the development of strong product and capital markets in East Asia would be a potential threat to American hegemony, given that five countries in East Asia finance the bulk of the American current account deficit. Together, Japan, China, Taiwan, South Korea, and Hong Kong control about 50 percent of the world's foreign exchange reserves. The credit extended by them has ensured that Americans have the means to continue buying their products. But if these countries were to rely more heavily on each other for trading, central banks in East Asia would have less incentive to buy American government paper. A quick recall of foreign investment in the United States could make external adjustment painful and provide a real blow to the American economy. Second, the end of the dollar's key currency status would cancel the United States' ability to draw in goods and capital at low cost and reduce the "free ride" it receives on the net foreign asset position. Third, decoupling in the security arena would remove political incentives to support American hegemony and put a magnifying glass to economic incentives to derail American hegemony.

Some progress has been made in all of these areas. First, there are blueprints for deep integration in East Asia that could have important consequences for American hegemony. If economic integration paves the way to political union, countries in the region would become less dependent on the United States' willingness to absorb imports and protect allies. After decades of outward-oriented policies, the future of

East Asia could become more inward-looking. Not only would financial resources be diverted away from the United States, but an East
Asian union anchored around a Sino-Japanese axis could represent a
viable alternative to American power. Second, pooling of sovereignty in
Europe has turned the European Union into a commercial, monetary,
and military power that in future could challenge American hegemony.
Commercially, the European Union is on a par with the United States.
Monetarily, the euro was successfully launched in 2002 and is a contender to the dollar for reserve currency status. Third, and less widely
publicized, the European Union is committed to a European Security
and Defense Policy (ESDP) and has taken on a military identity.

The size advantages highlighted by the model in chapter 3 and the
new trade theories explored in chapter 4 are extremely illuminating
in this regard, and provide a consistent and useful explanation for
why countries are coalescing around free trade agreements. Small
countries have caught on to the benefits tied to a large market, and
enhanced their bargaining power by banding together on a regional
basis. Not all initiatives will have consequences for American power,
but European and East Asian regionalisms represent a potential cap on
American dominance. If allies no longer perceive tangible benefits from
American hegemony, at a time when alternatives to American power
exist, the United States' capacity to use power assets to advantage will
come under fire. Yet while the significant momentum towards regional
groupings witnessed in the postwar era could eventually produce a
world order in which the United States is no longer centripetal, a careful analysis reveals that tighter cooperation is needed to muster a credible threat and restructure the top of the power hierarchy.

In the first part of this chapter, I explore the trend towards greater
trade among East Asian countries. A central question is whether the
strengthening of commercial links among countries in the region
will redefine their role in the international economy and reduce their
dependency on the United States. Whether or not the regional push
in East Asia will result in a customs union without borders, or even a
single all-embracing FTA, is hugely important for the United States'
future capacity to process external liabilities and gradually correct
external imbalances. If commercial ties within East Asia increase
significantly, and spearhead other forms of economic and political
cooperation, the big five may find less incentive to keep their currencies undervalued in order to sustain exports to the American market.

There are already signs that East Asian economies are relying more on each others' markets for trade (recall table 5.3). Japan and South Korea had grown less dependent on the American market by the early 1990s and China has recently displaced the United States as Japan's most important trade partner. China, Indonesia, and Malaysia, on the other hand, have increased their exports to the United States.

A flurry of regional agreements – forty or so – have been concluded or are currently being negotiated in East Asia. Plans for an East Asian-wide customs union are also in the pipeline. While an exclusive East Asian FTA, comprising Japan, China, South Korea, and ASEAN, would dramatically shift the economic power balance, such a trading bloc is unlikely to succeed. The main inhibiting factors are the nature of trade taking place in the region, a reluctance of countries in East Asia to cede sovereignty, and the primacy of security over economic objectives. Each of these roadblocks has its own logic.

First, in order for East Asian countries to increase bargaining power, they must lessen their dependency on markets in Europe and North America. Currently, however, much trade taking place within East Asia is in intermediate inputs with final goods destined for overseas markets.

Second, the only way to increase bargaining power through regionalism is to offer other countries a sizeable and coherent market, which East Asian countries are unlikely to do because of the sovereignty implications attached to such a project. Even the relatively low level of integration that a customs union represents requires that states forego certain basic prerogatives, such as maintaining independent tariff regimes. Countries in East Asia are, however, exceptionally averse to ceding sovereignty. In the future, China may provide just the import pull needed to loosen ties to North America and Europe; but, for now, a rising China, and the perception that it is refurbishing the hierarchy of regional value-added, is the most important brake on integration in East Asia. While an economic power shift is unavoidable, regardless of whether regional cooperation takes place or not, Japan – the world's second largest economy – is in a position to compete, and will carefully guard its economic status in the region and the world.

Third, although rivalry between Japan and China for regional dominance has spurred regionalism in East Asia, an East Asia-wide agreement without the participation of Australia, New Zealand, and the United States is unlikely for security reasons. Japan, South Korea, and ASEAN countries continue to rely on American security provision, and are not interested in being "protected" by China. They want an outside security option because of China's democratic deficit; but democratizing China would only raise prospects of realignment, since the transition to democracy would likely be a political earthquake with negative economic repercussions.

The second part of this chapter analyzes the prospects for the dollar to lose its status as key currency. Here, the euro is the dollar's litmus test. With the onset of the euro, private and official investors were expected to diversify out of dollars and into euros on the order of $500 billion to $1 trillion; some thought that this would send American interest rates sky high, cripple an economy already burdened by debt, and weaken the dollar.[1] With a market of twelve countries following Greece's entry in 2002, the euro-zone countries were close to achieving the scale necessary for key currency status. When the euro was put into circulation in 2002, the amount of financial transactions denominated in euros increased significantly. Almost instantaneously, more bonds were denominated in euros than in dollars. And some saw the extraordinary potential for the euro-zone to enhance the depth, breadth, and liquidity of its financial markets.[2] Seven years on, the most obvious predictors of change – the wealth encapsulated in the euro area, the greater use of the euro in trade and capital markets, the European Central Bank's zealous commitment to price stability, and the euro's appreciation towards the dollar – all point to a growing role for the euro as medium of exchange, store of value, intervention and reserve currency. Today, the euro-zone comprises sixteen countries and has quickly approached the size of the American economy in terms of GDP, trade, and finance. These are the original Baffling group (Belgium, Austria, France, Finland, Luxembourg, Ireland, the Netherlands, and Germany) with Italy, Portugal, and Spain, who were joined by Greece in 2001, Slovenia in 2007, Cyprus and Malta in 2008, and Slovakia in 2009.

Acquiring key currency status is often seen as harder than holding on to it, however, because factors like inertia, scale economies, and network externalities contribute to the incumbent's resilience.[3] The

---

[1] Bergsten 1999, 27.   [2] Hartmann and Issing 2002.
[3] Eichengreen 1998; Portes and Rey 1998; McKinnon 2002; Bergsten 2002; Cohen 2003; Chinn and Frankel 2005.

incumbency advantage is particularly strong in areas where gains can be made from reducing information costs as in foreign exchange trading where the dollar is predominantly used, whereas it is less strong in areas where gains can be made from spreading risk as in portfolio optimization.[4] The dollar persists because investors are risk averse (inertia), because transaction costs are lower for the dollar (scale economies), and because the more the dollar is used the more it makes sense for additional investors to use it (network externalities). The liquidity of the dollar – the ease with which it can be exchanged for goods, services, and assets in any part of the world – creates a bias to continue using it for commercial and financial transactions. Barriers to switching from one key currency to another exist because, for the most part, investors prefer to use whatever they have used in the past. These self-reinforcing advantages will tend to favour the international currency in use, in this case the dollar. Despite these incumbency advantages, there is clearly some point at which the euro could start to seem more attractive than the dollar.

In order to replace the dollar as world currency, the euro must be widely used as medium of exchange, unit of account and store of value. Specifically, it must be used more widely than the dollar. As we will see, the euro has made significant headway in challenging the dollar in all these respects. As I will demonstrate, however, the trade area, where the euro-zone now excels over the United States, is where the challenge for key currency status will be most difficult. First, the composition of the euro-zone's trade speaks against its adoption as unit of account. Second, euro-zone countries can be expected to run into political difficulties in effectively accommodating trade deficits, a task that has become closely associated with key currency status. Notwithstanding America's current weakness, I argue that different preferences for monetary and fiscal policy inside the euro-zone, and the need to coordinate these, will make it difficult to accommodate and correct large-scale imports over the long term. I also find that taking on the role of the world's preferred import destination is bound to exacerbate internal differences and complicate decision-making. Further enlargement is not likely to help.

In the third and last part of the chapter, I review prospects for Europe to flex its military muscle and become a self-regulating power

[4] Kenen 2002, 348.

without protection from Washington. There have been several intia-
tives to establish a credible military force in Europe by adopting a
Common Foreign and Security Policy (CFSP). The first attempt was
the French plan for a European Defence Community (EDC), a sugges-
tion that was mostly a reaction to American insistence that Germany
re-arm.[5] Ditched in the French National Assembly, the EDC failed,
but the French campaign for a CFSP continued. The Fouchet Plan was
the second major initiative. It became hostage to the confrontation
between federalists like Belgium and Holland, and inter-governmen-
talists like France, who had an additional ulterior motive with security cooperation, namely to balance American power.[6] Half a decade
into the fray, these dividing lines are as thick and impenetrable as
ever, leaving precious little evidence that Europe can create an independent military force with bite.

Geographically coherent regionalism in East Asia

ASEAN began as a declaration between Indonesia, Malaysia, the
Philippines, Singapore, and Thailand in 1967, and was an attempt to
create peace and stability in the region. It was not until the 1970s that
cooperation was extended to the economic domain, and new members
joined (Brunei, Vietnam, Cambodia, Laos, and Myanmar).[7] Although
a preferential trade arrangement (PTA) was achieved in 1977, a free
trade area was more difficult to achieve, since ASEAN countries trade
similar goods and depend on the same markets to offset their products. Eventually, however, concerns about the regionalization of the
world economy led to concrete steps to enhance the group's external
competitiveness and a free trade area (AFTA) was realized in 1993.[8]
By adopting a flexible and voluntary approach, whereby ASEAN-6
(the five original members and Brunei) implemented tariff reductions
according to schedule – while developing members (Vietnam, Laos,
Myanmar, and Cambodia) were given a longer time line – ASEAN
reduced average tariff rates from 111.4 percent to 3.2 percent between
1993 and 2000, and raised intra-ASEAN exports by 120 percent during the same period.[9] While these results are impressive and the free

---

[5] Hoffmann 2000, 190.   [6] Hoffmann 2000.
[7] Lay 2004, 937–9.   [8] Ong 2003, 64.
[9] Lay 2004, 963–4.

trade area has empowered ASEAN countries in negotiations with Japan and China, ASEAN's share of world trade is not sufficiently high to have a significant impact on international bargaining dynamics. The group's share of world exports only amounts to 7 percent, its share of global imports to 6 percent, and it only attracts 4 percent of the United States' FDI, and no more than 2 percent of the European Union's FDI.[10]

North East Asia has been slow to embrace regional cooperation for a variety of reasons, most importantly due to its dependency on extra-regional markets for trade.[11] An FTA linking Japan, China, and South Korea would, if realized, represent nearly 90 percent of East Asia's production, but South Korea is the only country backing the initiative, and its support is entirely motivated by a desire to avoid competition with ASEAN in key sectors (agriculture, air services, and labor-intensive goods).[12] As to the key players, Japan has been reluctant to entertain anything but bilateral deals outside of the WTO framework. China, on the other hand, has strengthened ties to ASEAN as a strategy in preparing for an East Asia-wide agreement, signaling its intent to bypass a North East Asian FTA.

There are currently two dialogues on how to create a bridge linking the southern and northern parts of East Asia. The "ASEAN plus one" (APO) talks provide a framework wherein ASEAN members pursue talks with Japan, China, and South Korea on a bilateral basis. Agreement exists to achieve an FTA with China (ACFTA) by 2010 and an ASEAN Japan Economic Partnership (AJEP) by 2012. Shortly after plans were announced to create an FTA between China and ASEAN, Japan moved to match the initiative. Instead of fortifying the region's inter-continental bargaining power, competition between a prospective ACFTA and AJEP may actually create an opportunity for the United States to play the two blocs off each other by giving preferential access to one side in exchange for concessions that make it difficult to create a bridge between the two FTAs. The United States could, for instance, offer AJEP preferential access with the proviso that intellectual property rights are enforced within the AJEP.

Multilateral talks between ASEAN, Japan, China, and South Korea, are held in the context of the "ASEAN plus three" (APT) process. If

---

[10] Lee and Park 2005, 21.   [11] Desker 2004, 16.
[12] Stubbs 2002, 441.

successful, these negotiations, which aim to establish an exclusive East Asia wide initiative, will dramatically improve the region's bargaining power. By threatening to withhold access to such a sizeable market, East Asia would be in a position to extract concessions from the United States or the European Union, or at least prevent them from extracting concessions. In other words, East Asia will have gained a credible threat vis-à-vis the United States and the European Union. But an East Asia-wide process is also the most problematic from an economic and security point of view. When the idea of an exclusive East Asian zone was first proposed by Malaysia's prime minister, Mahathir Mohamad, in the form of an East Asian Economic Grouping (EAEG) in 1990, the United States persuaded Japan and South Korea to turn it down.[13] When the first exploratory meetings were held in 1995, American opposition had however receded. The United States' first choice is inclusive regionalism not an independent East Asian bloc. In line with this thinking, Japan's former Prime Minister Koizumi proposed an alternative "ASEAN plus five" (APF) route, involving Australia and New Zealand, which would eventually include India and bring the United States into its orbit, thinning the lines to APEC.[14] The initiative is widely supported. Most countries prefer Asia-Pacific regionalism to exclusive East Asian regionalism; only China and Malaysia have reverse preferences.[15] Yet re-creating APEC in another guise will keep East Asian countries under American tutelage. Clearly, East Asia does not have a credible alternative with which to threaten the United States with market closure, if that alternative comprises the United States. Why do East Asian countries' preferences converge on alternatives that dilute their bargaining power? Why can't they sail off into the sunset on their own?

While the trend towards greater intra-regional trade in both South and North East Asia is clear, the American market is still needed to offload final goods. Much of the trade in the region is in component parts and takes place in the context of an intraregional hierarchy of production which defies the celebrated image of a "flying geese pattern."[16] Up until recently, it was assumed that technologies migrated to less industrialized countries in a V-shaped hierarchy, in which Japan was assumed to be the lead goose. After having imported

[13] He 2004, 114; Hund 2003, 394, 400.   [14] Hund 2003.
[15] Lay 2004 946–9.   [16] Bernard and Ravenhill 1995.

capital goods (and the technologies embedded in them), semi-developed countries would build up their own industrial capacity and eventually export the products they had previously imported. But this pattern is not borne out empirically. What has emerged instead is a strict division of labor, a "trade triangle" through which countries in the region import component parts from Japan, and with the involvement of Japanese affiliates assemble final products destined for the US market.[17] Unless production becomes regionalized or globalized in ways different from today, there is little reason to believe that East Asia's dependence on the American market will subside.

Japan is the second largest exporter of component parts while five countries in East Asia – Singapore, Hong Kong, Japan, Malaysia, and China – are the world's largest importers of component parts.[18] Trade in intermediate goods is growing faster than in any other region, and accounts for roughly one-fifth of trade in manufactures.[19] The rapid expansion of trade in component parts limits the extent to which China can substitute for the American market over the long term. China has tried to put its market on offer as an alternative export outlet in order to increase East Asia's autonomy and more effectively influence the regulatory framework governing world trade.[20] China's demands on the world trade organization are very specific. China is expected to challenge the informal character of WTO decision-making by tossing out closed room sessions which exclude small states, and by championing reform on a slew of issues ranging from the use of anti-dumping rules to the application of labor and environmental standards that have all raised the ire of developing countries.[21] But envisaging China as the region's future export outlet raises problems. ASEAN countries have already (between 1995 and 2000) lost important market shares to China in the United States and Japan, especially in goods they specialize in. The only way to recoup these losses is by expanding exports to China.[22] From the "hub–spoke" perspective on regionalism, however, we know that industrial concentration is more likely to occur in hubs like Japan and China than in spoke countries like ASEAN.[23]

---

[17] Bernard and Ravenhill 1995.   [18] Cai 2004, 586–8.
[19] Cai 2004.   [20] Ong 2003, 61.
[21] Holst and Weiss 2004, 1256, 1263.
[22] Tongzon 2005, 204. ASEAN specializes in electronics, engineering, primary products, resource-based manufactures, textiles, and clothing.
[23] Baldwin 2003.

According to the hub–spoke perspective, being in the center is productivity raising and export enhancing since a hub with a big market to offer, like Japan or China, can more easily gain access to foreign markets. The benefits of locating in the hub outweigh the benefits of lower production costs in the smaller spoke countries. Of course, this geography of industrial location contradicts the well-known presumption in the political economy literature that firms will position themselves wherever costs are lowest. The hub-spoke theory is still applicable to China, since it is both a hub and a low-cost producer. Firms therefore have every advantage in locating in China, which will most certainly evolve into a lead exporter of component parts. With China strengthening production of component parts over the long term, ASEAN countries may in future have to count on exporting agriculture and services to a wealthier China.[24] We should therefore expect considerable intra-regional rivalry in the very area where trade is expanding the most, i.e., in component parts. For these reasons, there will continue to be stronger complementarities between countries in East Asia and the United States than among East Asian economies for some time to come.

Another major obstacle is East Asian countries' reluctance to pool sovereignty. Deeper integration in East Asia is a step towards greater interference with national decision-making authority with lasting effects. The unwillingness of countries in East Asia to move in this direction presents an insurmountable barrier to accelerating integration in the region, and severely hampers East Asia's bargaining power, since both economic and political gains from greater scale should tend to be higher the more economies are integrated and policies harmonized.

Sovereignty implications

Bargaining power is a function of market size, and the more unified the market, the more credible the offer of market access, and the easier it becomes to attract FDI as investors seek to exploit complementarities between national economies. But deepening integration beyond an FTA, establishing a community with a single market, removing barriers to capital and labor, can only take place if states

---

[24] Ng and Yeats 2001, 87–8.

are willing to accept a gradual erosion of sovereignty. In East Asia, however, the aversion to cede sovereignty is so entrenched that it is even unlikely that countries will be able to agree on a common external tariff (CET). Aside from political factors, large tariff dispersions, as well as differences in wealth and development, will make implementing a common external tariff very difficult.[25]

Moreover, because the nation-state has a fragile base and is still young in East Asia, most states experience important challenges in maintaining stability, internally or externally, sometimes both.[26] Therefore, what undergirds Asian regionalism (nationalism, statism, and Asian values) is qualitatively different from European-style regionalism (individual freedoms, democracy, human rights, and pooled sovereignty).[27] Most East Asian countries have a long way to go before fundamental rights are protected by the state and there are currently no indications of a shift to the European brand of regionalism. To the contrary, states took the opportunity to tighten authoritarian rule in support of the "war on terror" that Washington unabashedly tied to bilateral trade deals during the Bush era.[28] Nor are there particularly strong affinities between East Asia and the European Union. East Asian countries prefer American hegemony to European dominance and are more likely to accept American infringement on their policy autonomy. There are two reasons for this. First, only Americans are capable of providing the security "good". Second, countries in East Asia have resisted European-style regulation ever since the Europeans tried to force agreement on the so-called "Singapore issues" at Cancun.[29] The way of organizing world trade envisaged by Europeans is perceived as a permanent and unwanted move towards increased domestic regulation. In contrast, the constraints imposed by Washington, while increasingly unpopular, are viewed as transient, and tolerated for broader security reasons.

Domestic bargaining dynamics will also tend to sideline ASEAN. Since exporters stand to gain a lot from accessing "hub" markets, they will organize to defeat import-competing interests but will be less motivated to access smaller "spoke" markets.[30] Possible solutions do not bode well for East Asian regionalism. So-called "anti-spoke

[25] He 2004, 107, 118–22.   [26] Beeson 2004.
[27] Beeson 2004.   [28] Desker 2004, 22.
[29] Ng and Yeats 2001.   [30] Baldwin 2003.

strategies" consist of forming a customs union or shadowing the hub –
that is signing on to free trade agreements with the hub and the hub's
partners.[31] Incentives to shadow the hub explain the spell of FTAs in
the region. The resulting "wildfire of regionalism" comes at a cost,
however. The strategy is, on the one hand, extremely demanding from
a negotiating perspective. On the other hand, the world trade system is
becoming increasingly complex with overlapping agreements and rules
of origin producing Bhagwati's infamous "spaghetti bowl" effect.[32]

Rules of origin are needed in a system where countries practice free
trade with each other but have differential access to countries outside
the free trade area. In other words, there is a qualitative difference
between a free trade area and a customs union with a common external tariff. Although rules of origin are also needed in a customs union
to determine whether goods produced by a foreign firm inside the
customs union should be subject to tariffs or re-exported duty-free
within the customs union, the problem is magnified in the case of a
free trade area. Unless there is a way of determining where a product originated, i.e., where it was primarily produced, goods could be
imported into a country with low external tariffs and re-exported
within the free trade area to countries with higher external tariffs.
Hence, the very idea behind rules of origin is to prevent the free trade
area from becoming a de facto customs union with a common external tariff. With interlacing FTAs, there is a need to keep track of the
country-content in each product and of which countries have preferential access to which goods based on content rules (i.e., is the good
primarily Japanese or South Korean?). Therefore, FTAs are more
unwieldy than CUs when it comes to administering rules of origin.

More significantly for East Asia, the proliferation of FTAs is dilut-
ing the region's bargaining power vis-à-vis other trade entities such
as the United States. The only way around this is to create a customs
union. This would make the spokes become part of the hub, giving
them access to whatever preferential treatment the hub has acquired.[33]
This is the optimal way of preventing spokes from being marginalized. But many countries in East Asia find themselves in a process
of nation-building and are very reluctant to renounce their new-won
sovereignty, which they would have to do in a customs union.

---

[31] Baldwin 2003.   [32] Bhagwati, Greenaway, and Panagariya 1998.
[33] Baldwin 2003.

As a third limiting factor, a regional dominance game, with intense competition for regional hegemony, is taking place between Japan and China, and will reduce East Asia's inter-regional bargaining power even further. As a direct response to China's initiative to establish an FTA with ASEAN, Japan pushed for an ASEAN-Japan Comprehensive Economic Partnership (AJCEP) in early 2002; the success of the ACFTA negotiations later that year put further pressure on Japan to achieve an FTA by 2012.[34] But Japan has shown little interest in consolidating an exclusive East Asia zone, and is hardly serious about an FTA with ASEAN. Japan is instead pursuing an ASEAN-5-Japan strategy, negotiating separate bilateral deals with Singapore, the Philippines, Malaysia, and Thailand, and is about to start talks with Indonesia.

China, on the other hand, is serious about widening cooperation across East Asia. From a Chinese perspective, an FTA with ASEAN is an important instrument in creating a pan-East Asian FTA. In fact, China, more than any other country in the region, imagines any preliminary arrangement – a purely Chinese FTA, a Chinese FTA with ASEAN, or a North East Asian FTA between China, Japan, and South Korea – as paving the way to an East Asian FTA (EAFTA).[35] The two main factors guiding China's FTA strategy are a desire to balance American power, and the realization that South East Asia sees the rise of China as a major threat.[36] Aware that neighbors worry about competing with a seemingly boundless territory and supply of labor, China's regional turn is a way of placating these concerns.[37] Chinese overtures have therefore been extremely conciliatory, the "early harvest proposal," for instance, offers to phase out tariffs on imports from ASEAN-6 five years ahead of schedule, and is clearly meant to win strong allies in South East Asia.[38] Similar gestures have been made in the security field: in 2001 China's prime minister Zhu Rongji reassured East Asian neighbors of the country's willingness to accede to both the ASEAN Treaty of Amity and Cooperation and the South East Asian Nuclear Weapon Free Zone (SEANWFZ), and agreed to "complete consultations with ASEAN on the norm of behavior in the South China Sea region."[39] The FTA with ASEAN will enhance China's bargaining power both regionally and internationally. By

---

[34] Cai 2004, 590–1.   [35] Hund 2003, 403.
[36] Cai 2004.   [37] Hund 2003, 403; Ong 2003, 59.
[38] Hund 2003, 395.   [39] Cai 2004, 593, 595.

negotiating with small states first, China has not only managed to improve her economic platform, but gained political leverage vis-à-vis Japan, and left its mark on the direction of East Asian regionalism.

Prospects for an exclusive East Asian community are bleak, however. Although China is intent on creating the economic foundations for an emerging "pole" to counter US unilateralism, Japan, South Korea, and ASEAN all have their reasons for opposing a division of the Pacific into East and West.[40] If North and South East Asia were to combine, South Korea would prefer an East Asian FTA with ties to New Zealand, and an alliance that would remain open to the United States, which South Korea sees as crucial in ensuring stability on its peninsula and in the wider region. For Japan, East Asian regionalism is highly contentious. To accept an economic powerhouse in the East without an American security guarantee is unthinkable.

Integration requires at least some degree of political convergence, as successful examples of regional cooperation in Europe and North America have shown. This presents a dilemma. For while states worry about authoritarian elements in Chinese rule, the transition to a democratic China will leave neighboring countries less secure, and the instability accompanying political liberalization is sure to have negative economic effects. Here economic and political calculations start to diverge. What matters most from an economic point of view is that transactions, not the source of protection, are secure. From a political perspective, however, where protection ultimately resides is of primary concern. Without democratic structures governing China, countries in East Asia, especially Japan, will continue to look to the United States. Exclusive integration encompassing South and North East Asia is therefore unlikely to succeed.

Euro power

In a first section below, I provide an empirical assessment of the relative use of the dollar and the euro across key currency functions. A second section examines the prospects of the euro overtaking the dollar as key currency country, given the various roles it will need to play. The special angle on its potential as world currency is the euro-zone's ability to absorb large and persistently high shares of world imports

[40] Hund 2003, 392.

as the United States has done in the last quarter-century. A third section examines possible ways for the euro-zone area significantly to outperform the United States on this score. There are basically two options. The euro-zone would either have to cope with external price instability, along with the associated risk to internal price stability, or expand by adding new members to the euro-zone. Both these scenarios have serious shortcomings.

An empirical assessment of dollar and euro use

A first step in reviewing the euro's prospects as key currency is to ask why we need one in the first place. As mentioned in the introduction to chapter 5, the overarching rationale for a key currency is to achieve efficiency and stability in international transactions.[41] An important implication of the following analysis is that reducing transaction costs is much more important than providing a means for spreading risk.

As I observed in chapter 5, a key currency has to effectively perform three main roles. It must serve as: (1) a medium of exchange; (2) a unit of account; and (3) a store of value. The key currency must play these roles in private and public international economic transactions, though for somewhat different reasons.

Medium of exchange
There is broad agreement that the initial test for a world currency is as medium of exchange in private markets and that the dollar continues to be the primary medium of exchange because of scale economies that favor dollar use. Here, the euro has made only modest progress.

Scholars infer which currencies are most widely used for international transactions by looking at foreign exchange trading. This is where the dollar has an especially strong lead.[42] By 2007, the frequency with which the euro appeared on one side of all currency transactions was actually down 0.6 percent, from 37.6 percent in 2001, whereas the dollar was down 4 percent from 90.3 percent, appearing 86.3 percent of the time on one side of foreign exchange transactions.[43] Scale

---

[41] Kenen 2002, 348.
[42] Chinn and Frankel 2005, 18; Cohen 2003; Hartmann and Issing 2002, 337; Kenen 2002, 349.
[43] Since two currencies are involved the percentage shares are out of 200: BIS 2007.

economies in currency use are difficult to break because it makes sense to continue using a currency with high turnover and low transaction costs, as opposed to switching to a start-up currency with high transaction costs. Still, in terms of currency in circulation, the euro surpassed the dollar in 2006, even though a much smaller portion of euros was used outside the euro-zone (10–20 percent) than dollars outside the United States (50–70 percent).[44]

The dollar also retains its lead as the currency with which central banks frequently intervene. This is simply due to the fact that most of their reserves are in dollars.

Unit of account

As unit of account, in private markets, the key currency is used to quote prices for traded goods (merchandises and commodities) as well as services. Thus, it makes sense for the key currency to be the largest country, economically speaking. It should command a high share of GDP, large trade shares, and a big financial market. These size measures bear on the attractiveness of pricing in a particular currency.

The available data suggests two procedures for assessing the international role of the euro for invoicing in trade. For instance, one can consider how much of the euro-zone's trade with countries outside the euro-zone is denominated in euros as opposed to dollars or some other currency. An alternative approach is to look at whether the trade of countries of the European Union (not members of the euro-zone), or candidate countries, or countries in other parts of the world is denominated in euros in excess of their share of trade with the euro-zone. In other words, to what extent is the euro used when euro-zone countries are not involved.[45] As can be seen from table 7.1, we see a marked increase in euro invoicing and a steady decline in dollar invoicing when using the first measure – i.e., use of the euro as compared to the dollar in the euro-zone's trade with countries outside the euro-zone.

---

[44] Walter and Becker 2008, 4.
[45] Because of data limitations, I will not be able to track the evolution of the euro's and the dollar's relative use as invoicing currency for a complete run of years.

Table 7.1 *Euro and dollar invoicing in extra-euro-zone trade*

	Euro-zone with countries outside euro-zone		
	1999	2004	Ql 2006
EUR (exports)	20.8	27.7	49.7
USD (exports)	55.4	49.1	44.0
Other (exports)	...	...	6.3
Total	...	...	100.0
EUR (imports)	...	...	35.2
USD (imports)	...	...	55.7
Other (imports)	...	...	9.1
Total	...	...	100.0

Source: Kamps 2006; ECB 2007a.

In terms of the second measure, how extensively non-euro-zone countries use the euro when invoicing trade with countries outside the euro-zone, the results are mixed. Table 7.2 shows how much more (or less) a country uses euros for invoicing than it trades with the euro-zone. For instance, in the first row of table 7.2, we see that, in 2004, the amount of Cypriot exports invoiced in euros was 4 percent higher than the amount of Cypriot exports to the euro-zone. This is an indication that euros are used for invoicing purposes with countries outside the euro-zone. A negative figure on the other hand, as in the case of Denmark, reveals that in 2004 the amount of Danish exports invoiced in euros was 10 percent lower than the amount of Danish exports to the euro-zone. This suggests that Denmark does not use euros to invoice exports to other countries to any great extent and that some exports to the euro-zone are invoiced in dollars or some other currency. Except for Denmark, Poland, and the United Kingdom, the countries of the European Union tend to use euros for invoicing even when they are not trading with euro-zone countries. By 2004, other European countries, including accession countries, for the most part also used euros to a greater extent than indicated by their trade with the euro-zone. However, this result does not extend to Ukraine or to countries in other parts of the world. They are not using euros for invoicing

Table 7.2 *Non-euro-zone countries' invoicing in euros, 2001 and 2004*

	Exports		Imports	
	2001	2004	2001	2004
Non-euro area EU countries				
Cyprus	...	4%	...	0%
Czech Republic	7%	10%	10%	15%
Denmark	–11%	–10%	–15%	–16%
Estonia	...	32%	...	15%
Hungary	10%	...	18%	...
Latvia	11%	23%	1%	19%
Lithuania	2%	20%	3%	19%
Poland	–2%	13%	4%	10%
Slovenia	27%	35%	15%	13%
United Kingdom	–31%	...	–30%	...
EU acceding and accession countries				
Bulgaria	–3%	11%	10%	20%
Croatia	12%	20%	23%	29%
Romania	–6%	8%	9%	19%
Turkey	...	8%	...	2%
Other European countries				
FYR Macedonia	...	38%	25%	35%
Ukraine	–13%	–9%	...	–6%
Other countries				
Australia	–6%	–6%	–6%	–8%
Indonesia	–9%	–9%	–4%	–3%
Japan	–4%	...	–7%	...
Pakistan	–17%	...	–8%	...
South Korea	–9%	...	–7%	...
Thailand	–9%	...	–5%	...

Source: Author's calculations based on ECB 2005b, Goldberg and Tille 2006.

purposes in any significant way. One can, however, note that in all cases – except for Australia and Indonesia (on the export side) and the Czech Republic, Slovenia, and Australia (on the import side) – there was an *increase* in the use of the euro for invoicing between

2001 and 2004.[46] Contrasting tables 7.2 and 7.3, we see that, by 2006, Ukraine and Asian countries were still mostly invoicing in currencies other than the euro when trading with the euro-zone, albeit to a lesser extent than in 2004.

The main picture that emerges is a narrowing of the gap in the use of the euro as invoicing currency relative to other currencies, primarily the dollar. However, the euro's role as invoicing currency only predominates in Europe. Thus, while the euro is still widely used for quoting prices of prospective and current members of the European Union, the dollar is used beyond its immediate trading bloc and has a particularly strong lead in primary commodities.[47]

Part of the reason for the dollar's resilience as key currency is simply due to the size of the American economy along various dimensions, its share of world GDP, its share of world trade, and its share of world capital markets, as well as the breadth, depth, and liquidity of its capital markets. However, its size advantage is quickly eroding. In 2008, America's share of world GDP was 24 percent, while the euro-zone's share was 22 percent.[48] Also, the euro-zone's share of world exports has been higher than the United States' since the euro's inception, and its share of world imports surpassed the United States' share in 2007 by 6 basis points.[49] As I will explain later, the euro-zone's import capacity is of particular importance for key currency status.

According to recent developments in the economics literature, there are nonetheless reasons to believe that the dollar will continue to be the most widely used invoicing currency. The starting point for that literature was the advantage of using currencies with low transaction costs, which were used as medium of exchange for invoicing.[50] This explained the role of the American dollar as vehicle currency, i.e., its use between trading partners even when the American market was neither the producer nor the destination country. But which currency is likely to prevail in the choice between the producing country's currency or the destination country's currency? Here, the default position

---

[46] The data is not available for both years for all countries so there may be other exceptions as well.
[47] Kamps 2006, 6, 31.
[48] Author's calculations based on IMF 2007b, 139.
[49] Based on author's calculations using EUROSTAT 2009a, 2009b.
[50] Swoboda 1968.

Table 7.3 *Non-euro-zone countries' invoicing in euros, 2006*

	Exports	Imports
	2006	2006
Non-euro area EU countries		
Bulgaria	8%	28%
Cyprus	1%	4%
Czech Republic	10%	8%
Estonia	25%	13%
Latvia	31%	25%
Lithuania	31%	20%
Romania	15%	24%
Slovakia	43%	31%
Slovenia	33%	15%
EU candidate countries		
Croatia	18%	21%
FYR Macedonia	22%	33%
Turkey	9%	7%
Other countries		
Indonesia	–8%	–2%
Thailand	–7%	–3%
Ukraine	–7%	–5%

Source: Author's calculations based on ECB 2008a and Goldberg and Tille 2006.

is that producers prefer to price in their own currency in order to eliminate exchange rate risk and the ensuing price uncertainty.[51] As Kamps suggests, McKinnon points to an incentive for exporters of substitutable goods to price in local currency.[52] They want to prevent consumers switching to comparable local products when their (home) currency depreciates. This connects price uncertainty with highly differentiated goods and demand uncertainty with less differentiated goods.[53] More recent work takes the size of the destination country into account in thinking about how the exporting country plans to

[51] Grassman 1973.
[52] Kamps 2006, 10; McKinnon 1979, 82–3.
[53] It is assumed that demand is more sensitive to price, the more highly differentiated the good.

reduce demand uncertainty for less differentiated goods. By invoicing in the currency that most of the competition in the destination country is using, exporters can avoid the higher average marginal costs associated with demand uncertainty.[54] This "herding effect," which is empirically salient, implies that vehicle currencies will be used in small markets, where foreign firms constitute most of the competition, whereas the local currency will be used in large ones, where domestic firms are the principal rivals.[55] Given the higher share of goods with a low degree of differentiation in world trade, the dollar's continued lead over the euro can in part be attributed to its high share of world imports even though (as I will discuss more fully) the euro-zone actually accounted for a slightly higher world import share in 2007.

Another reason for the dollar's resilience is its continued use as vehicle currency. Primary commodities tend to be priced in vehicle or local currency. The dollar is used as a vehicle currency because the United States is a major center for commodity exchange, facilitating global spot and future market assessments.[56] Invoicing in local currency occurs because developing countries sell their resources to many countries and find it difficult to estimate the risks involved with pricing in their own currency in these multiple relations.[57] Kamps gets around the dearth of bilateral data on invoicing by deducing which currency is most widely used as vehicle currency from the share of differentiated products in world trade.[58] She reports a negative relationship between the share of differentiated products in world exports and the share of world exports invoiced in dollars and a positive association between the share of differentiated world exports and the share of world exports invoiced in euros, suggesting a greater relative role for the dollar as vehicle currency, since these tend to be in goods with a lower level of differentiation.[59]

Officially, governments will track the value of the key currency in order to determine the price of their own currency, either by fixing their exchange rate against the key currency, by pegging to it, or more loosely by considering its value when delineating monetary policy. There are two ways to gauge a currency's use as quotation currency in official markets. One looks at either which currency is most widely used as pegging

---

[54] Bacchetta and van Wincoop 2005.   [55] Goldberg and Tille 2006.
[56] McKinnon 1979, 76–7.   [57] Krugman 1991b, 177.
[58] Kamps 2006, 22.   [59] Kamps 2006, 28, 31.

currency or at which has the strongest gravitational pull.[60] According to the first measure, the most recent ECB report suggests that the euro was used as pegging currency in forty out of 100 pegs.[61] For comparison, roughly sixty currencies are pegged to the dollar.[62] Small changes in the euro's bilateral exchange rates (low volatility), and increased foreign sensitivity to changes in the euro's price, are both indicators of its gravitational pull. Using this measure, the euro's role is growing within the European Union, and also in relation to the currencies of Australia, Canada, New Zealand, South Africa, Brazil, and Chile.[63]

Store of value

The key currency should offer private and official actors a good store of value. Given the sharp decline in the dollar over the past five years, we should expect increasing use of the euro as store of value. But, of course, this is an empirical question, which can be investigated by examining where value is being stored. The relative size of capital markets is an indication of what private actors are using as investment vehicle, whereas the currency composition of central bank reserve holdings tells us which currency governments are choosing to store value.

The size of European capital markets increased significantly with the onset of the euro. The euro-zone's share of world capital markets was considerably smaller than the United States' share (25 percent vs. 36 percent) in 2001, whereas their share was larger in 2008 (29 percent vs. 26 percent).[64] But, as can be seen in figure 7.1, looking at the aggregate size of capital markets masks important differences in the two entities' respective size advantages. The euro-zone's lead in overall capital market share is entirely due to a 20 percent higher share in world bank assets than the United States. In the graph, all data points are shares of the world total. The black line measures stock market capitalization. The thick lines are consistently used for the euro-zone, the thin lines (with a marker) for the United States. Since the thin black line lies significantly above the thick black line, it is clear that the United States has a considerable lead in equities. Similarly, the euro-zone's share of debt securities, as measured by the thick dotted line, lies below the United States' share (thin dotted line). On the other hand, the euro-zone has a notable edge when it comes to bank-based

---

[60] Galati and Wooldridge 2006, 11.   [61] ECB 2007, 40.
[62] Walter and Becker 2008, 4.   [63] Galati and Wooldridge 2006, 11–12.
[64] IMF 2003c, 121; IMF 2007b, 139.

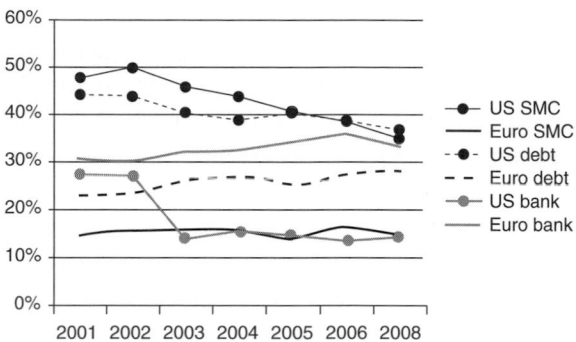

Figure 7.1 World capital market shares
Note: SMC = stock market capitalization.
Source: Author's calculations based on IMF 2003c, 2007b, October 2009.

financing reflected by the higher placement of the thick grey line for the euro-zone than the thin grey line for the United States.

Much of the debate about the euro's future prospects surrounds its role in the bond market. In 1999, the share of international debt securities issued in euros was 29 percent, as compared to 47 percent of the outstanding amount issued in dollars.[65] Within the span of seven years, it started to look as though the positions were beginning to reverse. By 2006, the euro's share had increased to 47 percent against the dollar's 36 percent.[66] While some saw the higher issues of euro-denominated debt securities (as compared to dollar-denominated ones) as a substantial achievement, others were more skeptical. Cohen, for instance, pointed out that a greater supply of euro-denominated debt securities would have to be matched by a corresponding demand for them.[67] The euro's lead may also reflect the fact that more euro-denominated assets are traded within the euro-zone.[68] There are three possible measures of the supply of debt securities: narrow, broad, and global.[69] The narrow measure reports debt securities issued in euros outside the euro-zone, the broad measure includes euro-denominated securities originating in the euro-zone as long as they target the international financial market, and the global measure includes all issues even those intended for the domestic market. To evaluate the international role of the euro, the most accurate measure is the amount of

[65] IMF 2004, 186; IMF 2007b, 146.   [66] IMF 2004, 186; 2007b, 146.
[67] Cohen 2003, 580.   [68] Chinn and Frankel 2005, 17.
[69] ECB 2005a.

issues denominated in euros outside the euro-zone, i.e., the narrow measure. This is the measure the ECB uses to gauge the international role of the euro.[70] According to this measure, and up until 2006, dollar-denominated bonds (44 percent) still accounted for a higher share than euro-denominated bonds (31 percent).[71]

The underlying differences in the components that make up the size of capital markets, referred to earlier, are important. Although the euro-zone has an advantage in bank-based financing, the United States' position in the equity and bond market is significant because securities financing is more fungible than financing through bank loans.[72] The United States also stands apart in issuing very liquid short-term obligations.[73] This liquidity advantage is not as strong as it used to be. Interest rate swaps denominated in euros now have a higher turnover than those denominated in dollars.[74] In addition, with the unfolding crisis in structured financial products, Galati and Wooldridge were right in anticipating the dangers associated with the United States' advantage in higher quality credit ratings for corporate bonds, which was mainly due to its larger share of collateralized (asset- and mortgage-backed) securities.[75] The greater emphasis on securities financing – as it relates to non-equity and particularly complex debt securities – can hardly be viewed as an advantage today.

In terms of the official sector, central banks will also hold their reserves in the currency that is the better store of value, although they may also factor in other motives, such as market access or maintaining positive allied relations, in choosing a particular reserve currency.

Here, change has been modest. Even though multiple currencies are used for reserve purposes, 64 percent of official reserves were held in dollars in 2008, as compared to 27 percent in euros (see table 7.4). These are, however, shares out of allocated reserves for which the composition is known and so do not include China's reserves, which are mostly held in dollars. China is estimated to hold nearly $2 trillion worth of foreign exchange reserves, and even though the entire amount is not held in dollars, a significant portion is likely held in dollars, so the dollar share of world reserves is likely much larger than reported in the table below.

[70] ECB 2007a.
[71] ECB 2007a.
[72] Eichengreen 1998, 500; Hartmann and Issing 2002, 320.
[73] Eichengreen 1998, 500.   [74] Galati and Wooldridge 2006, 14.
[75] Galati and Wooldridge 2006, 13.

Table 7.4 *Currency share of world (foreign exchange) reserves*

	1996	1999	2002	2005	2008
USD	62.1%	71.0%	67.1%	66.9%	64.0%
Euro	...	17.9%	23.8%	24.0%	26.5%
Deutsche mark	14.7%	...	...	...	...
Swiss franc	0.3%	0.2%	0.4%	0.1%	0.1%
Yen	6.7%	6.4%	4.4%	3.6%	3.3%

Note: Share of allocated reserves where currency composition is known.
Source: Author's calculations based on IMF 2009a.

The euro's prospects as world currency

Even though the euro lags behind the dollar in fulfilling key currency tasks, it is quickly catching up. What are the main arguments for and against the euro unseating the dollar? This question attracted a lot of interest at the time of the euro's inception. Economists were essentially divided into three camps. Some scholars saw the dollar's role as heavily entrenched.[76] Others believed the euro would displace the dollar.[77] A third intermediary position predicted serious competition for the dollar and a possible bipolar currency order.[78] With the euro below parity to the dollar until 2003, the debate petered out until a sustained wave of euro appreciation sparked a new round of debate. Two themes dominate the debate about whether the euro can eclipse the dollar in the near future, the impact of the euro-zone's enlargement and the dollar's long-term depreciation.[79] With the unfolding financial crisis and concomitant strengthening of the dollar, yet another round of debate might be in store.

Most scholars agree that a major limiting factor for the euro is the dollar's incumbency advantage, the "hysteresis" effect (from history) of being the key currency country.[80] There are three related components of this advantage: scale economies, network externalities, and

---

[76] Cohen 2003; Eichengreen 1998; Kenen 2002; McKinnon 1979.
[77] Bergsten 2002. [78] Wyplosz 1997.
[79] Chinn and Frankel 2005; Cohen 2007.
[80] Bergsten 2002, 310; Chinn and Frankel 2005; Cohen 2007; Hartmann and Issing, 2002, 327–30; McKinnon 1979, 356.

Germany.[84] Noreng views Germany as representative of other euro-zone countries and sees strong motivations for them to price in euros in order to prevent higher real oil prices as a result of dollar appreciation.[85] However, in reality, there has been a secular rise in the value of the euro vis-à-vis the dollar, canceling incentives for the euro-zone to promote euro invoicing of oil. But it is the non-euro-zone countries, Norway and the United Kingdom, that have the market power to price oil in euros and Noreng suggests that they have economic incentives to do so to stabilize oil revenues and mitigate unfavorable terms of trade effects from a rising euro.[86] Norway and the United Kingdom trade extensively with the European Union. The share of their exports that go to the EU-27 group is 81 and 57 percent respectively, for imports the corresponding figures are 69 and 55 percent.[87] If a larger portion of imports from the EU-27 is highly differentiated than exports to the group of EU-27 countries, more imports will be invoiced in euros than exports, causing a potential problem if the euro rises. This is more likely the case for Norway, which has a much higher share (72.6 percent) of fuel and mining products in overall exports than the United Kingdom does (14.8 percent).[88] However, an examination of spot prices for Brent crude oil (the North Sea benchmark) and the respective countries' exchange rate to the dollar between 1999 and 2008 shows that there was only one year, 2001, when the rise in the price of oil did not compensate for the decline in the dollar.[89] The overall pattern during this period is for the dollar exchange rate to appreciate with oil price increases before depreciating. Krugman showed that this is because oil exporters tend to invest the surplus in dollar assets before they start spending it on (American) goods.[90] So, while there may be some motivation for them to price oil in euros, they do not seem to have a strong interest to do so. The inefficiency and instability of pricing in multiple currencies also speaks against a large-scale shift into euros as invoicing currency for oil.[91] Finally, as in the case of Saudi Arabia, neither the United Kingdom nor Norway

---

[84] I will not try to sort out the direction of causality in this chapter, i.e. whether oil prices influence the dollar exchange rate or whether the dollar exchange rate influences oil prices. Noreng 1999, 43, 49.

[85] Noreng 1999, 49.   [86] Noreng 1999, 50, 53–54.

[87] WTO 2009b.   [88] WTO 2009b.

[89] Author's calculations based on EUROSTAT and EIA data.

[90] Krugman 1980.   [91] Looney 2004, 32.

has any political incentive to break their strategic alliance with the United States.

Store of value

Are euro-zone countries likely to offer a currency for international use that is a better store of value than the American dollar? One dimension of this is the ability to maintain price stability, since that will offer investors reassurance of future purchasing power. However, as Cohen points out, the ability to deliver strong growth is equally important in assessing how well a particular currency is able to serve as store of value, since the value of the assets in which currencies are stored (for the most part) depend on growth.[92]

Many see the euro-zone's ability to deliver price stability as its greatest promise, particularly at a time when the United States has failed to offer external price stability and internal price stability remains at risk.[93] However, thinking through the implications of credibly committing to price stability in the long-term exposes major sources of weakness in the euro-zone. To see this, consider how the capacity to absorb a large share of world imports bears on key currency status. This requires us to cut to one of the most important reasons for the persistence of the dollar as key currency, namely the capacity of the United States to provide an open market where countries can sell their export products.[94] In order for the euro-zone to become more attractive than the US market, its import absorption capacity should exceed the United States' by quite a bit more than a few basis points. How might the euro-zone countries increase their share of world imports? Although the import/export ratio depends on a variety of factors, there are two principal ways this could happen. A first possibility is that extra euro-zone imports rise significantly as the euro area expands to include more members. Second, if we were to see large-scale diversification into the euro, the current sixteen-member euro-zone's buying power would rise and we should expect import shares to swell above export capacity, in ways similar to the American

[92] Cohen 2003.
[93] Bergsten 2002, 312; Chinn and Frankel 2005; *Wall Street Journal,* March 25, 1998.
[94] Although we are not entirely outside the box, since the ability to sustain high and regular trade deficits is related to the key currency's store of value function.

experience. I now consider each of these avenues for the euro-zone to consistently challenge the United States as the world's first importer.

The relative size of the euro-zone

One way to enhance the euro-zone's share of world imports and capital markets is to include new members. Although I will concentrate on the potential to increase the area's buying power, it is important to note that both are important, since large-scale merchandise imports require large-scale capital imports. What are the possibilities and implications of embracing new members?

Incorporating the United Kingdom within the euro-zone is widely believed to significantly enhance the euro's prospects as key currency.[95] Crucially, the United Kingdom is, with New York, the world's leading financial center, and its inclusion would be a big boost to the size, depth, and liquidity of the euro-zone's financial markets. When scholars first started discussing the future potential of the euro as key currency, the prognosis for an extended fifteen-member euro-zone was based on including the United Kingdom, Sweden, and Denmark. However, between 2001 and 2009, it was Slovenia, Cyprus, Malta and Slovakia who joined. Integrating countries with advanced capital markets, such as the United Kingdom, Sweden, and Denmark, in addition to those already admitted, can only occur by trading off some efficiency since the euro-zone would at the very least consist of nineteen members. But not everyone agrees that size is a constraint. Under some scenarios, notably a continued decline of the dollar, the euro is expected to supplant the dollar even if the United Kingdom stays out of the euro-zone, provided that between twelve and fourteen other member states join and the dollar continues to depreciate sharply.[96]

Expansion also poses familiar collective action problems.[97] The Eurosystem of Central Banks (ECSB) comprises the ECB and the national central banks (NCBs) of the European Union, whereas what is called the Eurosystem consists of the ECB and the national central banks of the euro-zone. The ECB's decision-making body is the Governing Council, which consists of the Executive Board (President, Vice-President and four other members) and the national central bank

---

[95] Bergsten 2002; Chinn and Frankel 2005; Cohen 2003.
[96] Chinn and Frankel 2005, 56.   [97] Olson 1965.

governors, which amount to sixteen members, for a total of twenty-two members of the Council. The ECB is elevated above national central banks, who are entrusted with operationalizing ECB policy decisions. For example, when conducting open market operations such as "refinancing operations" (repurchase agreements), national central banks gather bids to sell securities, the ECB then ranks the bids and determines the interest rate by settling on the amount of assets to be bought; the list is then transmitted to the respective central banks, who in turn let the national banks know who won the bid.[98] Despite the fact that the system is "deconcentrated" rather than decentralized, transactions remain more byzantine and risky than those that take place through the Fed, since coordination is required between local banks and the NCB and among the NCBs themselves.[99]

Although a consensus is hammered out within the Council, each country technically has a vote. This has triggered concerns about the ECB's ability to maintain price stability through a one-size-fits-all policy that clearly does *not* fit all, a problem that will grow deeper as new members join. Decision-making will be hampered as the euro-zone grows and the Governing Council includes thirty-one instead of twenty-two members. Inefficiency is not all one can expect. The preference for low interest rates in low-growth economies is bound to collide with the need for higher interest rates to combat inflation in high-speed economies. This tension will be hard to avoid. The voting reform proposed by the ECB will do little to avoid a clash. Currently, simple majority is the decision rule used in the Governing Council where each member has a vote. The governors of the national central banks cannot take orders from their respective governments but, apart from this rule, there is nothing that prevents them from voting in line with the national interest; indeed there is much evidence that this is precisely what they do.[100]

With nine states expected to join, the Council would amount to thirty-one members, but voting rights are capped at twenty-two (the six Executive Board members have permanent rights). For comparison the Federal Reserve's Open Market Committee has twelve members with voting rights. Under the new system, sixteen votes are divided among Council members while the Executive Board retains

[98] Rolnick 2001.   [99] Cecchetti and O'Sullivan 2003.
[100] Heisenberg, 2003, 406–7.

its six votes. A rotation model has been proposed in order to enhance decision-making. The model has been highly criticized for being inefficient, undemocratic, and lacking in transparency, and for departing from the "one country one vote" principle, thus encouraging countries to take national positions.[101] In December 2008, the ECB issued a statement saying that it will wait to implement the rotation model until three new countries join the euro-zone and the Governing Council reaches a total of nineteen members.[102] However the ECB chooses to deal with decision-making in the context of a sizeable and growing body of decision-makers, there is bound to be a trade-off between effectiveness and representation.

Institutional constraints on the ECB

With regard to the ECB itself, there are two main institutional constraints that work against the euro-zone's ability to rival the depth, liquidity, and stability of the American securities markets. First, the ECB is only mandated to manage liquidity periodically through repurchasing agreements (repos), not regularly through open market operations, and as a result it cannot influence large turns in interest rates.[103] The Fed intervenes daily, the ECB weekly, and the ECB must deal with a wide range of assets, whereas the Fed only transacts in government securities.[104] Second, the Maastricht Treaty does not give the ECB lender-of-last-resort functions or the authority to supervise banks.[105] While national authorities have to liaise with the Eurosystem with regard to legislative changes pertaining to supervision, and the ECSB has a treaty obligation to "contribute to the smooth conduct of policies pursued by the competent authorities relating to the prudential supervision of credit institutions and the stability of the financial system," it is not directly responsible for supervision, and cannot provide lender of last resort functions.[106] According to Article 25§2 of the Treaty Establishing the Community, "the ECB may perform specific

---

[101] Belke 2003; Gros 2003; Heisenberg 2003; Meade 2003.
[102] Press release, December 18, 2008.   [103] Eichengreen 1998, 501–2.
[104] Cecchetti and O'Sullivan; Pollard 2003.
[105] Eichengreen, 501–2. The ECB buys securities from banks with cash that the bank agrees to repurchase within a few weeks through so called repos. Bank supervision rests with an agency that refers back to the respective ministries of finance, not the ECB.
[106] Rolnick 2001.

tasks concerning policies relating to the prudential supervision of credit institutions and other financial institutions with the exception of insurance undertakings."[107] The Fed's wider range of supervisory authority, as compared to the ECB, is something the ECB itself sees as a problem. The present situation, in which supervisory authority is mostly carried out by national central banks and authorities, is a constraint on the ability of the euro-zone to reach the depth of the American market for securities (equities in particular).[108] Reform is currently being considered but any proposal by the European Union's executive commission will need support in the European Parliament and consensus among all twenty-seven member states.

It is sometimes maintained that moral hazard and "too big to fail" concerns have defused calls to transfer supervisory and lender-of-last-resort responsibilities from national authorities to the ECB.[109] Moral hazard in this case translates into excessive risk-taking on the part of national authorities because they believe the ECB will come in and mop up negative consequences. "Too big to fail" refers to an inclination to save large banks for fear of economy-wide repercussions. But if the true concern is to curb risk-taking, supervision and lender-of-last-resort tasks might as well have been transferred to the ECB, since (national) central banks are for the most part responsible for bank supervision in the euro-zone economies, and the central bank alone can provide lender-of-last-resort assistance. More likely, preventing the nation-state from being purged of too much sovereignty lies behind the decision to refrain from locating these duties with the ECB. This is a real constraint on monetary policy and makes it difficult for the euro-zone to compete with the United States. Even if one concedes that the discontinuity between monetary policy and bank supervision insulates the ECB from pressure by large financial institutions and therefore makes sense for bank-based financial systems, it is not ideal for securitized financial markets that need hefty liquidity injections to avoid cataclysmic gyrations in asset prices.[110] Unless the ECB is ready to provide lender-of-last-resort functions, the United States' lead in security-based finance (see figure 7.1) is likely to persist.[111]

---

[107] Chatterjee 2003, 232.   [108] Cohen 2003; Eichengreen 1998, 500–4.
[109] Rolnick 2001.   [110] Eichengreen 1998, 502–3.
[111] Eichengreen 1998, 503.

When thinking about the prospects of the euro overtaking the dollar, it is useful to recall what spurred cooperation over the euro in the first place. The first solid initiative for monetary cooperation came in the late 1960s. The 1969 "Barre Plan" called for coordination of economic policies and financial assistance to mitigate the effects of fluctuating exchange rates. It was followed by the "Schiller Plan," which suggested an alignment of interest rate policies and monetary growth, and proposed the creation of a European central bank to guarantee price stability.[112] The "Werner Plan" of 1970 envisaged a three-stage scheme that would result in monetary union and a single currency by 1980, designs that were scuttled by the breakdown of Bretton Woods, the oil crisis, and the economic stagnation of the early 1980s.[113] Tighter monetary cooperation in Europe evolved as a strategic response to the macro-economic environment of the 1970s, and the struggle against inflation. Immediately after Bretton Woods collapsed, the dollar became hostage to inflationary pressures, and European governments looked for different ways to foster price stability, which eventually paved the way to an independent monetary arrangement anchored around the D-mark.[114] After the botched attempt with the "snake in the tunnel," which tied European currencies to the D-mark, the European Monetary System (EMS) was set up in 1979 to stabilize exchange rates within fixed margins through cooperation in the Exchange Rate Mechanism (ERM).[115] Finally, the 1989 "Delors report" outlined three stages which would lead to European Monetary Union, ideas that were formalized in the 1992 Maastricht Treaty and which led to the single currency in 1999.[116] By the time of the euro's inception, however, the United States had been embroiled in a decade-long fight against inflation and established an eminent track record at that.[117]

At the heart of the ECB's monetary policy strategy is an emphasis on price stability with two mechanisms in place for analyzing threats to price stability – the first and second pillars. The first pillar establishes a reference value for the growth of the broad monetary aggregate M3, which in 2001 was fixed at 4.5 percent. The second pillar includes a wide array of indicators, exchange rates, the yield curve,

[112] Cyr 2003, 985.   [113] Kaikati 1999, 175.
[114] McKinnon 2002, 356–8.   [115] Kaikati 1999, 175.
[116] Cyr 2003, 988.   [117] McKinnon 2002, 358–9.

surveys, and macro-economic forecasts upon which to base monetary policy decisions. Since prices in the euro-zone have fallen within this parameter despite the fact that actual growth in M3 has persistently gone over the reference value, the relevance of the first pillar in controlling inflation is indeed questionable.[118] According to the ECB, price stability can be maintained as long as the "harmonized consumer price index" (HICP) does not increase more than 2 percent each year. But to be fair, the Fed too has stopped watching M3. The greatest weakness is that the monetary strategy of the ECB, particularly the lack of transparency regarding the relative importance of the first and second pillars in shaping monetary policy has undermined the ECB's credibility and led to suspicions that it is simply following the Fed.[119] This lack of a clear international strategy is something that was admitted by the ECB on its tenth anniversary.

Price stability
Some scholars see recurrent and prolonged periods of sizeable American trade deficits along with associated and fairly high net external liabilities as presenting fertile ground for a euro take-over.[120] A stable currency, which is expected to appreciate, is viewed as more attractive as store of value than a falling one.[121] Indeed, the problems that the United States encountered in trying to maintain internal price stability in the mid 1970s up until the early 1980s is seen as having contributed to the emergence of a fixed exchange rate regime within Europe, whereas America's success with controlling inflation in the 1990s is viewed as having entrenched the dollar's role in the world economy.[122] Consequently, the depreciation required to adjust current account imbalances (and associated external liabilities) through export growth and valuation effects could undermine confidence in the dollar as store of value.[123] But this perspective fails to scrutinize the future pull of the euro beyond its appeal as a hedge against a

---

[118] Rich 2005.   [119] Frisch 2003, 16–19.
[120] Bergsten 2002, 312; Chinn and Frankel 2005.
[121] Hartmann and Issing 2002, 321.
[122] Bergsten 2002, 308; McKinnon 2002, 358–9.
[123] As the study points out, however, there is no statistically significant relationship between the net international investment position and reserve currency status; in part this is due to the large role of the United States in the sample. See Chinn and Frankel 2005, 29–30.

falling dollar. To be sure, the slide in the dollar will cause investors to flee into euros, and many of them already have. But although the euro may be an attractive hedge, there are structural obstacles with a transfer into euros. So, this strategy has limited range.

How might diversification into euros play out? The euro would increasingly acquire a store of value function for private actors and official investors might follow suit. The value of the euro would rise, imports would become more affordable and exports less competitive. This is the direction in which a strong euro has taken the currency block. The euro-zone's trade balance with the outside world was in deficit for the first time in 2006 and the euro-zone's share of world exports has consistently declined since 2002, whereas its share of world imports experienced a one-time decline in 2002 and then remained constant.[124] Thus, so far significant diversification has taken place independently of the euro attaining key currency status.

Although there is some empirical evidence that the euro-zone is tending towards trade deficits, as a result of large-scale diversification into the euro, the United States established itself as key currency when exporting dollars on capital account, so why would it not be possible for the euro-zone to do so as well rather than export dollars on current account, as I have assumed? One reason has to do with the move from fixed to flexible exchange rates, which creates greater pressure, and indeed incentives, for the key currency to fluctuate. There is greater stress on the key currency country to run trade deficits under floating rates since the capital inflow that results in appreciation makes the relative purchasing power of the key currency country more obvious. There are also greater incentives on the key currency country to accept large and persistent trade deficits because subsequent depreciation facilitates the process of external adjustment through capital and exchange rate gains.[125] The interests of the key currency country also intersect with the interests of other countries, particularly in East Asia, that pursue a strategy of export-led growth.[126]

So, how would the euro as primary world currency differ from the dollar as major world currency? While the dollar's decline in the last five years has mostly taken place vis-à-vis the euro, the dollar's

[124] These calculations are based on Eurostat 2008; GOFT 2008; WTO 2008.
[125] Gourinchas and Rey 2005a; Lane and Milesi-Ferretti 2006.
[126] Dooley, Folkerts-Landau, and Garber 2003.

depreciation could in principle be diffused across a wider range of countries, including countries in East Asia. Consequently, instability in the key currency's (i.e., dollar) exchange rate need not imply the same scale of instability in the exchange rate of other major currencies (i.e., the euro). Another difference between being a major and a primary currency is the incentives facing official actors to prop up the key currency for political reasons. If the euro were the key currency, we should expect countries to intervene in the foreign exchange market in order to prolong the region's buying power. Here, political factors play a role. In the postwar era, economic and security reasons have often overlapped in official investors' decisions to hold dollar reserves. Apart from strengthening America's capacity to absorb imports, major purchasers of American Treasury bills – France, Germany, Japan, and other East Asian countries (even China for the moment) – have prospered under the United States' security guarantee. The euro-zone, on the other hand, is nowhere near as potent a military force.

Another reason for the dollar's staying power is that the United States is in a better position to act effectively in the face of economic shocks. Unlike the euro-zone, which can only achieve a massive fiscal stimulus by drawing on national budgets in a concerted effort, the US government can tap the federal budget. Although supplementary spending in the United States is conditional on congressional approval, the absence of a "European taxpayer" is a constraint on fiscal policy under normal, as well as harder, times. As for a monetary response, the Federal Reserve is entrusted with two goals, to combat inflation and to promote growth, allowing it to ease interest rates in order to safeguard the second objective. This brings us back to Cohen's point about the significance of the Federal Reserve's dual mandate to promote price stability and growth. By contrast, the ECB has a very strict mandate to ensure price stability. Quite apart from the disadvantage this creates when managing shocks, as made plain by the present financial crisis, its special focus is good for countries who prioritize inflation-fighting but not for those who need lower interest rates to feed growth. Striking a balance between these different needs will prove especially difficult when attempting to boost competitiveness in the wake of ongoing deficits. If adjustment takes place through a long-term descent in the value of the euro, we are back to the American example and a key currency that does not fare better in terms of external price stability. Some inflation may also creep in through the trade channel, and so internal price stability may also be at risk. If, on the other hand, adjustment is to occur through higher interest rates and price pressures within the euro-zone (to induce sub-stitution towards domestic goods), unemployment will rise. Without the option of pursuing beggar-thy-neighbour policies in the form of competitive devaluations against each other (or the rest of the world), the less competitive euro-zone countries will be particularly exposed. While the euro area as a whole could adopt protectionist policies, and calls for such measures reverberate quite strongly today, doing so would vitiate one of the main functions that the key currency country is expected to play, namely to maintain an open market where coun-tries can offload their products. The real question, therefore, boils down to whether Europeans are prepared to adjust to periods of vari-able job security, and the associated social unrest, to the same extent that Americans have.

If the problems that currently haunt the dollar are inherent to key currency status, we should not expect the euro to oust the dollar as key currency but for the dollar to retain its number one position or for a bipolar key currency system eventually to emerge.

Fiscal policy

Prospects for price stability, and the cohesion of any currency union, also depend on fiscal policy. To ensure price stability, countries enter-ing the euro-zone must meet the four convergence criteria outlined in the Maastricht Treaty. A country must have successfully participated in the exchange rate mechanism (ERM) two years prior to entry, the budget deficit must be less than 3 percent of GDP, government debt must be less than 60 percent of GDP, the inflation rate must not exceed the average of the three top performers by more than 1.5 per-cent, and long-term interest rates must not rise above 2 percent of the interest rate prevailing in the three countries with the lowest inflation rate.[127] Unlike the conditions for entry, the ongoing requirements for participation in the euro-zone are not seriously enforced and do not have strong enough sanctions to back them.

Once countries have qualified for entry, not much constrains their fiscal policy. Originally, governments were supposed to suffer

[127] Rehman 1998, 52–3.

sanctions if they failed to comply with the provisions of the Stability and Growth Pact (SGP). But countries were not sufficiently deterred to run big deficits, and could easily dodge implementation of the excessive deficit procedure (Article 104c of the Maastricht Treaty), which called for fines of up to 0.5 percent of GDP to punish bad behaviour. After core members like Germany and France failed to follow the prescriptions for deficit reduction, the SGP was revised at the European Summit in March 2005, and the rules established to police fiscal discipline significantly watered down. Now countries can gain time in adjusting deficits by pointing to slow growth. They can also justify increased government spending by invoking any number of factors, ranging from education to other public goods intended to unite Europe. Governments are also granted a longer time-line to battle deficits. This new-won flexibility has left the market suspicious that the Maastricht promise, not to pull a bail-out stunt if countries run into trouble with the excessive deficit procedure, amounts to little more than cheap talk. The slippery slope that would set in if countries started to think that the ECB might lend a helping hand to save a defaulting government, and more dramatically if markets started to suspect a moral hazard problem, might well end in sixteen currencies.

Differences in countries' initial fiscal position, and thus ability to accommodate external shocks through fiscal measures, was accentuated with the ongoing financial crisis and is no longer an abstract academic discussion. Germany received a slap on the wrist from the ECB after it announced that it would assist countries with rising fiscal deficits. Rising spreads on ten-year bonds for countries facing difficulties with fiscal discipline – Greece, Ireland, Italy, Portugal, and Spain – have fuelled rumours that some states may actually break away from the euro.

The problems tied to ensuring fiscal discipline, and the politics of the euro area at large, cannot be dissociated from the economics of currency union. The ultimate yardstick for assessing the viability of sharing a currency is how closely the group constitutes an "optimal currency area."[128] However, the fact that business cycles are not synchronized, and capital and labour markets not perfectly integrated, suggests that the euro-zone does not qualify as the "optimal currency

[128] Mundell 1961.

area" envisaged by Robert Mundell.[129] This is a serious impediment to the long-term viability of the euro area, since price stability depends on the credibility of the ECB's anti-inflation stance, and more fundamentally the ability of the euro-zone to absorb asymmetric shocks in one region without triggering destabilizing consequences throughout the entire area. The inability of European capital and labour markets to smooth out regional differences is usually borne out by comparing them to their American counterparts. In the United States, a common language and culture makes it relatively simple to pick up and leave whenever a better opportunity presents itself elsewhere, and there are no impediments to the free movement of capital either. In contrast, the euro area is fraught with visible and invisible barriers impeding capital and particularly labour to flow freely across borders. It remains to be seen whether the ECB is able to prevent asymmetric shocks and, in case they nonetheless occur, whether it is capable of limiting their damaging effect. Once a region is hit by a shock, preventing a contagion spread of economic malaise to other regions, or stimulating growth in one region without over-heating other regions, will not be easy.

Variation in how different regions are able to cope with a common monetary policy over the long term makes it difficult to believe that all members of the ECB's Governing Council can remain committed to an aggressive anti-inflationary stance. As soon as a common monetary policy starts to produce large differential effects within the euro area, politics within the Council will become disorderly. This will strain the inflation-fighting capacity of the ECB in two ways.[130] First, with a divided Council, the ECB will not be able to fight inflation as adamantly as the Bundesbank did. Second, with the market watching, governments may learn that, even if they over-spend, some mechanism will eventually kick in to rescue them from past profligacy in order to prevent contagion, producing the classic moral hazard problem referred to earlier, and a huge loss of credibility for the ECB and its commitment to price stability.

Limits to pooling sovereignty

History reveals that lasting monetary unions have been political unions. A single currency has been more likely to emerge and

[129] Kaikati 1999, 182.
[130] Fratianni, Hauskrecht, and Maccario 1998, 484–5.

persist when political unification has been the driver of monetary union. The experience of Switzerland, Germany, and Italy in the mid-nineteenth century, as well as Belgium–Luxembourg in 1921, are good examples of this, whereas the Latin monetary union and the Scandinavian monetary union, in the latter half of the nineteenth century, remind us that monetary union may fail despite political union.[131] How far will the euro-zone countries go in merging politically to allay fears that different countries want different things? Their ability to cede sovereignty to create a semblance of underlying unity is in fact limited by statute. While a complete overhaul of the way decisions are made within the Eurosystem in favour of a "centralized" solution is required to formulate a coherent monetary policy, Article 5 of the Nice Treaty[132] explicitly forbids further transfers of sovereignty from national governments in the monetary realm.[133] The Lisbon Treaty is a step in the right direction for twenty-seven countries to realize a common monetary policy.

A credible monetary policy cannot be hammered out unless national authorities are entirely cut loose from monetary policy and fiscal discipline is enforced. Political union, if not inescapable, seems hard to dodge. The second theme to be raised in the following section is the prospect of the euro being backed by military power. To rival the dollar, the euro will have to build a credible military apparatus capable of protecting foreign investments in the euro-zone. This would allow the European Union to collect the kind of security premium the United States has enjoyed. If the European Union wants to tower over the United States economically and politically, it will need an armed force capable of protecting European foreign investments and policing world order.

Military revival

While heightened cooperation to create an autonomous military power has been attributed to trepidation over American foreign policy, the

---

[131] Capie, 1998, 451–5, 458; Kaikati 1999, 172–3.
[132] The "Enabling Clause" of the ECSB Statute, Articles 10.2 and 10.6.
[133] Belke 2003.

initial impulse for concerted action in security affairs came in the 1990s, when the effects of the dissolution of the Soviet empire were first being felt. At this time, the United States too saw the militarization of Europe as desirable, at least in so far as American resources would be freed for deployment elsewhere. The diminishing strategic relevance of Europe relative to the Middle East and Asia in the post-Cold War era sent a signal to European states that they needed to put their own house in order. Following unification, this meant accelerating cooperation in the security realm to contain Germany.[134] Another major reason for collaborating on security matters was the perceived need to deal with a volatile Russia and the need to manage relations with Soviet client states.[135]

The Maastricht Treaty (1992) created a pillar for a Common Foreign and Security Policy (CFSP) but true progress in establishing the European Union as "military actor" began with the incorporation of the "Petersberg tasks" in the Amsterdam Treaty (1997) as part of the Union's "acquis," including the appointment of a high-profile High Representative for the CFSP (Javier Solana), and the creation of a Policy Planning Unit. The "Petersberg tasks," which originated under the Western European Union (WEU) in 1992, have both a civilian and military component. They include humanitarian rescue operations and peacekeeping missions, as well as crisis management and peace enforcement. The "Petersberg tasks" were incorporated into the European Union framework as a reaction to France's failure to garner adequate support to dispatch WEU forces during the Bosnian crisis.[136] The debacle in the Balkans in the late 1990s showed Europeans just how dependent they were on American air force, "logistics, intelligence, and communications."[137] The lack of a credible military apparatus had the European Union immobilized and humbled by the United States' technological superiority at a time when some of the most demeaning human rights abuses in the postwar era were being committed on European soil. Stripped of the latest advances in airpower, "airborne command-and-control capabilities, air-to-air refuelling, capacities to suppress enemy air defence and all-weather strike capabilities, as well as communications systems interoperable with the more advanced US systems," Europeans were marginalized on their

---

[134] Jones 2003.   [135] Hoffmann 2000, 191.
[136] Treacher 2004.   [137] Gordon 2000.

own turf.[138] The United States' ambivalence about whether to intervene at all, and their prioritization of airpower once they did, forced
Europeans to scrutinize their dependence on the American military
and contemplate increasing NATO contributions in a bid for greater
influence.[139] Slighted by the Balkan experience, and with the dysfunctional nature of the WEU out in the open, member states decided to
cannibalise the WEU at the European Council meeting at Cologne in
June 1999. The Petersberg tasks were thus incorporated in the Treaty
of the European Union (Treaty of the European Union, Article 17).

Even before the Kosovo intervention, Prime Minister Tony Blair
had caught on that the European Union would never gain influence
within NATO unless they were better able to contribute to the organization's military operations.[140] His meeting with the French Prime
Minister, Jacques Chirac, in 1998 at St. Malo is considered a water-
shed in European defence cooperation. To boot, the shifting stance
of countries like Germany, Spain, Italy, Sweden, and Finland had
already lowered barriers to collective action in defence, and persuaded
Blair to prop up European defence cooperation instead of cooperating with France on a bilateral basis. With the change of heart came a
court decision authorizing German forces to join international peacekeeping missions, Spanish participation in NATO's integrated force,
Italian leadership in the concerted effort to address the 1997 Albanian
crisis, and neutral countries' acceptance of the EU mandate to execute
the Petersburg tasks.[141] After the decision to usurp the WEU in the
summer of 1999, European member states – save Denmark, which
had an opt-out clause on security cooperation since 1993 – agreed to
realize the so-called "Headline Goals" by 2003. The purpose of these
goals was to create a European Rapid Reaction Force (ERRF) capable
of deploying up to 60,000 troops within sixty days over a one-year
period. The decision to realize this objective was taken at the Helsinki
European Council meeting of December 1999. Three committees were
set up at Helsinki: the PSC (Political and Security Committee), the
EUMS (European Union Military Staff), and the EUMC (European
Union Military Committee). Significant developments were made to
create decision-making structures for defence and security policies at

[138] Giegerich and Wallace 2004, 166.
[139] Gordon 2000.   [140] Gordon 2000.
[141] Treacher 2004.

the European Council meeting at Nice in December 2000, and it was decided that the interim committees would become permanent. From now on, the EUMS is mandated to advise and report to the EUMC, the EUMC is to report to the PSC, and the PSC to liaise with the High Representative of the CFSP.[142]

Given these developments, how well equipped is Europe to fight? Although the European Union's military capabilities are often characterized as being insignificant, armed force was used in 2002 and 2003 to keep and maintain the peace in Afghanistan, Rwanda, Sierra Leone, the Ivory Coast, Kuwait, Iraq, Georgia, Tajikistan, Bosnia, Kosovo, and Macedonia.[143] Measured in hard military capabilities, the European Union is the second most significant power in the world.[144] Thus far, the EU has concluded four small-scale operations – Concordia, Artemis, Proxima, and the EU Police Mission in Bosnia (EUPM) – and is currently involved in another operation in Georgia as well as Bosnia and Herzegovina.[145] The 2003 Concordia mission in Macedonia was a Berlin-plus operation that made use of NATO assets and planning capabilities. Proxima followed up with a police mission to Macedonia (2003–04), while the EUPM to Bosnia (2003–05) was a civilian Petersberg operation, and operation Artemis (2003) a self-sufficient (UN-mandated) expedition to resolve ethnic rivalry in the Democratic Republic of Congo.[146] Recently, Operation Althea (2004) replaced NATO's stabilization force (SFOR) to maintain order in Bosnia.

Collective action problems in creating an autonomous and credible force

These capabilities notwithstanding, European military power is neither autonomous nor credible. The Nice Declaration (2000) explicitly recognizes that Europe has the ambition to ensure an autonomous capacity to use force. But what precisely this means varies across member states. For countries like Britain, the whole point of enhancing defence cooperation has been to reinforce NATO and to gain greater influence within the organization. For countries like France, the desire for an independent force capable of balancing American

---

[142] Shepherd 2003, 45.   [143] Haine 2004.
[144] Ulriksen 2004.   [145] Whitman 2004, 446.
[146] Whitman 2004, 446.

power has been a foreign policy trademark since De Gaulle. In 2001, the French Chief of Defence Staff, General Jean-Pierre Kelche, made it very clear that building a European military capability was not only about Europeans gaining more influence within NATO, but about acquiring independent structures for military command, control, and planning.[147] Superimposed on this question is the equally divisive issue of whether the Union is assuming a federal structure or not. Both France and Britain struggled to dilute the Commission's influence over defence policy and have tried to keep both the European Parliament as well as national parliaments at arm's length.[148]

The fundamental problem the European Union must confront is that it consists of countries with different conceptions of what circumstances merit the use of force, a point brought home in the rift over Iraq II in December 2003. When the United States started to ratchet up the pressure on allies to enlist in the war – claiming "you are either with us or against us" – some were confirmed in their view that a serious alternative to NATO was needed, while others joined the "coalition of the willing." Out of the Union's current twenty-seven members, twelve countries did not support the war; the most fervent opponents to the war were France, Germany, Belgium, and Luxembourg. Yet while most European countries remain cognizant of the high political price dependence on American protection entails, six years into the war, not even the staunchest proponents of balancing think they have more to lose than gain from American hegemony. Even France has come around, and toned down the posturing and jockeying for power that was so striking in the run-up to the invasion. Today, French ground forces are committed to postwar reconstruction and institution-building in Iraq. In part, this volte face is due to fear of being stuck on the fringes of international politics but is also motivated by real affinities and historic ties with the United States; after all, the longest-standing military alliance is the one between them. Asperity between Europe and the United States may resume, but unless tensions across the Atlantic become more portentous than the discord that exists among member states, American military power will not be seriously challenged.

Military cooperation within the Union remains competitive. In a bid for greater influence within the Union, Italy contributed more

---

[147] Winn 2003, 56.   [148] Treacher 2004, 65.

troops in 2003 than France or Germany.[149] Moves of this sort pre-clude collaboration among members, which to be effective will require some form of leadership. But small states have fiercely resisted any form of "directoire" by the likes of France, Germany, or Great Britain. Yet cooperation on security and defence policy is impossible if all countries are required to agree at every stage. The touchy nature of organizing an independent force has subjected ESDP decisions to a unanimity constraint (through the Nice Treaty), effectively giving each state blocking power.[150] To overcome the collective action prob-lems that arise in large groups, and prevent a watered down agree-ment with minimal contributions, a group of countries that obtain a qualified majority in the European Council have been authorized to deepen security and defence cooperation.[151] This opportunity was created at a meeting held in December 2003, and exploited by Britain, France, and Germany, who proposed (and in September 2004 received approval for) EU "Battle Groups," consisting of 1,500 troops.[152] With the Council's approval, such a grouping could be given a green light to engage in "permanent structured cooperation." Pending a qualified majority vote by participating member states, new members could then be added to the alliance.[153]

The lack of a war-fighting capability and a strategic concept

The European Union does not possess a standing army. When classi-fied as the second largest military power in the world, the rank is based on outstanding commitments not on any form of integrated force. Currently, member states' ERRF commitments consist of 100,000 troop commitments, 400 aircrafts, and 100 naval vessels.[154] But this is simply a pool of reserves which national governments – who retain full control over whether and what forces will be engaged in any EU operation – promise to make available should the need arise. How this "need" will be assessed is still wide open. While Article 11§1 of the Maastricht Treaty outlines the broad contours of the CFSP, a strategic concept for the ESDP to identify when intervention is necessary, and what means to use, has yet to materialize.[155] The European Security Strategy (ESS) of 2003 points to priority areas but is not sufficiently

---

[149] Giegerich and Wallace 2004, 173.   [150] Wessel 2003, 277.
[151] Haine 2004, 111.   [152] Whitman 2004, 448.
[153] Whitman 2004, 448.   [154] Shepherd 2003, 44.
[155] Biscop 2002, 477–9.

clear about when states should mobilize and what level of force to use.[156] The three corners of the European Union's foreign and security policy are according to the ESS, to promote "good governance" in contiguous areas, to support "an international order based on effective multilateralism," and to combat both traditional and new security threats. The principal threats are according to the ESS – international terrorism, the proliferation of weapons of mass destruction (WMDs), and failed states. But agreement on how to tackle different threats is sorely lacking. As uncertainty about when to get embroiled in a war-fighting mission unravels there is risk of backlash from the public and traditional neutrals – Sweden, Finland, Austria, and Ireland – who may start to suspect a crawling militarization of the Union.[157] The reassurance offered Ireland at the European Council meeting at Seville in 2002 – that the Nice Treaty would not endanger its neutrality – will do little to still such fears.

Given the differences in defence strategies, military traditions, language, and the fierce rivalry that exists between states and different services within the military itself, it is difficult to see how countries will be able to agree on a strategic concept.[158] For example, France and Italy have been the most eager to link war-fighting capabilities to peace enforcement, acknowledging the need for a militarized component to accompany stabilization initiatives, while Britain and the Netherlands have been much more ambivalent, and Germany and Sweden the most opposed to securitization. A military doctrine uniting all twenty-seven member states does not exist, and is even less likely to emerge with thirty member states at the negotiating table. Without a clear strategic concept, the European Union is most likely to make progress where it already has, in devising enhanced procedures and pooling resources to manage external crisis operations.

It is not merely that the commitments made to the ERRF are pledges which can be broken or that the tasks of the fifteen brigades envisaged in the Headline Goals are not adequately outlined, equally important is the fact that estimated troop levels fail to take support functions into account. Units have to be rotated between pre-deployment, deployment, and post-deployment recovery; as a result 180,000 troops are needed to provide an armed force of 60,000.[159] If a pool of

[156] Ulriksen 2004.   [157] Biscop 2002, 477–9.
[158] Ulriksen 2004, 468.   [159] Shepherd 2003, 42.

reserves of this size were set aside for foreign operations, a fifth of the forces not conscripted for service or out on mission would be usurped by the ERRF.[160] For all these reasons, and since many units are simultaneously engaged elsewhere via NATO, the United Nations or in ad-hoc coalitions with the United States, the ERRF does not amount to a credible war-fighting machine.[161]

A major limiting factor for Europe's ability to acquire global reach is that its force is primarily land-based and that whatever aircraft carriers or satellite systems exist completely lack the sophistication of those possessed by the United States.[162] When it comes to command, control, communications, and intelligence, the United States has strategic lift and all-weather strike capabilities, precision-guided munitions, roll-on roll-off ships, deployable communications and leading satellite systems for intelligence, surveillance, target acquisition, and reconaissance (ISTAR) – leaving the European Union in a technological backwater.[163] As a future strategy, the European Union can either duplicate and challenge American capabilities or accept American military doctrine and "plug and play" into the command, control, and information structures, which have allowed the United States to rule the commons – space, ocean, and air.[164] Although France, Britain, Germany, Italy, and Spain are developing satellite surveillance systems and communication satellites that could eventually be used to guide missiles, it is not likely that the EU will ever be able to control the commons in the manner that the United States does.[165] The satellite intelligence system, Galileo, which will cost almost $4 billion, has been launched as an alternative to the United States' Global Positioning System (GPS), and is not very popular with the Americans who fear that terrorists will be able to use it to detect troop movements.[166] Neither is it likely that the European Union will be able to match the United States' capacity for combat in various hotspots around the world. Only in very specific situations, for instance when it comes to fighting in littoral zones, mine warfare, winning "hearts and minds," peacekeeping, or post-conflict reconstruction, is the Union able to outclass the United States.[167] Despite its considerable deployments abroad, the European Union is not capable of acting autonomously but must rely

---

[160] Winn 2003, 50.   [161] Ulriksen 2004, 459–60.
[162] Winn 2003, 55.   [163] Shepherd 2003, 48–9.
[164] Ulriksen 2004, 460–2.   [165] Ulriksen 2004, 463.
[166] Winn 2003.   [167] Ulriksen 2004, 463–4.

on NATO for "transport, support, and protection," which it will likely continue to do unless defence budgets are increased, and progress made in information technology.[168]

If the European Union aims to acquire a military capable of autonomous action, operating independently of NATO, this can only be achieved at considerable cost. Some of these shortages can be overcome through a division of labour, asset pooling, and joint procurement.[169] The obvious drawback to pooling and specialization is that it is politically sensitive. Specialization requires a high level of trust among member states, since it requires concentrating lethal capabilities with a handful of players while others focus on low-level capabilities.[170] Geography may also speak against specialization for certain assets, in so far that they impede rapid mobilization. Moreover, as long as member states have different security priorities, there is the more serious threat of a potential resource veto with a strict division of labour. Small defence budgets and the comparative dearth of resources dedicated to research and development also limit procurement of a high-tech defence capability.[171] Attempts to become a full-fledged military power with the latest in weapon technology will sit uneasily with efforts to balance budgets and could very well endanger the ECB's commitment to price stability.[172] In a climate of high unemployment and slow growth, raising taxes to prop up the Union's military base will resonate badly with a public that still views the euro with great scepticism. The sneak approach used by member states to increase deployments has kept the question of where an integrated European force is headed out of public purview, and left both national parliaments and the European parliament in the dark.[173] Raising taxes to acquire better weapon systems will bring the issue of whether a European common defence is desirable into the open, and possibly expose politicians to a plebiscitary veto. Moreover, to match the competitiveness of the American defence industry will take more than a few successful joint ventures and mergers such as European Aeronautic, and probably a move away from the tradition of public ownership in this area.[174] Moreover, as benefits with asset pooling

---

[168] Haine 2004.   [169] Haine 2004, 111.
[170] Shepherd 2003, 49.   [171] Shepherd 2003, 49.
[172] Hoffmann 2000, 196.   [173] Giegerich and Wallace, 178. Bono 2004, 451.
[174] Winn 2003, 54–5.

and joint procurement continue to grow with European expansion, so
will coordination and cooperation problems among member states.

NATO: the ties that bind

When Europe severed the ties to the WEU, it appeared as if the ESDP
(European Security and Defence Policy) could emerge as a separate
force to be reckoned with outside NATO's purview. But decoupling
European defence from NATO has been difficult.

Indeed, going back to St. Malo, one of the main objectives with
improving defence cooperation was to elaborate a European pillar within NATO, thus establishing a European Strategic Defence
Identity (ESDI). As long as developing European military capability
was tantamount to reinforcing the transatlantic alliance, the United
States backed the effort. Under the Clinton administration, Madeleine
Albright summed up the United States' position on European defence
plans by referring to the "Three Ds" – decoupling, discrimination, and
duplication. There was to be no decoupling of Europe from the United
States, or discrimination against NATO allies outside the Union, or
unnecessary duplication of capabilities. A joint working group on
capabilities – the Capabilities Commitment Conference (CCC) met at
Brussels in November 2000 – to ensure that the efforts of NATO and
the EU would be complementary and that a European army was not
established.[175] The CCC also brought up the thorny issue of whether
NATO had a "right of first refusal" over the European contingent
within NATO, or the ERRF for that matter, a proposition vehemently
opposed by France.[176]

A "Berlin plus" agreement was elaborated at the Washington
Summit in April 1999. The agreement ensured that the EU could
access NATO planning capabilities and assets. It also identified
European command options and found ways to incorporate EU-led
operations in NATO defence planning. The precise ways in which
the EU would access NATO assets, and preserve decision-making
autonomy in view of extensive consultation procedures, was discussed at the European Council meeting held at Feira in June 2000.
Difficulties in disentangling the relationship between NATO and EU
members delayed agreement another two years. Especially Turkey
worried that the creation of a European pillar within NATO would

[175] Cornish and Edwards 2001, 593.   [176] Shepherd 2003, 43.

give non-NATO members of the EU access to NATO assets, and that non-EU members of NATO would be discriminated against.[177] These hurdles were finally overcome in December 2002 when the "EU-NATO Declaration on ESDP" was announced. NATO would give access to assets and planning capabilities even when it was not directly involved, and non-EU members of NATO would become full participants in the ESDP whenever possible.[178] The final draft of the "Berlin plus" agreement was signed in March 2003.

At present, European defence cooperation is operationally tied to NATO through the Partnership for Peace agreement, and future strategies linked to NATO through Peace Support Operations (PSO). The PSO places higher emphasis on peace enforcement, civil-military relations, and "coalitions of the willing" that do not derive their legitimacy from international law.[179] This arrangement has been convenient for both the United States and the European Union. It has allowed the United States to stick to mini-lateral solutions and for the European Union to get involved in post-conflict reconstruction operations that the United States manages poorly.[180]

The future of European defence cooperation
In the final analysis, it seems very likely that the European Union will remain dependent on American defence capabilities. Despite the progress made with the CFSP and the ESDP, Europe is not united on defence and security policy. There is nothing in the CFSP that obliges member states to adopt a common foreign and security policy; they are simply obliged to consult.[181] Neither does the ERRF amount to a "European army," it is merely a collection of earmarked forces. Nor is collective defence, thus far the privilege of NATO, envisaged. As a military actor, the European Union is neither autonomous nor credible. Its bargaining power will remain limited in security affairs, as it continues to depend on American war-fighting capabilities.

The European Union does, however, have a certain kind of structural power – the power to inculcate a preference for peaceful conflict resolution tools in its own members, in potential members, and those who depend on economic and political assistance.[182] The EU can use

---

[177] Wessel 2003, 279.   [178] Wessel 2003, 279.
[179] Bono 2004, 459–60.   [180] Bono 2004, 450.
[181] Wessel 2003, 287.   [182] Andréani 2000, 487.

its own institutional setup to advantage, for example, through delay tactics in accession negotiations, and exercise significant agenda-setting power in international negotiations. But it does not have the centralized command structures required to change state behaviour by credibly threatening force; the best the EU can hope for is to use its "soft power" to morph states into democracies.[183] The European Union still sees itself as a "civilian power," fostering international peace and security by advocating respect for human rights and promoting liberal norms through diplomatic channels. "Hard power" has only been invoked to eradicate conflict in its immediate neighbourhood, or as a means to strengthen its own identity.[184]

The division of labour that has emerged between the European Union and the United States is mutually beneficial. The European Union provides the legitimacy that American leadership lacks by involving its institutions in humanitarian relief operations, postwar stabilization, "security sector reform," and sporadic peace enforcement.[185] Forging a vision which encompasses the dreams and aspirations of all member states, one which all states, and ultimately the citizens of those states, will be prepared to fight and die for, is a precursor of any security strategy. With Europeans committed to resolving conflict through peaceful means, who will die for the Union? Several surveys conducted among officers reveal that they still identify with the country they come from, and are not willing to sacrifice their lives for the Union.[186] The street is fiercely anti-militarist and was increasingly dissatisfied with American power projection under the Bush era. The only way the European Union will find it worthwhile to prove itself militarily through a full-fledged and independent military capability is if some of that frustration spills over to government quarters and politicians prepare to endure the wrath of a peace-loving public.

Conclusion

In theory, East Asian and European regionalism could put an end to American privilege. If countries in East Asia, who have extended a long credit line to the United States in order to promote exports, were to rely more on each other for trade, they might suddenly stop

---

[183] Rynning 2003, 487.   [184] Larsen 2000.
[185] Bono 2004, 452–53.   [186] Mérand 2003.

investing – and sell off a large chunk of the assets they currently hold – in the United States. Most trade in East Asia is, however, in component parts. For some time to come, countries in East Asia will therefore remain dependent on the American market to absorb final goods and the transition to more independent policies will more likely be slow and gradual than abrupt. The rise of China will not fundamentally change the relationship between East Asia and the United States. China is in some respects still a developing country and cannot exert the kind of import pull that the United States does. Excessively dependent on foreign investment, China's future growth trajectory is precarious. The call of the governor of the Chinese central bank, Zhou Xiaochuan, for an end to the dollar as world currency because of the quantitative easing pursued by the Federal Reserve, and the expected depreciation of the dollar in its wake, belies China's position in the world economy as a consumer of American government bonds, and a country with interests in a commercial development strategy. A few currency swaps – like the ones with Argentina, South Korea, Malaysia, Indonesia, Hong Kong, and Belarus – to make invoicing in yuan possible, is not going to significantly change demand for dollars. Moreover, if China continues to grow, she will compete with other countries in the region for a market in component parts. The regional drive that we are now witnessing could very well be thrown into paralysis as a result of this economic rivalry. A cohesive East Asia-wide union could be one way of reassuring ASEAN countries that they will not be marginalized by China and Japan. But both sovereignty considerations and the running political contest between China and Japan are insurmountable roadblocks for achieving such a union. East Asian regionalism may limit the extent of American advantage but not dissolve it entirely.

The European Union has much more potential to displace American power although it is currently far from doing so. The arrival of the euro has already capped the United States' ability to reap disproportionate gains somewhat. Nevertheless, the problems I anticipate for the euro-zone to assume trade-related key currency tasks, the battle for influence within key European institutions, real differences among euro economies, and the unlikely participation of Britain in the euro-zone prevent the euro-area from harvesting the kind of benefits the United States currently enjoys. In the early millennium, the European Union had the opportunity to create an autonomous military force with punch. As the ESDP was being elaborated it became increasingly difficult to reconcile the different military traditions and ambitions of member states. Today, European military capability is again buried under NATO command structures and not sufficiently independent from NATO assets. The independent force that exists is a hotchpotch of revocable commitments, which lack credibility. If the European Union is serious about balancing American power, a political union with an impregnable security force is inescapable.

8 | Conclusion

After sixty years of securing superpower status, and forty years of power sharing with the Soviet Union, the United States is the dominant power in the world today. Common sense tells us that it is good to be the unrivalled Great Power of the international system, king among states. But an important body of theory argues that being a small state is better than being the largest economic and military power. This book is an attempt to demonstrate that what most people believe intuitively is right after all. The single largest state benefits disproportionally from international cooperation.

There have, of course, been moments in the postwar era when other states have come out ahead, times when the United States has failed to influence other states, and when the economic and political foundations of American power have seemed shaky. For example, the United States did relatively poorly when the two smaller Great Powers (the European Community and Japan) were equally sized and together combined as much economic power as the United States did alone. Interestingly, this goes some way in explaining American support for accelerating European integration on other than ideological or cultural grounds. Since a strong Europe is more conducive to American interests than the diffusion of power between Europe and Japan, consistent with the international context from the mid-1970s until the early 1990s, America's encouragement of European collaboration can be said to have a rational basis. Variations in the distribution of power such as these, and their effect on states' relative impact, suggest that the United States does not fare better than other states in every conceivable situation, but is better off in a sufficient number of cases to support the claim about disproportional gains accruing to the strongest as opposed to weaker states. What explains the United States' ability to benefit disproportionally, when collaborating with other states, is a number of structural advantages, and the positive synergies between these, across different domains.

First, as we have seen, America's key currency status produces disproportionate commercial gains by creating long-term pressures for import growth and trade deficits. Trade benefits accrue to American consumers, producers, and the American government as a result of the United States being the dominant monetary power, i.e. the supplier of the key currency for international trade, financial transactions, and reserves.

Second, America's commercial power provides American financial hegemony with policy flexibility. Actors and agents in the international economic system have a myriad of incentives – the general demand for safe and liquid assets, weak domestic capital markets, reimbursement of dollar-denominated debt, and the fear of a ricochet effect following large-scale dollar sales – to hold assets in the United States. Another very important motivation to accumulate dollar assets is heavy reliance on American product markets. This gives the United States the power to defer adjustment and absorb real resources. Moreover, foreign dependence on American capital and product markets allows the United States to shoulder as little of the cost as possible when the time for adjustment comes.

Third, and finally, America's military preponderance facilitates commercial expansion, and also secures and raises the appeal of American asset markets, thus boosting American buying power. The US government has supported American foreign direct investment and, consequently, the outward extension of American firms. This has been done by using military might to defend property rights abroad and by using government clout to advocate on behalf of American firms, exerting pressure on foreign governments to guarantee the safety of American plants and personnel. In various ways, government endorsement has encouraged risky high-yield foreign direct investment that would have been prohibitively costly without a political safety net. Military preponderance facilitates commercial expansion and makes American capital markets more attractive by reinforcing the perception of the United States as a safe investment venue. Although this security premium is difficult to measure, chapter 6 provides a tentative indicator by pointing to a positive correlation between capital inflows and military successes as well as between capital outflows and military defeats. As background noise, foreign military interventions and extended deterrence have carved out a unique leadership role, and created systemic dependence on the United States, putting it in favor with the powers that count. Once upon a time, American naval and military power even contributed to creating the conditions for key currency status.

A surprising result, confirmed in the model developed for this book, is that relative weakening can be advantageous, and that the United States actually acquires greater leverage and a greater capacity to reap disproportionate benefits under certain phases of decline. The presence of automatic stabilizers to cushion America's fall is also borne out by the empirical evidence from negotiations within the trade regime as well as cooperation in monetary affairs. Thus, while the United States has declined relative to other countries along some dimensions, this decline is not a function of American benevolence – the propensity to shoulder costs, greater than benefits, on behalf of other states in the system.

At this stage, most people will wonder how to explain American decline, if, as I claim, the United States benefits disproportionally from international cooperation most of the time. The answer is that power hierarchy not only depends on America's capacity to benefit from its position within the international structure, but is contingent upon its internal and foreign policies, as well as the internal and foreign policies of other states. A series of domestic policy mistakes could, in other words, constitute a source of decline and place America on a downward trajectory, creating a de facto relative advantage for competitors. The financial crisis, which was caused by high-risk financial products and lending practices in the United States, is an example of how different sectors in the United States failed to get their economic house in order, and could still play itself out in a nasty way, deepening American decline. But, so far, the big shocker is not just how the financial crisis rocked the world, but how it strengthened the dollar and lowered American borrowing costs. Made in America (despite foreign banks' complicity), the catastrophe's consequences are a supreme irony. Besides money fleeing to the dollar rather than from it, we also see massive government spending, which is expected to weaken the dollar over the long term, leaving Great Powers like China to absorb the costs. The dynamics of the financial crisis confirm, the thesis of this book, that the strongest Great Power has structural advantages that others do not, and, more specifically, that the United States is able to pursue, and more remarkably gain from, policies that would bring other countries to the brink of disaster. This in itself is proof of a capacity to benefit from international cooperation where others cannot. While this financial crisis will pass, there were signs of the United States' extraordinary ability to draw in foreign investment despite large and persistent trade and fiscal deficits, long before the credit crunch made an appearance. Significant capital inflow was sometimes combined with considerable unproductive use of domestic resources, indicating an unusually wide "policy error" window. This point should not be overstated, however. While the United States has a more comfortable margin of error than other countries, it is subject to the same economic laws that rule the market for goods and financial products. Domestic profligacy and policy blunders cannot indefinitely persist without triggering capital flight and a destabilizing decline in the value of the dollar.

What are the limits of America's advantage and privileged position? If being the dominant power provides tangible economic and security benefits and greater degrees of freedom, why don't others seek these advantages for themselves? Well, they do. Internal developments in other states, China in particular, have contributed to America's relative decline. China does not want to be just another Great Power on the block. It has its eyes set on superpower status. Superficially, it may not look like China is pulling any punches. Grumbling overtly, and from high places, the Central Bank governor recently asked for the dollar's special role in the world economy to be dismantled, calling for an artificial key currency in the form of Special Drawing Rights (SDRs) managed by the IMF instead. With so much invested in American dollar assets, they are irked by the expansion of the monetary base in the United States to cope with the crisis. But they are stuck and must be careful what they wish for. Who is going to absorb Chinese exports – the reason why so much of their money is tied up in American assets in the first place – if the dollar is dethroned as key currency?

Over the long term, many scholars see China ejecting the United States from its privileged position. I do not see this happening any time soon, perhaps not at all. An East-Asian union axed around China or Japan is a more likely possibility, with some progress already made in that direction, although such cooperation is constrained by mutual rivalries on both the economic and political planes.

Collective action among European states has done more to undercut America's relative size advantage than collaboration among East

Asian states. Furthermore, the European Union is, I think, more likely to displace American power. The reason is simple. Cooperation in Europe cuts to the heart of core superpower functions. The European Union has a large product market where other countries can offload their exports. A European currency union has been in force for a decade, supplying the euro, a currency widely used, with the potential of becoming the primary currency. Significant advances have also been made in the field of security cooperation.

Despite these portents, even the European Union is unlikely to take over America's role in the world economy. While it is possible that the euro will crowd the dollar out to the extent that a symmetrical, multiple, key currency system, is introduced, the euro is unlikely to replace the dollar as key currency. On the security dimension, there is no prospect for the European Union to rival the United States in the foreseeable future. It is even unclear whether the political will exists to create a rival autonomous capability. The second Bush presidency did much to speed up security cooperation, but the initiative quickly petered out, and one wonders how much transatlantic discord would be needed to create a critical security force when policies so disliked in European quarters could not generate stronger developments. This gets to the crux of what keeps American hegemony alive.

Transforming the current power structure is not only about America's relative weakening, but also about other states' incentives and capacities to organize. Currently, they are too dependent on America. They cannot project power because they do not have the autonomy to define and pursue their interests. Both East Asia and Europe rely on America economically and militarily, Europe less so economically than in the past. But, as we have seen, economic and security functions intersect. This makes it virtually impossible to reach the top, without assuring self-sufficiency in both domains. Of course, in our globalized world, no actor can turn its back on all others in the system. Everyone is interdependent to some extent, although not everyone is dependent to the same extent. Recognizing shared dependence is important for all actors but, for any single actor with the ambition to rule the world, paying attention to the differential vulnerability that comes with relative dependence is imperative. If other Great Powers become serious about closing the American era, they will not be able to continue to depend on the American system for their economic well-being and basic security. Those longing for another world order may be disappointed with them for lacking the political will to stand on their own feet. However, a crisp lesson from this exploration of the determinants and consequences of American power may very well be that, while breaking away from an inequitable system which is exploitative is hard, breaking away from an inequitable system which is not, is harder. The substitution of American leadership is slowed by the way American power is exercised. Not quite benevolent, the current world order is, for the most part, mutually beneficial. Everyone benefits from cooperation, although not everyone benefits equally, and the gains from cooperation are asymmetrically distributed at the crest. This leads me to predict that rapid decline is not on its way. America will bounce back, preserving its unique position in the international system for the foreseeable future.

References

ABS. 2005. 5302.0 – Balance of Payments and International Investment Position, Australia, Dec. 2004. Canberra: Australian Bureau of Statistics.

    2006a. 5302.0 – Balance of Payments and International Investment Position, Australia, Dec. 2005. Canberra: Australian Bureau of Statistics.

    2006b. 5302.0 Table 79. Levels of Foreign Investment in Australia – Financial Year. Canberra: Australian Bureau of Statistics.

    2006c. Australian Demographic Statistics. Canberra: Australian Bureau of Statistics.

Aggarwal, Vinod K., and Cédric Dupont. 1999. Goods, games, and institutions. *International Political Science Review* **20**(4): 393–409.

Aggarwal, Vinod K., Robert O. Keohane, and David B. Yoffie. 1987. The dynamics of negotiated protectionism. *American Political Science Review*. **81**(2): 345–66.

Aggarwal, Vinod K., and John Ravenhill. 2001. Undermining the WTO: the case against open sectoralism. *Asia Pacific Issues* **50**: 1–6.

Alesina, Alberto, and Enrico Spolaore. 2003. *The Size of Nations.* Cambridge, MA: MIT Press.

Allianz. 2008. *EM Outlook 2009.* London: Dresdner Kleinwort.

Andréani, Gilles. 2000. Why institutions matter. *Survival* **42**(2): 81–95.

Bacchetta, Phillippe, and Eric van Wincoop. 2005. A theory of the currency denomination of international trade. *Journal of International Economics* **67**: 295–319.

Bacevich, Andrew J. 2002. *American Empire: The Realities and Consequences of U.S. Diplomacy.* Cambridge, MA: Harvard University Press.

Baker, James A., and Lee H. Hamilton. 2006. Iraq Study Group Press Conference Transcript.

Baldwin, Richard E. 2003. *The Spoke Trap: Hub and Spoke Bilateralism in East Asia.* Geneva: The Graduate Institute of International Studies.

Barro, Robert J. 1986. Government spending, interest rates, and budget deficits in the United Kingdom, 1701–1918. *National Bureau of Economic Research* **2005**: 1–36.

Bayard, Thomas O., and Kimberly Ann Elliott. 1993. *Reciprocity and Retaliation in U.S. Trade Policy.* Washington DC: Institute for International Economics.

BEA. 2007a. Balance of Payments: Table 1. US International Transactions. Washington, DC: US Department of Commerce.

2007b. Balance of Payments: Table 1. US International Transactions Washington: US Department of Commerce.

2007c. Current-dollar and "Real" GDP. Washington, DC: US Department of Commerce.

2007d. Table 2. International Investment Position of the United States at Yearend, 1976–2006. Washington, DC: Bureau of Economic Analysis, US Department of Commerce.

2007e. U.S. International Transactions 1960–present. Washington, DC: US Department of Commerce.

2008a. International Investment Position of the United States at Yearend, 1976–2007. Washington, DC: US Department of Commerce.

2008b. U.S. International Transactions Accounts Data. Washington, DC: US Department of Commerce.

2009a. Current-dollar and "Real" GDP. Washington, DC: US Department of Commerce.

2009b. International Investment Position of the United States at Yearend, 1976–2007. Washington, DC: US Department of Commerce.

2009c. International Investment Position of the United States at Yearend, 1976–2008. Washington, DC: US Department of Commerce.

2009d. U.S. International Transactions Accounts Data. Washington, DC: US Department of Commerce.

2009e. U.S. International Transactions Accounts Data, 1960–2008. Washington, DC: US Department of Commerce.

Becker, Gary S. 1997. *Accounting for Tastes.* Cambridge, MA: Harvard University Press.

Becker, Gary S., and Kevin M. Murphy. 2001. *Social Economics: Market Behavior in a Social Environment.* Cambridge, MA: Harvard University Press.

Beeson, Mark. 2004. U.S. hegemony and Southeast Asia. *Critical Asian Studies* **36**(3): 445–62.

Belke, Ansgar. 2003. The rotation model is not sustainable. *Intereconomics* **38**(3): 119–24.

Bergsten, C. Fred. 1975. *The Dilemmas of the Dollar.* New York, NY: New York University Press.

1999. America and Europe: clash of the titans? *Foreign Affairs* **78**(2): 20–34.

2002. The euro versus the dollar: will there be a struggle for dominance? *Journal of Policy Modeling* **24**(4): 307–14.

Bernard, Mitchell, and John Ravenhill. 1995. Beyond product cycles and flying geese. *World Politics* **47**: 171–209.

Bertaut, Carol C., and Ralph W. Tryon. 2007. Monthly estimates of U.S. cross-border securities positions. *International Finance Discussion Papers* 910.

Bhagwati, Jagdish. 2004. Don't cry for Cancun. *Foreign Affairs* **83**(1): 52–63.
2008. The selfish hegemon must offer a new deal on trade. *Financial Times,* August 19. London.

Bhagwati, Jagdish, David Greenaway, and Arvind Panagariya. 1998. Trading preferentially: theory and policy. *The Economic Journal* **108**(449): 1128–1.

BIS. 2007. Triennial Central Bank Survey of Foreign Exchange and Derivatives Market Activity in 2007 – Final results. Basel: Bank for International Settlements.

Biscop, Sven. 2002. In search of a strategic concept for the ESDP. *European Foreign Affairs Review* 7: 473–90.

Blackhurst, Richard. 1998. "The capacity of the WTO to fulfill its mandate", in Anne O. Krueger (ed.), *The WTO as an International Organization.* Chicago, ILL: University of Chicago Press.

Bono, Giovanni. 2004. The EU's military doctrine: an assessment. *International Peacekeeping* **11**(3): 439–56.

Boyer, Mark A. 1989. Trading public goods in the western alliance system. *Journal of Conflict Resolution* **33**(4): 700–27.

Brander, James A. 1995. *Strategic Trade Policy.* Cambridge, MA: National Bureau of Economic Research.

Brawley, Mark. 1995. Political leadership and liberal economic subsystems: the constraints of structural assumptions. *Canadian Journal of Political Science* **27**(1): 85–103.

Brewer, John. 1989. *The Sinews of Power: War, Money and the English State, 1688–1783.* New York, NY: Alfred A. Knopf.

Buchanan, James M. 1994. "Introduction", in James M Buchanan and Yong J. Yoon (eds.) *The Return to Increasing Returns.* Ann Arbor, MI: Universitiy of Michigan Press.

Buchanan, James M., and Yong J. Yoon. 1994. *The Return to Increasing Returns.* Ann Arbor, MI: University of Michigan Press.

Bulow, Jeremy, and Kenneth Rogoff. 1989. Sovereign debt: is to forgive to forget? *American Economic Review* **79**(1): 43–50.

Cable, James. 1994. *Gunboat Diplomacy 1919–1991.* Basingstoke: Macmillan.

Cai, Kevin G. 2004. Chinese changing perspective on the development of an East Asian free trade area. *The Review of International Affairs* **3**(4): 584–99.

Calvo, Guillermo, and Carmen Reinhart. 2002. Fear of floating. *Quarterly Journal of Economics* **117**: 379–408.

Capie, Forrest. 1998. Monetary unions in historical perspective: what future for the euro in the international financial system. *Open Economies Review* 9(0): 447–65.

Carpenter, Ted Galen. 1992. "Direct military intervention", in Peter J. Schraeder (ed.) *Intervention into the 1990s*. Boulder, CO and London: Lynne Rienner.

Cavallo, Michele. 2004. Exchange Rate Movements and the U.S. international balance sheet. *FRBSF Economic Letter* 25.

CBO. 2005. *Why Does U.S. Investment Abroad Earn Higher Returns than Foreign Investment in the United States?* Washington DC: Economic and Budget Issue Brief.

Cecchetti, Stephen G., and Róisín O'Sullivan. 2003. The European Central Bank and the Federal Reserve. *Oxford Review of Economic Policy* 19(1): 30–43.

Chamberlin, Edward. 1933. *Theory of Monopolistic Competition*. Cambridge, MA: Harvard University Press.

Chatterjee, Charles. 2003. The European Central Bank. *Journal of International Banking Regulation* 4(3): 225–36.

Chinn, Menzie, and Jeffrey Frankel. 2005. Will the euro eventually surpass the dollar as leading international reserve currency? *National Bureau of Economic Research* **11510**.

Cho, Sungjoon. 2004. A bridge too far: the fall of the Fifth WTO Ministerial Conference in Cancun and the future of trade constitution. *Journal of International Economic Law* 7(2): 219–44.

Cline, William R. 1995. Evaluating the Uruguay Round. *World Economy* 18(1): 1–23.

2005. *The United States as a Debtor Nation*. Washington, DC: Institute for International Economics.

Cohen, Benjamin J. 1971. *The Future of Sterling as an International Currency*. London: Macmillan.

Cohen, Benjamin J. 1977. *Organizing the World's Money: The Political Economy of International Monetary Relations*. New York: Basic Books.

2003. Global currency rivalry: can the euro ever challenge the dollar? *Journal of Common Market Studies* 41(4): 575–95.

2005. The Macrofoundation of Monetary Power. In *EUI Working Paper*. Florence: European University Institute.

2007. Enlargement and the international role of the euro. *Review of International Political Economy* 14(5): 746–73.

Conybeare, John A. C. 1984. Public goods, prisoners' dilemmas and the international political economy. *International Studies Quarterly* 28(1): 5–22.

1987. *Trade Wars*. New York: Columbia University Press.

Cooper, Richard N. 2001. Is the U.S. current account sustainable? Will it be sustained? *Brookings Papers on Economic Activity* 1 (217–226).

Cornish, Paul, and Geoffrey Edwards. 2001. Beyond the EU/NATO dichotomy: the beginnings of a European strategic culture. *International Affairs* **77**(3): 587–603.

COW. 2007. *Correlates of War Project: MID-level Data and Documents.* Urbana, IL: Department of Political Science.

Crystal, Jonathan. 2003. Bargaining in the negotiations over liberalizing trade in services: power, reciprocity and learning. *Review of International Political Economy* **10**(3): 552–78.

Curcuru, Stephanie E., Tomas Dvorak, and Francis E. Warnock. 2008a. Cross-border returns differentials. *Quarterly Journal of Economics*: 1495–530.

2008b. The decomposition of the U.S. external returns differential. *IMF Conference on International Macro-Finance*.

Cyr, Arthur I. 2003. The euro: faith, hope and parity. *International Affairs* **79**(5): 979–92.

Deardorff, Alan V., and Robert M. Stern. 1983. Economic effects of the Tokyo Round. *Southern Economic Journal* **49**(3): 605–24.

Desker, B. 2004. In defence of FTAs: from purity to pragmatism in East Asia. *The Pacific Review* **17**(1): 3–26.

Despres, Michael P., Charles P. Kindleberger, and Walter Salant. 1966. The dollar and world liquidity: a minority view. *The Economist,* February 5. London.

Destler, I. M. 1995. *American Trade Politics*, 3rd edn. Washington, DC: Institute for International Economics.

Destler, I. M, and C. Randall Henning. 1989. *Dollar Politics: Exchange Rate Policymaking in the United States*. Washington, DC: Institute for International Economics.

Dixit, Avinash K., and Joseph E. Stiglitz. 1979. Monopolistic competition and optimum product diversity: reply. *American Economic Review* **69**(5): 961–63.

Dooley, Michael, David Folkerts-Landau, and Peter Garber. 2003. An essay on the revived Bretton Woods system. *NBER* 9971.

Doremus, Paul N., William W. Keller, Louis W. Pauly, and Simon Reich. 1998. *The Myth of the Global Corporation*. Princeton, NJ: Princeton University Press.

Drahos, P. 2003. When the weak bargain with the strong: negotiations in the World Trade Organization. *International Negotiation* **8**(1): 79–109.

Dunning, John H. 2002. *Theories and Paradigms of International Business Activity*. Cheltenham: Edward Elgar.

Eaton, Jonathan, and Mark Gersovitz. 1981. Debt with repudiation: theoretical and empirical analysis. *Review of Economic Studies* **48**(2): 289–309.

ECB. 2005a. *Review of the International Role of the Euro*. Frankfurt am Main: European Central Bank.

2005b. *Review of the International Role of the Euro.* Frankfurt am Main: European Central Bank.

2007a. *Review of the International Role for the Euro.* Frankfurt am Main: European Central Bank.

2007b. *Review of the International Role of the Euro.* Frankfurt am Main: European Central Bank.

2008a. *The International Role of the Euro.* Frankfurt am Main: European Central Bank.

2008b. 18 December 2008 – ECB Governing Council decides to continue its current voting regime. *Press Release.*

2009. *Exchange Rates: Bilateral.* Frankfurt am Main: European Central Bank.

Eichengreen, Barry. 1998. The euro as a reserve currency. *Journal of the Japanese and International Economies* **12**(4): 483–506.

Eichengreen, Barry J., and Ricardo Hausmann. 1999. Exchange rates and financial fragility. *NBER* 7418.

Ekelund, Robert B., and Robert D. Tollison. 1997. *Microeconomics: Private Markets and Public Choice.* Reading, MA: Addison-Wesley.

English, William B. 1996. Understanding the costs of sovereign default: American state debts in the 1840s. *American Economic Review* **86**(1): 259–75.

Ethier, Wilfred J. 1982. National and international returns to scale in the modern theory of international trade. *American Economic Review* **72**(3): 389–405.

2008. *External and Intra-European Union trade: Statistical Yearbook – Data 1958–2006.* Luxembourg: Office for Official Publications of the European Communities.

EUROSTAT. 2009a. *Exchange Rate Database.* Luxembourg: Statistical Office of the European Communities.

2009b. *External Trade Database.* Luxembourg: Statistical Office of the European Communities.

Farrell, Diana. 2004. *A New Look at the U.S. Current Account Deficit: The Role of Multinational Companies.* San Francisco, CA: McKinsey Global Institute.

Feldstein, Martin. 2008. The dollar–oil link. *The International Economy,* Summer, 15.

Finger, Michael J. and Sumana Dhar. 1994. "Do rules control power? GATT articles and arrangements in the Uruguay Round", in Alan V. Deardoff and Robert Stern (eds.) *Analytical and Negotiating Issues in the Global Trading System.* Ann Arbor, MI: University of Michigan Press.

Forbes. 2008. "The Global 2000", in *Forbes.* New York.

Foreign Affairs and International Trade Canada. 2006. *Investment Income.* Foreign Affairs and International Trade Canada.

Fratianni, Michele, Andreas Hauskrecht, and Aurelio Maccario. 1998. Dominant currencies and the future of the euro. *Open Economies Review* **9**(1): 467–92.

FRBS. 2009. "Exchange rates", in *Economic Research*. St. Louis, MO: Federal Reserve Bank of St. Louis.

Friedrich, Klaus. 2002. Imports as deterrence: American consumers rule, *International Herald Tribune*.

Frisch, Helmut. 2003. The euro and its consequences: what makes a currency strong? *Atlantic Economic Journal* **31**(1): 15–31.

Frohlich, Norman, and Joe A. Oppenheimer. 1970. I get along with a little help from my friends. *World Politics* **23**.

Funabashi, Yoichi. 1988. *Managing the Dollar: from Plaza to the Louvre*. Washington, DC: Institute for International Economics.

Gabszewicz, Jean J. 1999. *Strategic Interaction and Markets*. New York, NY: Oxford University Press.

Galati, Gabriele, and Philip Wooldridge. 2006. The Euro as a Reserve Currency: A Challenge to the Pre-eminence of the US Dollar? *BIS Working Papers*. Basel: Bank for International Settlements.

Garrett, Geoffrey. 1998. Global markets and national politics: collision course or virtuous circle? *International Organization* **52**(4): 787–824.

Giegerich, Bastian, and William Wallace. 2004. Not such a soft power: the external deployment of European forces. *Survival* **46**(2): 163–82.

Gill, Stephen. 1990. *American Hegemony and the Trilateral Commission*. Cambridge: Cambridge University Press.

Gilpin, Robert. 1975. *U.S. Power and the Multinational Corporation*. New York, NY: Basic Books.

1981. *War and Change in World Politics*. Cambridge: Cambridge University Press.

GOFT. 2008. *Ranking of Germany's Trading Partners in Foreign Trade*. Cologne: Federal Ministry of Economics and Technology.

Goldberg, Linda S., and Cédric Tille. 2006. "Vehicle currency use in international trade", in *International Research Function*. New York, NY: Federal Reserve Bank of New York.

Goldstein, Judith. 1986. The political economy of trade: institutions of protection. *American Political Science Review* **80**(1): 161–84.

Gordon, Philip H. 2000. Their own army? *Foreign Affairs*: July/August 12–17.

Gourinchas, Pierre-Olivier, and Hélène Rey. 2005a. From World Banker to World Venture Capitalist: U.S. External Adjustment and the Exorbitant Privilege. *NBER Working Paper* 11563.

2005b. International Financial Adjustment. *NBER Working Paper* 11155.

Gowa, Joanne S. 1989. Rational hegemons, excludable goods, and small groups: an epitaph for hegemonic stability theory? *World Politics* **41**(3): 307–24.

Graber, D.A. 1959. *Crisis Diplomacy: A History of U.S. Intervention Policies and Practices.* Washington, DC: Public Affairs Press.

Grassman, Sven. 1973. Currency distribution and forward cover in foreign trade. *Journal of International Economics* 6: 215–21.

Gray, H. Peter. 2004. *The Exhaustion of the Dollar.* New York, NY: Palgrave Macmillan.

Grieco, Joseph M. 1988. Anarchy and the limits of international cooperation. *International Organization* 42: 485–507.

1990. *Cooperation Among Nations.* Ithaca, NY: Cornell University Press.

2002. "Modern realist theory and the study of international politics in the twenty-first century", Michael Brecher and Frank P. Harvey (eds.) *Realism and Institutionalism in International Studies.* Ann Arbor, MI: University of Michigan Press.

Grieco, Joseph M., Robert Powell, and Duncan Snidal. 1993. The relative-gains problem for international cooperation. *American Political Science Review* 87(3): 727–43.

Gros, Daniel. 2003. An opportunity missed. *Intereconomics* 38(3): 124–29.

Gros, Daniel, and Stefano Micossi. 2008. European banking on borrowed time. *Financial Times,* September 20. London.

Grossman, Gene M., and Elhanan Helpman. 1994. Protection for sale. *American Economic Review* 84(4): 833–50.

Gruber, Lloyd. 2001. Power politics and the free trade bandwagon. *Comparative Political Studies* 34(7): 703–41.

Grunberg, Isabelle. 1990. Exploring the "myth" of hegemonic stability. *International Organization* 44(4): 431–77.

Haass, Richard N. 1999. *Intervention: The Use of American Military Force in the Post-Cold War Era.* Washington, DC: Brookings Institution Press.

Hagan, Kenneth J. 1973. *American Gunboat Diplomacy and the Old Navy, 1877–1889.* Westport, CT: Greenwood Press.

Haine, Jean-Yves. 2004. Idealism and power: the new EU security strategy. *Current History* 103: 107–12.

Harrison, Jason, and John Hawkins. 2007. How international investment income flows affect Australia's balance of payments.

Hartmann, Philipp, and Otmar Issing. 2002. The international role of the euro. *Journal of Policy Modeling* 24(4): 315–45.

He, Baogang. 2004. East Asian ideas of regionalism: a normative critique. *Australian Journal of International Affairs* 58(1): 105–25.

Healy, David. 1976. *Gunboat Diplomacy in the Wilson Era: The U.S. Navy in Haiti, 1915–1916.* Madison, WI: University of Wisconsin Press.

Heckscher, Eli. 1950. "The effect of foreign trade on the distribution of income", in *Readings in the Theory of International Trade,* 272–300. London: George Allen and Unwin Ltd.

Heisenberg, Dorothee. 2003. Cutting the bank down to size: efficient and legitimate decision-making in the European Central Bank after Enlargement. *Journal of Common Market Studies* **41**(3): 397–420.

Hicks, John R. 1994. "The assumption of constant returns to scale", in James M. Buchanan and Yong J. Yoon (eds.) *The Return to Increasing Returns*. Ann Arbor, MI: The University of Michigan Press.

Higgins, Matthew, Thomas Klitgaard, and Cédric Tille. 2006. "Borrowing without debt? Understanding the U.S. international investment position", in *Federal Reserve Bank of New York Staff Reports*. New York, NY: Federal Reserve Bank of New York.

Hindley, Brian, and Patrick Messerlin. 1993. "Guarantees of market access and regionalism", in Kym Anderson and Richard Blackhurst (eds.) *Regional Integration and the Global Trading System*. New York, NY: Harvester Wheatsheaf.

Hiscox, Michael J. 2002. *International Trade and Political Conflict*. Princeton, NJ: Princeton University Press.

Hoekman, Bernard M., and Michael M. Kostecki. 2001. *The Political Economy of the World Trading System*. New York, NY: Oxford University Press.

Hoffmann, Stanley. 2000. Towards a common European foreign and security policy. *Journal of Common Market Studies* **38**(2): 189–98.

Holst, David Roland, and John Weiss. 2004. ASEAN and China: export rivals or partners in regional growth? *The World Economy* **27**(8): 1255–74.

Hood, Miriam. 1975. *Gunboat Diplomacy 1895–1905: Great Power Pressure in Venezuela*. London: George Allen & Unwin Ltd.

Howard, David H. 1989. Implications of the U.S. current account deficit. *Journal of Economic Perspectives* **3**(4): 153–65.

Hund, Markus. 2003. ASEAN Plus Three: towards a new age of pan-East Asian regionalism? A skeptic's appraisal. *The Pacific Review* **16**(3): 383–417.

Huntington, Samuel P. 1988/1989. The U.S.: decline or renewal? *Foreign Affairs* **67**: 76–96.

IBRD. 2009. World Development Indicators Database. Washington, DC: World Bank.

Iida, Keisuke. 2004. Is WTO dispute settlement effective? *Global Governance* **10**(2): 207–25.

Ikenberry, G. John. 2001. *After Victory: Institutions, Strategic Restraint, and the Rebuilding of Order after Major Wars, Princeton Studies in International History and Politics*. Princeton, NJ: Princeton University Press.

2004. Liberalism and empire: logics of order in the American unipolar age. *Review of International Studies* **30**(4): 609–30.

2005a. Power and liberal order: America's postwar world order in transition. *International Relations of the Asia-Pacific* 5: 133–52.

2005b. Why Bush grand strategy fails. Unpublished Paper.

IMF. 1997. *International Capital Markets: Developments, Prospects, and Key Policy Issues.* Washington, DC: International Monetary Fund.

2003a. *External Debt Statistics: Guide for Compilers and Users.* Washington, DC: International Monetary Fund.

2003b. *World Economic Outlook: Public Debt in Emerging Markets.* Washington, DC: International Monetary Fund.

2003c. *Global Financial Stability Report: Statistical Appendix.* Washington, DC: International Monetary Fund.

2004. *Global Financial Stability Report: Statistical Appendix.* Washington, DC: International Monetary Fund.

2007a. *International Financial Statistics. Total Reserves Minus Gold.* Washington, DC: International Monetary Fund.

2007b. *Global Financial Stability Report: Statistical Appendix.* Washington, DC: International Monetary Fund.

2008a. *International Financial Statistics.* Washington DC.: International Monetary Fund.

2008b. *Global Financial Stability Report: Statistical Appendix.* Washington, DC: International Monetary Fund.

October 2009. *Global Financial Stability Report: Statistical Appendix.* Washington, DC: International Monetary Fund.

2009a. *Currency Composition of Official Foreign Exchange Reserves (COFER).* Washington, DC: International Monetary Fund.

2009b. *IFS Online: Balance of Payments.* Washington, DC: International Monetary Fund.

2009c. *IFS Online: Country Exchange Rates.* Washington, DC: International Monetary Fund.

2009d. *IFS Online: International Investment Position.* Washington, DC: International Monetary Fund.

2009e. *IFS Online: National Accounts.* Washington, DC: International Monetary Fund.

2009f. *IFS Online: Total Reserves Minus Gold.* Washington, DC: International Monetary Fund.

Irwin, Douglas A. 1996. *Against the Tide: An Intellectual History Of Free Trade.* Princeton, NJ: Princeton University Press.

Jackson, John H. 1997. *The World Trading System: Law and Policy of International Economic Relations,* 2nd edn. Cambridge, MA: The MIT Press.

Johnson, Chalmers. 2000. *Blowback.* New York, NY: Metropolitan Books.

2004. *The Sorrows of Empire.* New York, NY: Metropolitan Books.

Johnson, Harry G. 1953. Optimum tariffs and retaliation. *Review of Economic Studies* **21**(2): 142–53.

Jones, Seth G. 2003. The European Union and the security dilemma. *Security Studies* **12**(3): 114–56.

Jupp, Kenneth. 2000. European feudalism from its emergence through its decline. *American Journal of Economics and Sociology* **59**(5): 27–45

Kaikati, Jack. 1999. The euro versus the U.S. dollar: an overview. *Journal of World Business* **34**(2): 171–92.

Kamps, Annette. 2006. The euro as invoicing currency in international trade. *Working Paper Series*. Kiel: ECB.

Kenen, Peter B. 2002. The euro versus the dollar: will there be a struggle for dominance? *Journal of Policy Modeling* **24**(4): 347–54.

Kennedy, Paul. 1987. *The Rise and Fall of the Great Powers: Economic Change and Military Conflict from 1500 to 2000*. New York, NY: Random House.

Keohane, Robert. 1982. The demand for international regimes. *International Organization* **36**(2): 325–55.

   1984. *After Hegemony: Cooperation and Discord in the World Political Economy*. Princeton, NJ: Princeton University Press.

Kindleberger, Charles P. 1973. *The World in Depression 1929–1939*. Harmondsworth: Penguin.

   1981. Dominance and leadership in the international economy. *International Studies Quarterly* **25**: 242–54.

   1986a. Hierarchy versus inertial cooperation. *International Organization* **40**(4): 841–47.

   1986b. International public goods without international government. *American Economic Review* **76**(1): 1–13.

Klein, Michael, Bruce Mizrach, and Robert G. Murphy. 1991. Managing the dollar: has the Plaza agreement mattered? *Journal of Money, Credit, and Banking* **23**(4).

Kouparitsas, Michael. 2005. Is the U.S. current account sustainable? *Chicago Fed Letter,* **215** (June): 1–4.

Krasner, Stephen D. 1979. The Tokyo Round: particularistic interests and prospects for stability in the global trading system. *International Studies Quarterly* **23**(4): 491–531.

Krueger, Anne. 1999. The developing countries and the next round of multilateral trade negotiations. *World Economy* **22**(7): 909–32.

Krugman, Paul R. 1979. Increasing returns, monopolistic competition and international trade. *Journal of International Economics* **9**: 469–79.

   1980. Oil and the Dollar. *NBER Working Paper* **554**: 1–18.

   1986. *Strategic Trade Policy and the New International Economics*. Cambridge, MA: MIT Press.

1991a. *Currencies and Crises*. Cambridge, MA: MIT Press.

1991b. *Geography and Trade, Gaston Eyskens Lecture Series*. Leuven: Leuven University Press.

Krugman, Paul R., and Maurice Obstfeld. 2000. *International Economics: Theory and Policy*, 6th edn. Reading, MA: Addison Wesley Longman.

Lake, David A. 1993. Leadership, hegemony, and the international economy: naked emperor or tattered monarch with potential? *International Studies Quarterly* 37: 459–89.

Lake, David A., and Angela O ' Mahony. 2004. The incredible shrinking state. *Journal of Conflict Resolution* 48(5): 699–722.

Lal, Deepak. 2004. *In Praise of Empires*. London: Palgrave Macmillan.

Lambelet, Jean Christian, and Urs Luterbacher, with Pierre Allan. 1979. Dynamics of arms races: mutual stimulation vs. self stimulation. *Journal of Peace Science* 4(1): 49–66.

Lane, Philip R., and Gian Maria Milesi-Ferretti. 2006. The external wealth of nations mark II: revised and extended estimates of foreign assets and liabilities, 1970–2004, in *IMF Working Paper*. Washington, DC: International Monetary Fund.

    2008. Where did all the borrowing go? A forensic analysis of the U.S. external position, in *IMF Working Paper*. Washington, DC: International Monetary Fund.

Larsen, Henrik. 2000. Concepts of security in the European Union after the cold war. *Australian Journal of International Affairs* 54(3): 337–55.

Lay, Hong Tan. 2004. Will ASEAN economic integration progress beyond a free trade area? *International and Comparative Law Quarterly* 53(4): 935–67.

Lee, Jong-Wha, and Innwon Park. 2005. Free trade areas in East Asia: discriminatory or non-discriminatory? *The World Economy* 28(1): 21–48.

Leontief, Wassily. 1953. Domestic production and foreign trade: the American capital position re-examined. *Proceedings of the American Philosophical Society* 97.

Levey, David H., and Stuart S. Brown. 2005. The overstretch myth. *Foreign Affairs* 84(2): 2–7.

Lewis, Karen K. 1999. Trying to explain home bias in equities and consumption. *Journal of Economic Literature* 37(2): 571–608.

Lipson, Charles. 1982. The transformation of trade: the sources and effects of regime change. *International Organization* 36(2): 417–55.

Looney, Robert. 2004. Petroeuros: a threat to U.S. Interests in the Gulf? *Middle East Policy* 11(1): 26–37.

    2007. The Iranian oil bourse. *Challenge* 50(2): 86–109.

Mann, Catherine L. 2002. Perspectives on the U.S. current account deficit and sustainability. *Journal of Economic Perspectives* 16(3): 131–52.

Mann, Michael. 2003. *Incoherent Empire*. New York, NY: Verso.

Marris, Stephen. 1987. *Deficits and the Dollar: the World Economy at Risk*. Washington DC: Institute for International Economics.

Marshall, Alfred. 1895. *Principles of Economics*, 3d edn. London: Macmillan.

Mataloni, Raymond J. 2004. A note on patterns of production and employment by U.S. multinational companies. *Survey of Current Business* 84 (March): 52–6.

   2008. U.S. multinational companies operations in 2006. *Survey of Current Business*, 88 (November): 26–47.

McCaughrin, Rebecca. 2004. Dispelling trade myths. *Morgan Stanley Global Economic Forum*, April 5.

McKenna, Barrie. 2005. Trade deficit clobbers greenback. *The Globe and Mail*, B1, January 13.

McKinnon, Ronald I. 1979. *Money in International Exchange*. Oxford: Oxford University Press.

   2001a. The international dollar standard and sustainability of the U.S. current account deficit. Paper presented at the Brookings Panel on Economic Activity: Symposium on the US Current Account.

   2001b. The international dollar standard and the sustainability of the U.S. current account deficit. *Brookings Papers on Economic Activity: Symposium on the Current Account*, 227–39.

   2002. The euro versus the dollar: resolving a historical puzzle. *Journal of Policy Modeling* 24(4): 355–59.

McKinnon, Ronald, and Gunther Schnabl. 2004a. The East Asian dollar standard, fear of floating, and original sin. *Review of Development Economics* 8(3): 331–60.

   2004b. The return to soft dollar pegging in East Asia: mitigating conflicted virtue. *International Finance* 7(2): 169–201.

Mead, Walter Russell. 2004. America's sticky power. *Foreign Policy*: 46–53.

Meade, Ellen E. 2003. A (critical) appraisal of the ECB's voting reform. *Intereconomics* 38(3): 129–31.

Mearsheimer, John J. 1994. The false promise of international institutions. *International Security* 19(3): 5–49.

Mérand, Frédéric. 2003. Dying for the Union? *European Societies* 5(3): 253–82.

Mill, James. 1844. *Elements of Political Economy*. London: Henry G. Bohn.

Milner, Helen. 1988. Trading places: industries for free trade. *World Politics* 40(3): 350–76.

Milner, Helen, and Jack Snyder. 1988. Lost hegemony? *International Organization* 42(4): 749–50.

Milner, Helen V., and David B. Yoffie. 1989. Between free trade and protectionism: strategic trade policy and a theory of corporate trade demands. *International Organization* **43**(2): 239–72.

Mundell, Robert A. 1961. A theory of optimum currency areas. *American Economic Review* **4**: 657–65.

    1998a. The case for the euro – II. *Wall Street Journal*, A.22, March 25.

    1998b. The case for the euro – I and II. *Wall Street Journal*, March 24.

    1998c. What the euro means for the dollar and the international monetary system. *Atlantic Economic Journal* **26**(3): 227–37.

National Statistics. 2006a. *Amendment United Kingdom National Accounts. The Blue Book* 2006. London: National Statistics.

    2006b. *United Kingdom Balance of Payments. The Pink Book 2006.* Basingstoke: Palgrave Macmillan.

Ng, Francis, and Alexander Yeats. 2001. "Production sharing in East Asia: who does what for whom, and why?", in Leonard K. Cheng and Henryk Kierzkowski (eds.) *Global Production and Trade in East Asia*, 63–109.

Niels, Gunnar. 2000. What is antidumping policy really about? *Journal of Economic Surveys* **14**(4): 467–92.

Noreng, Øystein. 1999. The euro and the oil market: new challenges to the industry. *Journal of Energy Finance and Development* **4**: 29–68.

Norrlof, Carla. 2008. Hegemonic privilege. Unpublished paper.

Nye, Joseph S. 1990. *Bound to Lead: The Changing Nature of American Power.* New York, NY: Basic Books.

Obstfeld, Maurice, and Kenneth Rogoff. 2005. The unsustainable current account position revisited. *National Bureau of Economic Research Working Paper* 10869.

Ohlin, Bertil. 1933. *Interregional and International Trade.* Cambridge: Harvard University Press.

Olson, Mancur. 1965. *The Logic of Collective Action.* Cambridge, MA: Harvard University Press.

Olson, Mancur Jr., and Richard Zeckhauser. 1966. An economic theory of alliances. *Review of Economics and Statistics* **48**(3): 266–79.

OMB. 2009a. *Budget of the United States Government Fiscal Year 2010.* Table 15.1 – Total Government Receipts in Absolute Amounts and as Percentages of GDP: 1948–2008. Washington, DC: The White House.

    2009b. *Budget of the United States Government Fiscal Year 2010.* Table 15.4 – Total Government Expenditures by Major Category of Expenditure: 1948–2008. Washington, DC: The White House.

    2009c. *Budget of the United States Government Fiscal Year 2010.* Table 15.5 – Total Government Expenditures by Major Category of Expenditure as Percentages of GDP: 1948–2008. Washington, DC: The White House.

Ong, Eng Chuan. 2003. Anchor East Asian trade in ASEAN. *Washington Quarterly* **26**(2): 57–72.

Pahre, Robert. 1999. *Leading Questions*. Ann Arbor, MI: University of Michigan Press.

Pakko, Michael R. 1999. The U.S. trade deficit and the 'new economy'. *Federal Reserve Bank of St. Louis Review* **81**(5): 11–20.

Palmeter, David. 1993. Protectionism and the rise of "unfair" trade. *Journal of World Trade* **27**(6): 187–90.

Perkins, Dexter. 1955. *A History of the Monroe Doctrine*. Toronto: Little, Brown and Co.

Pollard, Patricia S. 2003. A look inside two central banks: the European Central Bank and the Federal Reserve. *Federal Reserve Bank of St. Louis Review* **85**(1): 11–30.

Portes, Richard, and Hélène Rey. 1998. The emergence of the euro as an international currency. *National Bureau of Economic Research Working Paper* 6424.

Preeg, Ernst H. 2000. *The Trade Deficit, the Dollar, and the U.S. National Interest*. Washington, DC: Hudson Institute.

Puckett, A. Lynne, and William L. Reynolds. 1996. Rules, sanctions and enforcement under section 301: At odds with the WTO? *American Journal of International Law* **90**(4): 675–89.

Quinlan, Joseph, and Marc Chandler. 2001. The U.S. trade deficit: a dangerous obsession. *Foreign Affairs* **80**(3): 87–97.

Ransom, Harry Howe. 1992. Covert intervention, in Peter J. Schraeder (ed.) *Intervention into the 1990s*. Boulder, Co and London: Lynne Rienner.

Rehman, Scheherazade S. 1998. The euro as a global trade currency. *International Trade Journal* **12**(1): 49–64.

Ricardo, David. 1996. *Principles of Political Economy and Taxation*. New York, NY: Prometheus Books.

Rich, Georg. 2008. A proposal for extracting information from the ECB's second pillar. Unpublished Working Paper, March 17.

Robinson, Joan. 1933. *The Economics of Imperfect Competition*. London: Macmillan.

Rogowski, Ronald. 1989. *Commerce and Coalitions*. New Haven, NJ: Princeton University Press.

Rolnick, Arthur J. 2001. An interview with Tommaso Padoa-Schioppa. *The Region* **15**(4): 28–42.

Romero, Simon. 2009. Chávez reopens oil bids to west as prices plunge. *The New York Times*, January 15. New York.

Rueff, Jacques. 1972. *The Monetary Sin of the West.* New York: Macmillan.

Russett, Bruce. 1985. The mysterious case of vanishing hegemony; or, is Mark Twain really dead? *International Organization* **39**(2): 207–31.

Rybczynski, T.M. 1955. Factor endowments and relative commodity prices. *Economica* **22**: 336–41.

Rynning, Sten. 2003. The European Union: towards a strategic culture. *Security Dialogue* **34**(4): 479–96.

Schoenbaum, Thomas J. 1996. The theory of contestable markets in international trade: a rationale for "justifiable" unilateralism to combat restrictive business practices? *Journal of World Trade*: 161–90.

Schraeder, Peter J. 1992. "Paramilitary intervention", in Peter J. Schraeder (ed.) *Intervention into the 1990s.* Boulder, CO and London: Lynne Rienner.

Schultz, Theodore William. 1993. *Origins of Increasing Returns.* Oxford: Blackwell.

Setser, Brad, and Nouriel Roubini. 2005. How scary is the deficit? *Foreign Affairs* July/August.

Shepherd, Alistair J.K. 2003. The European Union's security and defence policy: a policy without substance? *European Security* **12**(1): 39–63.

SIPRI. 2009a. *The SIPRI Military Expenditure Database.* Solna: Stockholm International Peace Research Institute.

2009b. World and Regional Military Expenditure 1988–2008 (Table). Solna: Stockholm International Peace Research Institute.

Slaughter, Anne-Marie. 2004. A Dangerous Myth. *Prospect,* February 20.

Smith, Adam. 1991. *The Wealth of Nations.* New York, NY: Everyman's Library.

SNB. June 2007. R3 Auslandvermögen – Passiven. Switzerland's international investment position – liabilities. Swiss National Bank, *Monthly Statistical Bulletin,* June.

Snidal, Duncan. 1985. The limits of hegemonic stability theory. *International Organization* **39**(4): 580–614.

Soderberg, Nancy. 2005. *The Superpower Myth.* Hoboken, NJ: John Wiley & Sons.

Sraffa, Piero. 1926. The law of returns under competitive conditions. *Economic Journal* **36**: 535–50.

Statistics Canada. 2006a. *Canada's International Investment Position.* Ontario: Canada's National Statistical Agency.

2006b. *Canada's Population Clock.* Ontario: Canada's National Statistical Agency.

2007. *National Accounts: International Investment Position.* Ontario: Canada's National Statistical Agency.

Stegemann, Klaus. 2000. The integration of intellectual property rights into the WTO system. *World Economy* **23**(9): 1237–67.

Steinberg, Richard H. 2002. In the shadow of law or power? Consensus-based bargaining and outcomes in the GATT/WTO. *International Organization* **56**(2): 339–74.

Stiglitz, Joseph E. 2000. Two principles for the next round or, how to bring developing countries in from the cold. *The World Economy* **23**(4): 437–55.

Stolper, Wolfgang, and Paul Samuelson. 1941. Protection and real wages. *Review of Economic Studies* **9**: 58–73.

Stopford, John M., Susan Strange, and John S. Henley. 1991. *Rival States, Rival Firms: Competition for World Market Shares*. Cambridge: Cambridge University Press.

Strange, Susan. 1987. The persistent myth of lost hegemony. *International Organization* **41**(4): 551–74.

Stubbs, Richard. 2002. ASEAN plus three: emerging East Asian regionalism? *Asian Survey* **42**(3): 440–55.

Swoboda, Alexander. 1968. The euro-dollar market: an interpretation. *Essays in International Finance* 64.

Sylvan, David J. 1981. The newest mercantilism. *International Organization* **35**(2): 375–93.

Tanca, Antonio. 1993. *Foreign Armed Intervention in Internal Conflict*. Dordrecht: Martinus Nijhoff.

Tertrais, Bruno. 2004. The changing nature of military alliances. *The Washington Quarterly* **27**(2): 135–50.

Tille, Cédric. 2003. The impact of exchange rate movements on U.S. foreign debt. *Current Issues in Economics and Finance* **9**(1): 1–7.

Todd, Emmanuel. 2003. *After the Empire*. New York, NY: Columbia University.

Tomz, Michael. 2007. *Reputation and International Cooperation*. Princeton, NJ: Princeton University Press.

Tongzon, Jose L. 2005. ASEAN-China free trade area: a bane or boon for ASEAN countries? *The World Economy* **28**(2): 191–210.

Treacher, Adrian. 2004. From civilian power to military actor: the EU's resistable transformation. *European Foreign Affairs Review* **9**: 49–66.

Treasury. 2007. Major foreign holders of Treasury securities. Washington, DC: United States Department of the Treasury.

2009. Major foreign holders of Treasury securities. Washington, DC: United States Department of the Treasury.

Tyson, Laura D'Andrea. 1993. *Who's Bashing Whom? Trade Conflict in High-technology Industries*. Washington, DC: Institute for International Economics.

US Census Bureau. 2006. *U.S. and World Population Clocks*. Washington, DC: US Census Bureau

Ulriksen, Ståle. 2004. Requirements for future European military strategies and force structures. *International Peacekeeping* **11**(3): 457–73.

Soviet Union, military
        spending 20, 19
Spanish-American War 181
Special drawing Rights (SDRs) 250
Spolaore, Enrico 35
Sraffa, Piero, size of firms 64
S-shaped curve
    assumption of increasing returns
        41–4
    public goods benefits 40
stability 56
    and hegemonic decline 49–50
    see also hegemonic stability theory
Stability and Growth Pact (SGP) 231
Stegemann, Klaus 107, 108
Steinberg, Richard H. 103, 105, 107
Stern, Robert M. 105
Stiglitz, Joseph E. 64, 106
Stolper-Samuelson theorem 61, 62
Stopford, John M. 66
Strange, Susan 11, 18, 66
strategic debt 78
structural adjustment programs 87–8
Stubbs, Richard 199
sub-prime market, and defaults on
        mortgages 139
Swoboda, Alexander 211

Tanca, Antonio 187
technological diffusion, and
        hegemonic decline 50
technology differences
    and comparative advantage 60
    and division of labor 58
Term Asset-Backed Securities Loan
        Facility (TALF) 139
Tertrais, Bruno 168
Tille, Cédric 210, 212, 131, 134, 213
Todd, Emmanuel 52
Tokyo Round, *see* GATT
Tollison, Robert D. 65, 66, 71
Tomz, Michael 169
Tongzon, Jose L. 201
Torrens, Robert 59
Torres, President Juan of
        Bolivia 183
trade
    adjustment assistance 98
    deficits 1
        US policy 4, 5

    weakness of non-US countries 4
    laws 102
    sanctions 108
    sources of 8
    see also current account deficit;
        international trade regime
transaction costs, and key currency
        208, 211
Treacher, Adrian 234, 235, 237
Triffin dilemma 160
TRIPS Agreement 108
troubled asset relief package (TARP)
        139
Tryon, Ralph W., investment data
        147, 148
Tudjman, President of Croatia, *see*
        militarized disputes and US
        capital flows
Tyson, Laura D'Andrea 100, 109

UK
    investment in US 149, 151
        short-term 151
    net external liability 86
    US investment in 149–50
Ulriksen, Ståle 236, 239–40
UN authorization, and US military
        interventions 187
UNCTAD 85, 87
unemployment, and adjustment to
        economic shocks 230
unilateralism
    and US hegemony 186–7
    US military intervention 187, 188–9
United States Trade Representative
        (USTR) and trade law 102
Uruguay, US anti-communist
        intervention in 184
Uruguay Round, *see* GATT
US
    Caribbean interests, and
        enforcement of debt
        payments 170–1
    and lending 171
    decline, predictions of 3
    deterrent threats 160
    effect of economic collapse in
        165–6
    import share 90, 113
    lending 169–71